THEY WENT WEST...
True Tales of Frontier America

by
Sharon McKinzie

Illustrations by
Kinzie Lee Juergens

Copyright © 2017 by Sharon McKinzie

All rights reserved. No part of this publication may be reproduced, distributed, or transmitted in any form or by any means, including photocopying, recording, or other electronic or mechanical methods, without the prior written permission of the copyright holder, except in the case of brief quotations embodied in critical reviews and certain other noncommercial uses permitted by copyright law. For permission requests, write to the copyright holder, at the address below.

Printed in the United States of America by

H.V. CHAPMAN & SONS
BOOKBINDERS | PRINTING | PROMOTIONAL PRODUCTS

802 North Third Street
Abilene, Texas 79601
www.hvc-ram.com

ISBN: 978-1-940850-77-1
First Paperback Edition

10 9 8 7 6 5 4 3 2 1

The paper used in this publication meets the minimum requirements of ANSI/NISO Z39.48-1992 (R 1997) (Permanence of Paper). ∞

As always,
for Paul

TABLE OF CONTENTS

PREFACE ix

"Boss of the Plains" 1

A Camel Cavalcade 7

It's Five O'Clock..15

The Thorny Fence 21

The Little Wires That Could 27

Dinner Bell 33

The Saga of Liver-Eating Johnson 47

John, Galba, and Billy 53

"Timeless and Right" 57

Doom of the Donners 63

Dr. Sofie...73

The Boat 77

Bass Reeves..83

Harvey Girls..91

Chief Bacon Rind..99

The Trusted Trio	105
Alferd Packer	109
Teddy's Bear	115
Poker Alice	121
Pemmican	125
Gentleman Robber	129
Pleasant Pierre	133
"The Snowshoe Itinerant"	137
Butterfield	143
Postmen of the Plains and Prairies	151
Two Oceans United	161
Charley Parkhurst	171
Texas Rangers	175
The Unbroken Treaty	187
Schools and Golden Rules	193
30 Cents: The Story of Tombstone	205
The Gift	211
Ouray and Chipeta	215

Potato Creek Johnny 221

U.S. Marshals Service...225

The First Trail..229

Chips 233

Sky City 237

The Long Look West 245

ODDMENTS..249
Jim Bridger Couldn't Read a Lick...249
And Kit Carson Couldn't Spell...249
At the Rendezvous 249
A Full House 250
Bose and Britt..251
Stagecoach Etiquette 253
"Prunes" 253
A Rolling Darkroom 254
When "Cowboys" Weren't Real Cowboys..............................255
Wild About Texas 255
Plains Paper...255
Mountain Men 256
Deer vs. Turkey 257
Skeeters..257
Oliver's Casket 259
Dutch Oven 259
Indian Ponies 260
Manifest Destiny 261
GTT...261
A Bridger-Bright Idea 261
For the Love of Books 262
No Barriers 264
Ragtag Texians Blazed a Trail!..265

Ouray, Colorado	266
What $15 Million Bought... Then and Now	266
Louisiana: From "Territory" to "Purchase" to "States"	267
A Lifesaver	268
Doctor Sue	268
Wells Fargo	269
"California or Bust"	270
Captain and Captain	271
Li'l Braves 'n' Colts	271
Meeker Massacre	272
Sheriff or Marshal?	273
Cattle Drives	273
Tejanos	274
Ain't That There "Buffalo" a "Bison"?	275
First Ladies	276
Missouri River	277
One Bad Dude	279
South Pass	279
The Great American Desert	280
How Many?	280
Cows and Cliffs	281
Turntables, Roundhouses, and Wyes	282
The Mighty Three-and-a-Half	283
"Go West, Young Man..."	283
Ghost Towns	284
Salt	285
Winning the West	286
The Frontier Closes	286
BIBLIOGRAPHY	289
INDEX	329

PREFACE

They went West. Indeed, they did.

Less than thirty years after American independence and twenty-three after its successful revolution, the "back door" of our country cracked open with the exploratory party of Lewis and Clark into the great unknown, joining independent mountain men in vast reaches of the great West. By mid-century of the 1800s, an exodus from the established environs of the country slipped into full-swing. Once adventurers crossed the Allegheny and Appalachian ranges, the path westward opened like an unread book.

While the world itself was once a frontier, the archive of the American West is unique in history. Settler families in wagon trains, surveyors, trappers, prospectors and miners, mail and freight coaches, ships around Cape Horn, the Pony Express, the beginnings of rail and telegraph communication, soldiers and forts, cowboys and ranches, trade of all kinds, the search for a new opportunity and, perhaps, boundless acres of untilled land. And then there was the yen for sheer adventure, lawful or not.

Truly, the East with its cities, seaports, historic places, and green landscapes is beloved and appealing! Still, there is something about the West that draws this writer like metal to a magnet. And Western research proves a never-ending treasure hunt. Mountains, certainly, and crystal air. Forests of fir and pine. Badlands and Plains. Mines, deserts, canyons, and ghost towns. The Columbia rushing into the Pacific, while Might Mo leaves the Divide on its eastward journey.

People went West. And so shall we.

The writer expresses gratitude to supportive friends and beloved family members, who listen with interest (or politeness) to the myriad of stories from the West. (Paul gets the "full load." Thanks, sweetheart.) Also, special appreciation is extended to Carolee Juergens, ever helpful and enthusiastic.

"It's the last thing you take off and the first thing you notice."

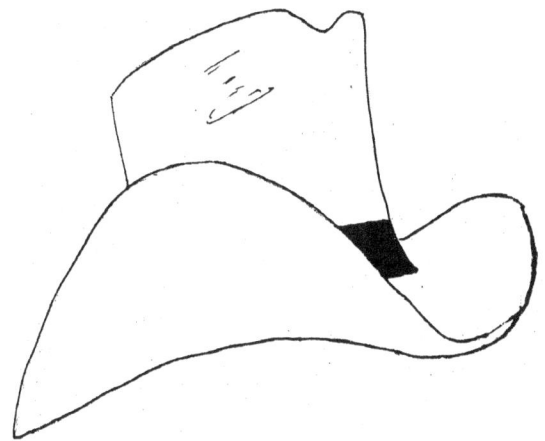

"BOSS OF THE PLAINS"

There's little doubt that head coverings of some ilk have graced noggins since the start of human history.

They weren't cowboy hats.

Fresh on the western frontier, men wore whatever they'd used in previous occupations and places. Top hats. Tams. Bowlers. Sailors. Civil-War caps. Derbies. Clearly needing alternatives, the mountain pioneers patched together temporary headgear of coon skins, wool, or beaver pelts – itchy, smelly, and sagging.

At age 30, John B. Stetson, ill with terminal tuberculosis, left his family enterprise in the East and hazarded a move to the wilderness for a drier climate and unpolluted air. Should he recover, exploration (and, perhaps, a little gold) promised a fine adventure.

He ended up changing the Western costume forever.

Back home in East Orange, New Jersey, John's father Stephen operated the reputable No Name Hat Shop, where toppers were fashioned for traditional city folk. Having grown up in the business, young John was, admittedly, ahead of the game in headwear design and workmanship. His experience proved fortuitous in far-off Colorado, where he found nasty weather and not a nugget of gold.

It started on a dreary Pike's Peak expedition when Stetson and his miserably-cold companions cobbled together a makeshift tent-like shelter of skins from the critters they'd shot for food. While the small hides were not waterproof, the so-called "fur blanket" provided welcome relief from the chill. Stetson's next step was to make actual tent cloth using the felting process his father employed in the hat factory.

Beaver or rabbit fur was shaved off the hides, fanned in the air, water-sprayed, and allowed to settle on the ground, where the fuzz made a mat that could be picked up and rolled. Repeated dipping in boiling water, followed by squeezing, caused the fur sheet to shrink and become pliable enough for manipulation into a soft blanket. Several pieces made a warm tent.

One day, in mischief, John shaped a blanket square into a tall-crowned, wide-brimmed hat similar to a Mexican sombrero. To accommodate wearers in the windy West, Stetson's crown and brim were not as lofty and wide as the south-of-the-border version. The uncommon headdress generated plenty of attention and a few laughs.

John wore his new "Stetson" on a hunt and liked it so well that it had a permanent place up top – until he sold it off his head for $5.00. By 1865, Stetson's future clearly was not in mining, so he headed back East to make his felt-cloth hats. Starting with $100 (and $10 in fur), he rented a small room in Philadelphia and employed two workers.

The rest, as they say, is history.

John's modified sombrero with its high, creased crown and wide brim formed the model "cowboy hat." Today, the Stetson brand offers a hundred styles for men and women. Hat shops employ hot steam to change the form of the brim or crown to suit a customer wanting to "twist a lid" (shape his own hat).

This "lid" has the right stuff – a simple safeguard against summer's merciless sun as well as the frozen punishment of brutal winter settings. It's all scientific. That spacious crown keeps the wearer's head in a moderate state of comfort, whatever the elements, and the brim mimics a shade tree. Stetson uses a mixture of furs for its hats, primarily rabbit, wild hare, and naturally-water-resistant beaver.

> "It kept the sun out of your eyes and off your neck. It was an umbrella. It gave you a bucket to water your horse and a cup to water yourself. It made a hell of a fan, which you needed sometimes for a fire, but more often to shunt cows this direction or that."
>
> Unknown wearer

"Ten-gallon hat?" Not likely. The typical cowboy headgear holds only a quart or two of water. Tall white hats were easy targets out there among armed miscreants, so a lower crown was preferred. "Gallon" is a misuse of the Spanish word *galon*, a braided hatband on a Mexican sombrero; a vaquero's *ten-galon* headpiece could sport 10 of those bands around the crown.

> "For the old-time cowboy it was more than a hat – it was a tool. You'd use it to fan the flames of your campfire. You'd use it to get you and your horse a drink... fill your hat with water, take a drink, give it to your horse. Not the other way around."
>
> Cliff Fowler

America's first cowboy star, Tom Mix, was shaded by the "Boss of the Plains." Stetsons caught on with Gene Autry, Roy Rogers and

Dale Evans, Buffalo Bill Cody, Annie Oakley, and the Lone Ranger. Add "J.R. Ewing," Garth Brooks, and "Lonesome Dove" stars Robert Duvall and Tommy Lee Jones. (Stetson purchasers often request the "Gus Crease" feature of Duvall's hat in the movie.)

John Wayne? Naturally. The Duke dubbed Stetson "the hat that won the West."

> "Everyone knows what a Stetson is. It's like Coke."
> Ricky Bolin

Presidents Lyndon B. Johnson and the George Bush duo sported Stetsons, of course, but so did Dwight Eisenhower and Ronald Reagan, on occasion. Texas Rangers wear them on duty, and U.S. Cavalry troops, during ceremonial events. Ranchers and cowboys – always. Guys, gals, and kids love 'em, too, and Country-Western artists consider their cowboy hats a part of the act.

When the *U.S.S. Maine* was recovered in 1912 (having been sunk in Havana Harbor in 1898), a Stetson hat was found in the wreckage. Fourteen years of mud, brackish water, and plant life were no match for the well-regarded headgear. It was undamaged.

> "Fits good. That's real important when the wind comes up. You don't want it blowing away. It's lightweight and durable. It's held up for a long time. I've cleaned it pretty often – three times in twenty years."
> Cliff Fowler

"Hats off!" to Stetson-wearers worldwide.

There is some speculation that *felting* was devised by the Apostle John, who might have collected sheep's wool stuck in bushes and stuffed it in his sandals, where the wool flattened in the heat and pressure of walking.

The sombrero may trace backward to nomadic Mongols swarming over Europe in the 14th century. The conquest failed, but their broad-brimmed hats were adopted by Spaniards and passed on to Mexican vaqueros in the Americas.

Like many factories across our land, Stetson Hats re-directed their resources toward products for the military during World War II – parachutes, heavy webbing, and safety belts. Additionally, the company generated advertising with patriotic messages such as "Idle Words Make Busy Subs," and "Keep It Under Your Hat."

John B. Stetson was a benevolent and progressive employer; the company's Christmas parties were legendary, with gifts of gloves, turkeys, candy, cash bonuses, stock shares, and hats, of course. He contributed generously to charitable causes, and his beneficence to DeLand University in DeLand, Florida, led to the school's name change to John B. Stetson University. Stetson Law School, Florida's first, was added in 1900. The university's sports mascot is "The Hatters."

"[The odor] is more easily imagined than described. No, as there are heights to which imagination cannot soar, so there are depths to which it cannot descend..."
A traveler in the Middle East

A CAMEL CAVALCADE

A parcel from the office of the President arrived for Mrs. Mary Shirkey of Victoria, Texas. The package contained an engraved goblet and a note of thanks for the socks. Socks?

The year was 1856. Weeks earlier, the Shirkey family had witnessed the eye-popping drama of nearly three dozen camels clomping off a docked ship. At the invitation of the man in charge, Major Henry Wayne, Mary had permitted her young daughter Pauline to ride one of the creatures a couple of miles.

As a souvenir, we suppose, Major Wayne offered Mrs. Shirkey some clippings of camel hair. How nice. Mary then came up with the *hair*-brained idea to knit the strands into *a pair of socks for President Franklin Pierce.*

The tangled mess stank to high heaven. Washing. Sunning. Exposure to the clean air of night. Nothing helped. The dismal product remained dismal. Major Wayne held his nose, composed a message, and *gamely* forwarded the odoriferous socks on to Washington.

> "The fleece from which these socks were knit consisted of the loose dead hair of the past year that I had clipped off. The fact of its being dead may have some influence upon the softness of the fabric woven from it."
> Henry C. Wayne, Major, U.S. Army

Dead and smelly, but soft.

Maybe the good officer was hinting at a novel commercial enterprise featuring camel pile as an alternative to woolen fabric.

Nothing doing! Reports surfaced that the Chief Executive, no more able to bear the stench than the nice lady in Texas, ditched the stinkers, but graciously thanked the giver.

Hold yer camel reins jest a minute. Humps in the land o' longhorns?

The whole country was obsessed with western movement. Land! Fortunes! Fresh air! Booming commerce! But it was hard to get there.

Never before had authorities faced such obstacles as those presented by the "tyranny of distance" in the remote and dangerous Southwest.

In 1848, 529,000 square miles had been ceded to America by Mexico in the Treaty of Guadalupe Hidalgo, comprising the territories of Arizona, Nevada, California, Utah, and portions of New Mexico, Wyoming, and Colorado. It was the federal government's task to survey, defend, govern, and supply the vast land grant, but the U.S. Army found itself stretched beyond its means in that big back yard. The challenges of desert terrain, hostiles, and a lack of forage and water were overwhelming. Rail travel in the West was not expected for decades. (Many chuckled at the idea of trains crossing the nation.)

U.S. Secretary of War Jefferson Davis nudged forward an idea which had been floating around in D.C. for a number of years. Perhaps an "army" of camels could overcome some of the headaches "out there." Davis himself had spent some time in the West on various assignments; other officials had seen camels in use overseas and weighed in favorably on the suggestion of importing the large beasts.

> "Possibilities unequaled and discouragements unexpected."
>
> Chris Emmett

Camels are known to thrive without water for long periods of time. They do not store water in their humps, but can swallow as much as 25 gallons when available. Fluid loss is prevented by a unique metabolism and body-cooling system; much of the vital liquid is naturally replenished by food plants.

A camel will eat almost anything in the wilderness and carry heavy loads in oppressive heat. Pads on the knees and chest permit kneeling for loading and unloading. And that oversized body! Just right for squelching predatory moves by wild animals and bloodthirsty men in the wilderness. With gentle treatment, the beasts were reputed to be cooperative and docile.

> "The animals seemed content to gnaw on ocotillo, creosote, prickly pear, and catclaw they found along the trail. And although they hauled barrels of water on the expedition for other animals, the camels themselves usually only drank when they came across a stream or a creek."
>
> Michael Morris

In 1855, Congress allocated $30,000 for purchase of camels from the Middle East. Major Wayne, on the naval ship *Supply*, carefully studied the characteristics and habits of the animals; he spoke with zoologists, veterinarians, and handlers along the Mediterranean. Finding healthy, vermin-free beasts was not easy, but at last he bought 33 Bactrian and Dromedary camels. Meanwhile, Lt. David Dixon Porter saw to it that the *Supply* was suitably outfitted with stables, hoists, slings, and special hatches – preparations that insured the comfort and safety of the camels during stormy days at sea.

After three months of what must have been a unique ocean voyage, the Major unloaded 34 camels at Matagorda Bay, near the Texas port of Indianola in 1856. One male had died aboard ship, but two calves were born, a net increase of one camel. The beasts, it was observed, were in better shape after the boat trip than before. Eight Greek handlers accompanied the unusual cargo.

The next year, a second shipment deposited 41 camels and five additional drovers. Safe in Texas, but *where* would those galumphing quadrupeds be permanently situated?

Wrangling over details led at last to the choice of Camp Verde, located beside an Army road from San Antonio to El Paso. The small encampment edged by Verde Creek was suitably remote, replete with ample grassland for grazing, and close to the Guadalupe River with its many feeder streams.

Wayne favored a lengthy time period for training and breeding the animals. (He had, after all, spent months learning about the care and welfare of camels.) Secretary Davis had immediate and far-reaching military purposes in mind. Because of his higher position, Davis prevailed.

But first, a test. A camel easily rose up with over 1200 pounds on its back. Then six camels carried 600 pounds of supplies each from San Antonio in half the time it would have taken 12 horses and six wagons. The officials were amazed!

The Camel Corps conquered rough mountain trails and wretched roads that wagons could not manage. Only slippery slopes and water crossings gave trouble; the desert dwellers did not know how to ford a stream. As pack animals, they proved their stamina, hauling heavy bundles thirty miles a day. Bactrians, with a single hump, supported a saddle. Loads on Dromedaries were secured between their dual humps.

Of primary importance to the Army was the construction of a 1200-mile wagon road from Texas to California. Military posts and supply stations along the new route were expected to give the nation its foothold in the Southwest. The camels would be utilized as beasts of burden in the layout of the road and thereafter as "ships of the desert" up and down the trail, transporting freight such as munitions, salt, dry goods, water, and mail.

Edward F. Beale, long familiar with the American West, was appointed by President Buchanan to survey and build the strip. In June of 1857, he set out with 44 soldiers, a train of mule-drawn wagons, 25 camels, and experienced camel drovers Greek George and Haiji Ali. ("Hí-gee Ah-leé"). In Texas, Ali's name morphed into "Hi Jolly."

At first, Beale balked at the presence of camels, but quickly came to appreciate their vigor, saying he'd rather have one camel than four mules. It's recounted that the kind-hearted Beale painstakingly learned some Arabic words for conversational use so the animals might "feel more at home!"

> "My admiration for the camels increases daily...they pack water for others for days under a hot sun and never get a drop, they pack grain and oats for a month and never get a grain. On the bitter greasewood and worthless shrubs, they not only subsist, but keep fat."
>
> Lt. Edward F. Beale

Beale's Wagon Road – America's first federal highway – was not grand by any scale. Only ten feet wide, with rocks pushed to the side, it was used during three decades as the main path for freight and military travel in the Southwest and by countless sheep and cattle herders until the completion of a rail line in 1883. Beale himself traversed the finished trail many times to make improvements.

Today, the old wagon road lives on! The Santa Fe Railroad, Route 66, and Interstate 40 closely follow its course.

Within four years, though, the Camel Corps experiment was over.

The American Civil War splintered the nation. Jefferson Davis took on the Presidency of Confederate states, and Texas seceded from the Union. The U.S. Army shut down Camp Verde, abandoned its camels, and recalled the post's soldiers to support the Northern cause.

During the war, some of the animals were useful in transporting goods within the blockaded state of Texas; a few hauled personal baggage and carried mail around the Southwest. Afterwards, most were sold or turned out to fend for themselves.

Loose camels in Arizona tolerated the soft sand and arid climate of that territory, and a few camel drivers had small enterprises, far away from the rocks and thorny brush of West Texas, which had contributed to the obstinance of the beasts. Sightings continued well into the 1900s, including a number of bizarre accounts of an oversized "Red Ghost" that upended cowboy camps and supposedly killed a woman at her water well before being shot by a farmer in his turnip patch.

Some said the camel experiment was crushed prematurely under the feet of bitter combat. In the end, though, overlooked cultural factors likely would have jinxed the program regardless of the nation's tumult.

Americans were *horsemen*, and they used mules as necessary. Not camels. When camels were thrust upon them, many men refused to have anything to do with them. Camels became increasingly impossible to load; the beasts simply won't move if the burden is too heavy. The ordeal of reluctant novices packing and unpacking tall, ungainly critters "with an attitude" can only be imagined. Injuries resulted for men and beasts alike; nervous camels and swearing men were a volatile mix.

The smell. Soldiers assigned to the beasts couldn't bear it. The men lost their tempers, and the camels responded by spitting and blowing out the bloody linings of their stomachs or shrieking at a pitch loud enough to "drive off a pack of wolves."

Businessmen balked at the competition posed by camels and feared financial disaster should their sales of horses, mules, and tack supplies drop precipitously. Likewise, farriers, blacksmiths, and the animals they supported were increasingly uneasy around the imposters. All that racket and the gawky mass of reeking, screeching monster beasts – well, it was just too much.

A decade beyond the camel experiment, train tracks crisscrossed the nation, connecting East and West.

Hello, Iron Horse.

Neither men nor domestic creatures gave any slack to the interloping camels. The animals must not have been in the conversation when old-timer Odie Faulk said, "Tolerate a mule, but respect a horse." We can only imagine his comments if camels had been mentioned.

A Los Angeles newspaper in 1858 noted that Beall's camels

"came to town, giving the streets quite an Oriental aspect...far-off associations where the desert is as boundless as the ocean and the camel is the ship thereof."

The Mexican Cession (529,000 square miles) identifies territory ceded to the U.S. in the Treaty of Guadalupe Hidalgo, 1848. It was the third-largest land acquisition in U.S. history; only the Louisiana Purchase (820,000 square miles) and the Territory of Alaska acquisition (586,000 square miles) were greater in size.

Hi Jolly resumed using his Greek name Philip Tedro after he became a naturalized American citizen. In 38 years following the camel program, he worked as an Army pack master, scout, and guide; he may have operated a freighting business and carried "Jackass Mail." Tedro died in Arizona in 1902.

Archaeologists maintain that camels inhabited part of the North-American continent in the far-ancient past, having migrated across the land bridge from Asia. Eventually, camels died out on this side of the world; the last of the native species disappeared in California 15,000 years ago.

"We had a good time before the wreck."
Frank Barnes, crew-member

IT'S FIVE O'CLOCK...

It was not your ordinary gimmick.

William George Crush was a passenger-services agent for the Missouri-Kansas-Texas Railway. His friendship with circus showman P.T. Barnum might explain Mr. Crush's comical stunt designed to bring in some cash for the railroad while entertaining the masses on a sunny day in September, 1896.

By an odd twist of history, "Crush" was George's actual surname; the one-day "city" he established in Central Texas bore his clever moniker.

In that ephemeral hamlet, on an appointed day, George Crush was set to host the intentional head-on collision of two locomotives bolting toward each other on the same track. "Katy" officials of the M-K-T *approved the zany plan*. Working secretly for days, a crew of 500 had constructed a four-mile spur alongside the north-south tracks of the Katy about 14 miles north of Waco.

With the emergence of high-speed rail travel in the late nineteenth century, transportation accidents were bound to be spectacular, and many were horrifying. On the other hand, so-called victimless wrecks drew enormous crowds seeking cheap amusement.

On September 15, passenger trains full of guests rolled into Crush, Texas, one after another, the cars having filled up so quickly that latecomers rode on top. The temporary town boasted more "population," estimated at 40,000, than the city of Dallas.

Giddy spectators were "wowed" by the amenities.

Free admission. Cool drinking water. Carnival booths and a medicine show. Cheap snacks on the grounds or dinner inside a lofty circus tent. Cut-rate train fares for transportation to and from Crush. Political speeches, of course. Grassy slopes for casual comfort of the seated masses.

(Dignitaries were accommodated on grandstands.)

All guests, though, were welcomed equally through a specially-built depot identifying "Crush, Texas."

"Oh, but it's going to be smashing!"
George Crush

Newspaper articles, posters, and promotional tours around the state had kept the fervor alive for months. Wrapped in bright banners, pop-star Engines 999 (green with red trim) and 1001 (red with green trim) were paraded up and down the M-K-T rail line, to the adulation of cheering fans.

A celebratory atmosphere, spiked with illegal alcohol and the near-mania of rising excitement, moved into late afternoon. Though the party site was in a dry precinct, liquor was smuggled in, giving dozens of special constables the predictable task of hauling unruly folks to a makeshift jail.

The ballyhooed locomotives stood nose-to-nose for pre-performance photographs. Each pulled six boxcars filled with railroad ties. Then, slowly, the engines backed up two miles in opposite directions for the final run.

Four o'clock. And they're... NOT... off!

The inevitable delay. Spectators crowding too close to the rails had to be pushed back repeatedly. Late-arriving trains full of onlookers stretched out the time. Then...

Five o'clock. And they're off!

> "The rumble of the two trains...was like the gathering force of a cyclone...the whistles of each blowing repeatedly and torpedoes that had been placed on the track exploding in almost a continuous round like the rattle of musketry."
> *The Dallas Morning News*

Good sense made a brief appearance in that both engineers and their crews jumped off just before impact.

Having reached a speed of 45 miles per hour each, the locomotives collided "like twin bombs." It took only two minutes.

> "Words and Kodaks [cameras] are powerless."
> Newspaper reporter

Though the crash occurred at the intended spot, the engines had been expected to rise separately upward on impact, trailing their cars safely behind like a folding hand fan. Either a serious miscalculation or a freak mishap caused the cars to jam together, resembling a duet of collisions into a solid wall.

Both boilers erupted at once. Scraps of iron, wood, and steel (stamp-size to driving-wheel size) sailed into the crowd bunched together behind the ropes. Scalding steam sprayed as far as 300 yards from the track.

Two young people were killed by "black clouds of death-dealing iron." A third spectator died after falling between two rail cars on his way home. Many others suffered traumatic injuries from heat or flying debris. A hundred yards away on a press platform, the official photographer was slammed by a bolt that pieced an eye and landed in his brain. (The pieces of metal were eventually removed and he returned to work, but his eye was lost.)

In his travels with the Katy, Agent Crush had witnessed several train mishaps and noticed that crowds gathered quickly at disaster sites. His scheme in Texas may have hatched from those memories, nourished by thoughts of money to be made from large groups of curious onlookers. Admission was free, but the excursion fares, though moderate, generated a nice profit for the Katy.

On a practical note, the crash was a quick way to rid the company of a pair of outdated 35-ton locomotives; newer engines had been enlarged to 60 tons. Some of the fifty "oldies" had been sent to gravel or logging operations, but too many remained, cluttering the rail yard.

By no means had preparations for the Crush event been ship-shod. The spot was carefully situated in a rural area along the Katy right-of-way to entertain thousands of observers seated a safe distance from the wreck. Two wells were dug and water piped to dozens of faucets for the crowd's convenience.

The two engines, with a third as backup, had been thoroughly checked for mechanical problems, while speed tests determined the exact point of collision. Engineers had assured the planners that the trains' boilers could not explode.

Rails connecting the spur to the regular line had been removed beforehand to avoid the possibility of out-of-control cars careening into the crowd. The cars themselves, usually connected by couplers, were chained together. A sturdy fence was erected; only news reporters and a few officials were allowed within 100 yards of the impact point.

So safe – it seemed.

By midnight on September 15, 1896, the town of Crush was no more.

William Crush was fired on the spot by the M-K-T, but unobtrusively rehired the next day. He shed his flamboyance and finished a 57-year career with the railroad company.

The usual lawsuits were settled by the Katy and all seemed forgiven. Travelers excitedly filled the company's trains for months to come.

The "Crash at Crush" entered the realm of oft-told tales.

In 1865, thirty-one years before Crush, an explosion ripped apart the *Sultana*, a steamship carrying an unknown number of Union soldiers up the Mississippi River. The men had been freed from Confederate prisons and were returning home, but the boat was grossly overloaded. 1700 died from the explosion or by drowning as the craft sank. At that time, it was the largest loss of life due to a maritime accident in our country's history.

Steam-engine boilers are pressure tanks with water heated by coal, wood, or oil fires, so that the water turns to steam; the expansion that results creates pressure through pipes to the pistons and cylinders of the engine's drive wheels.

Amazingly, planned train crashes occasionally were staged following the disaster at Crush, particularly a large event in California in 1913. In none of these succeeding stunts did boilers fail.

"Light as air, stronger than whiskey, cheaper than dirt."
John W. Gates

THE THORNY FENCE

John and Pete's long stagecoach ride ended in San Antonio on a February day. After settling in at the Menger Hotel, the two strolled about the old town whose colorful history weaves together Native, Spanish, Mexican, and Anglo settlement, the siege of Bexar, and the fall of the Alamo.

By 1876, San Antonio had emerged as the central point of cattle business in the Lone Star State, and a big enterprise it was, considering all of those Texas longhorns.

John Gates and Pete McManus had a product to sell, but they were *Yankees* and the product was "twisted fence wire having a transverse wire," or, more familiarly, barbed wire. Few Texans had seen such a phenomenon; you couldn't scrape together a handful who believed it had any merit whatsoever.

Just a couple of years previously, Joseph Farwell Glidden, a DeKalb, Illinois, farmer, had received a patent for his fence wire with sharp barbs.

"The Winner," he named it.

Glidden had observed a clever, but inefficient, spike-and-wire fence at the county fair and was convinced, in the entrepreneurial spirit, that he could do better. Back home, in answer to his wife Lucinda's request for a fence to protect her garden, Joseph borrowed the kitchen's coffee mill to make barbs and a grindstone to twist together two wires holding the sharp points.

Barbed wire was born.

Midwest farmers had been dismayed to find, as they moved onto the prairies and plains, scarce trees for fence wood and too few stones for walls. Newcomers planted hedgerows of thorny bushes such as Osage orange or briars, but scrubby natural fences were slow to grow tall enough for usefulness and they easily multiplied out of control, fueling prairie fires. Timber, had it been available, had its own drawbacks. Wood must be cut, gathered, and hauled; it was susceptible to insect infestation; like scrub, it was tinder for fire.

Early cattle operations in the West, as a result, were an open-range situation. Stock mingled freely, cattle drives passed unhindered to railroads in Kansas and Missouri, and Plains Indians roamed seasonally at will.

Glidden's wire changed all that.

He took in hardware merchant Isaac Ellwood as a partner in The Barb Fence Company. Glidden's uncomplicated product was readily suitable for mass production. Ten thousand pounds of barbed wire were sold in 1874, the first year of business, 13 million pounds in 1877, and 80.5 million pounds in 1880.

Zinc wire avoids rot; it's fireproof, long-lasting, and easily installed. Floods might dislodge the wire, but it won't fall apart. Though barbed wire's advantages are obvious, the average rancher expressed a stony indifference to a new way of fencing. In the big and cattle-heavy state of Texas, demand for barbed wire remained, overall, depressingly stagnant.

Enter John and Pete, sent southward to open a new market for "bob wire," in Texas-speak. They'd chosen the Alamo City for their crusade and purposely headed away from their luxury hotel to seek out ordinary, hard-working ranchers congregated in the saloons and lobbies of more modest facilities.

Gates' reputation as an enthusiastic talker notwithstanding, the man needed a dramatic presentation to sell the strange-looking wire to skeptical stockmen. One evening, he strolled into a glitzy medicine show featuring an energetic hawker named Doc Lighthall. The theatrics gave Gates an idea for a little drama in his own spiel.

John and Pete rented the old Military Plaza in the center of San Antonio, where they fastened four rows of their barbed wire onto widely-separated posts, forming a makeshift corral. Then they ushered in some wild Texas Longhorn cattle (anywhere from 35 to 125 head; reports, as usual, vary). The two "showmen" may have offered $10 to the owner of each bovine that broke through the fence, but it's a moot point because NO cattle escaped.

Not one.

Sales exploded. By late evening, a year's production was under contract!

Texas Panhandle cattle operations, due to their immense size, had embraced barbed wire early on. The Frying Pan, JA, and XIT ranches were showcase examples of the barbs' usefulness. 800 miles of wire encircled the XIT property; cross fences brought the total length to 1500 miles of wire fence.

> "...an area so vast that many wild creatures including buffalo, mustangs, antelope, and deer lived in it for years without ever knowing they were prisoners."
> Paul I. Wellman

Closing the open range was not always a smooth trail. In time, stockmen acknowledged the obvious benefits of enclosed pastures to keep their animals in and predators out. The bloodlines of their registered stock were safe-guarded in a secure pen that, as a bonus, served as a visual reminder of private land not open for sale or trespass. Farmers and planters gradually came to employ the reliable fencing to protect their animals, crops, and gardens.

Nonetheless, "free-grassers" objected to closed-off properties, and access to water was perennially an issue. Cattle drovers regretted giving up the practice of moving their herds over sweeping, unhindered spaces. Range wars and fence-cutting burdened law-enforcement agencies. In a serious turn of events, barbed-wire "drift fences" proved ruinous, threatening the future of the popular wire.

Each winter, northern cattle instinctively wandered southward toward Texas for shelter in valleys and canyons. To prevent overstocking of stressed grasslands and to avoid the yearly waste of time spent separating herds, Panhandle ranchers came up with the idea of attaching four or five strands of barbed wire onto east-west fence posts to prevent the southerly drift. By 1885, makeshift fences crossed the Texas South Plains from New Mexico to Oklahoma.

In December of that year, blinding blizzards forced wayward cows to the south, as usual, but this time they became entrapped against the new drift fences. Cattle by the thousands were lost – frozen, crushed, dehydrated, starved, or destroyed by predators. The "Big Die-Up" occurred again the next winter, when some ranchers lost up to 75% of their herds. After a few years, a varied design with less-vicious barbs and easier-to-see wire lessened the catastrophic losses. Gradually, those drift-prone cattle became more settled.

The other dilemmas solved themselves, as well. Closed-in pastures became routine. Line-riding cowboys became fence-riders (with pliers in their jeans pockets for repairs). New state laws prohibited fence-cutting. Cattle drives ended with the expansion of railroad transportation. Indians of the Plains moved to reservations, no longer free to ramble at will.

Sadly, not too many years after barbed wire found success on farms and ranches, it also gained popularity on the Europe's Western Front during World War I. By war's end, a million miles of wire had been laid as traps by both sides, enough to circle the earth forty times. Before tanks were developed to overcome the sharps and tangles of barbed wire, soldiers used rubber mats to walk on the wire or volunteered to lie down on the spikes as their comrades marched over their bodies.

On a lighter note, a former mayor of Cimarron, Kansas, describes his misadventure as a young rancher needing a bit of barbed wire. He deemed it acceptable, as many did, to "borrow" a top wire from the fence of a large cattle company in the area. As he was quietly unstapling and rolling his small bundle, he felt a tug and discovered that someone on the other side of the hill was collecting the same top wire. It was the town's Methodist preacher.

Joseph Glidden, who produced "not the first or last, but the most successful barbed wire," sold his business interests to partner Ellwood, who, in turn, transferred the company to another firm; eventually, U.S. Steel Corporation absorbed the enterprise and its patents. Thus, production of Joseph Glidden's "game-changing" wire shifted from a small workshop in DeKalb, Illinois, to a giant manufacturer in the East.

> "It takes no room, exhausts no soil, shades no vegetation, is proof against high winds, makes no snowdrifts, and is both durable and cheap."
>
> A fan of barbed wire

Glidden's patent for the machine adding barbs to wire was #157,124.

The South has its own way of pronouncing words, including "barbed wire." It's "bobbed wire" in the Deep South and "bob wire" in Texas and the Southwest.

A former teacher, inventor Joseph Glidden donated 63 acres of his land for Northern Illinois Normal School, which opened in 1928. The name was changed to Northern Illinois University in 1957.

John "Bet-a-Million" Gates was quite a promoter and gambler, acquiring the nickname from his outrageous bets, many of which he won. He once wagered a bundle on which raindrop would reach the bottom of a train window first. And with a partner, he's said to have bet $1 million on a horse named Royal Flush at the Goodwood Race Track in London. (Actually, the bet was $70,000 and the payoff was $600,000. No complaints.)

Gates liked fishing and duck hunting on the Texas coast; he invested heavily in the community of Port Arthur. Additionally, Gates was one of the founders of The Texas Company, shortened to "Texaco," and he provided operating capital and a shipping facility for the 1901 Spindletop oil strike.

"What kept crops and animals apart helped bring people together."

David B. Sicilia

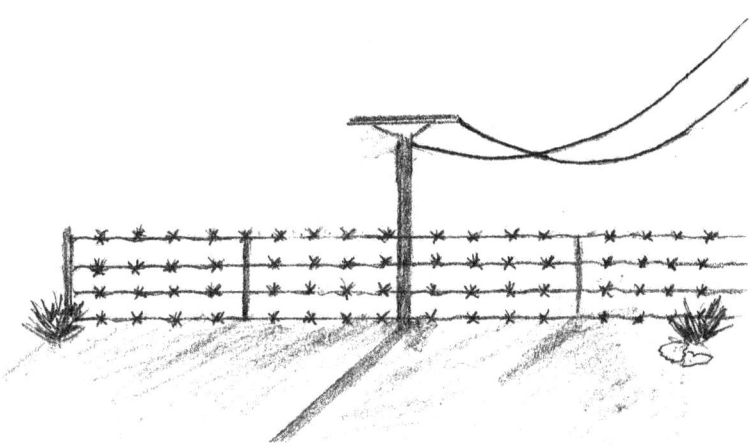

THE LITTLE WIRES THAT COULD

In a rather unique "twist," barbed wire was a harbinger of "talking wires" about to blossom in America's countryside, enabling hundreds of thousands of farmers to translate their *fencing* revolution to a *communications* revolution.

About the time the American West was being enclosed by miles and miles of Joseph Glidden's barbed fencing, Alexander Graham Bell transmitted a signal via thin wire to an adjacent room, and the telephone became reality – in major cities, that is.

Typical of the usual apathy toward an underserved populace desiring utility services, agrarian America was deemed unprofitable for the infrastructure necessary in telephone operations. In the 1880s, 70% of America's population was rural, leaving innumerable households silent in their isolation.

Leave it to enterprising farmers and ranchers to be part of the action! They simply used the barbed wire *out there on their fences* to "get 'er done."

> "Some savvy genius discovered that, if you hooked two Sears and 'Monkey' Ward telephone sets to the top wire of a barbed-wire fence, you could talk between the telephones as easily as between two 'town' phones connected by a slick wire through an operator's switchboard. A rural telephone system that had no operator, no bills – and no long-distance charges – was born."
>
> C.F. Eckhardt

Yep, savvy country folks figured that "wire is wire" and there you go. With free access and totally unconnected to Ma Bell, talk was indeed cheap.

It was the top fence wire that was used. Since most properties shared barbed fences or joined others at corners (with the wire intertwined for strength), a network was easy to set up. Crossing a gap or a road was accomplished by burying insulated wires or planting a couple of tall posts three feet into the ground to string wire overhead from a fence on one side to a fence across the way.

> "This network, owned by no one, was a model of democracy, openness, and free speech."
>
> Bob Holmes

Once Bell's patent on his telephone box expired, the sets could be purchased from mail-order catalogs. Those early-day machines were the now-antique wooden wall boxes with bells and cranks for initiating calls. Without a central switchboard, every phone in the network would ring at once because there were no individual telephone numbers. If talk was cheap, listening was even cheaper.

Each home was assigned its own signal – three short rings or two short and one long, for example. Everyone else was expected to hang up. Not a chance! It was lonely out there, so eavesdropping on a neighbor's conversation became an irresistible pastime.

> "Some folk quickly learned how to clear nosey neighbors from the line. Ol' Craig Moore, our early-day Trew Ranch foreman, was well known to cuss a lot. When he cranked out his call, Craig waited till everyone on the party line picked up their receivers, then announced, 'All you old biddies better hang up, 'cause I'm gonna talk about castrating a [expletive] stud horse.' The hang-up clicks that followed in rapid succession provided virtually unheard-of private conversation."
> Delbert Trew

The makeshift communications system was suddenly elevated into a genuine entertainment medium. (Social networking is nothing new.)

> "People would read the newspaper over the telephone. They'd have musical nights where someone would play a banjo [and] someone else would sing..."
> Rob MacDougall

> "Picnics, hayrides, and dances were planned and arrangements made. At the end of the social hour, a favorite song, such as 'Good Night, Ladies, Good Night, Gentlemen' was sung by all."
> Dick Violette

Maybe, in old movies, you've seen someone rush to the telephone box on the wall and rapidly turn the crank five or six times. That was the forerunner of our modern 9-1-1 system.

> "A shared line could even be a rudimentary broadcast system where a single long ring would signal a 'line

call,' an announcement of interest to everyone in the system – the weather report, livestock prices, a train's arrival time, or an emergency."

Rob MacDougall

Copper wire would've worked better than barbed-wire's zinc-covered steel, but, for the average farmer, the free use of his own equipment made a lot of sense. In rain or snow, however, phone signals grew dim with static because wires stapled directly to fence posts "grounded" the system, which remained inoperable until it all dried out.

Ingenuity again came to the rescue in the form of homemade insulators. While leather straps, corn cobs, and tire rubber acted in a pinch, the best ones were made of glass, and the local saloon had plenty of empty liquor and wine bottles out back. (At least they did before Prohibition. Glass snuff jars worked just as well during that time; lots of people had those.)

Here's the technique for a bottle insulator. Break off the neck. Stuff the bottle with cork or a wooden peg shaved to fit. Drill holes in the peg and nail it to the fence post. Wrap barbed wire around your new insulator and tie it with baling wire. Problem solved.

There were unexpected bonuses to the country network. If the cows got out, a family knew right away. The phone stopped working.

> "When a bunch of beef steers stampedes and goes through the barbed wire, [the rancher] will know that the line is in need of repair and that the steers are losing flesh by the pound."
>
> *Butte, Montana, Intermountain, 1901*

Large ranches made good use of barbed-wire communication lines to keep in touch with cowboys at far ends of the spread. (Predictably, the cowhands themselves became "telephone technicians" when there was trouble on the line.) Work schedules were confirmed, prairie fires reported, supply lists requested. In Montana, it was recorded that sheep men were notified of approaching winter storms at lambing time, and...

> "...in emergency cases, the rancher can call a physician or a minister, as the case requires. The latter is of particular importance... as some men down there still have the old habit of dying with their boots on."
> *Butte, Montana, Intermountain, 1901*

The major disadvantage of a fence-line system was the lack of a central operator and, therefore, no contact with the outside world. Ever-innovative, many rural networks evolved into telephone cooperatives, or "co-ops," which set up switch boards close to town. The operator, perhaps a farm wife who was paid for the job, would be able to hook up her rural network with the nearby regular system and the world beyond her kitchen.

But country folks went to bed at dark, including the operator, so callers expected to be off-line from early evening to early morning – *and* on Sundays, *and* if there was a big party Saturday night.

> "Barbed-wire fences still abound today to keep people out. For a few decades, though, barbed wire brought people, not apart, but together."
> Sarah Zhang

Eventually, by the 1920s, the formal telephone-company systems caught on to the clever chicanery of barbed-wire talk, and well they should. At the height, those tricky independent networks embraced three million happy members lapping up that open and free communication.

"Ma Bell," which for many years controlled nearly all the commercial telephone service in America, annexed the rural population to its for-profit networks. In some places, though, makeshift systems existed into the 1940s.

> "Any chore, no matter how important, could wait when the phone rang. Families fought for a listening position. We had a neighbor woman confined to a wheelchair who seemed able to stand when the phone rang. When invitations to a party went out, everyone who had eavesdropped showed up."
>
> Delbert Trew

Rural phone networks worked similarly to cooperatives, and America's farmers relish a long history with "co-ops." These beneficial organizations continue their important role in today's world of American agriculture, including production and marketing, credit unions, purchasing, and electric-power associations, all owned by the members they serve.

David B. Sicilia sums it up:

> "The transverse spur wire of Glidden soon became the most popular variety of fencing in the arid and semi-arid region stretching west from the 98th meridian to the Rockies...This ubiquitous fencing, in turn, became the infrastructure for an extensive web of "talking wires connecting thousands of American farmers."

"The quality of the meat depended on the appetite of the man."

Francis Aubrey

DINNER BELL

What's for dinner?

In the Old West, it was more than the casual query of modern times.

Out yonder, mealtime came up short when compared to the pleasant diversion of a cozy home kitchen. On a brighter note, nature offered a panorama of exotic flavors – the marketplace of all outdoors.

Those entering the frontier with full knapsacks found their provisions rapidly diminishing as days went by. For others, diets depended upon nature from the start. Hunting, fishing, and foraging were open to all, the odds of finding food mostly reliant on the seeker's skill.

In years to come, trading posts, bartering, and springing-up towns replenished supplies. America's first cannery opened in New

York in 1812; the industry steadily improved over the years, boosted by an ever-widening transportation network. Canned tomatoes in the Panhandle! Pork and beans headed west!

Modern food processing unfolded too late for the earliest adventurers into the American West and just a few years beyond Lewis and Clark's expedition.

With exquisite planning, President Jefferson's explorers had packed 193 pounds of dehydrated soup and seven tons of staples such as coffee, sugar, salt, flour, beans, dried apples, parched cornmeal, and lard. Beyond these stores, the acquisition of something to eat was an ongoing, repetitive quest.

Hunting in the wild offered a beneficial source of protein, whether the meat was consumed raw or dried. Modern nutritionists have determined that a diet of meat alone, with sufficient fat to provide calories, was capable of sustaining good health among the adventurers, without scurvy or a shortage of calcium.

Diaries reveal that the 33 travelers fed on hundreds of deer, 227 bison, 375 elk, 35 big-horned sheep, 3 grizzlies, 23 black bear, 113 beaver, 16 otter, 62 antelope, and one passenger pigeon. (Chewing fatty beaver tails seemed a treat.) Eighteen wolves were killed for safety reasons; a single one was consumed, likely out of desperation. Protein took a back seat during a brief "starving time" when the explorers were reduced to eating candles.

Many days, there were unnumbered hawks, crows, eagles, turtles, gophers, grouse, foxes, geese, ocean-shore brant, otters, rabbits, plovers, coyotes, and the occasional muskrat. Fishing yielded trout and, on the West Coast, seal, mussels, salmon, crabs, and whale blubber, the latter offered by Native-American Clatsop.

Not so tasty were 12 horses and 190 dogs purchased from Natives. Nearly every trapper, explorer, hunter, or Indian fighter at some time would be in the quandary of deciding whether he needed his horse or mule more for transportation or for food. "Food" usually won out if the situation was truly dreadful. Mule meat was new to most men and some could not tolerate it.

"When times get hard, any meat is good."
J. Frank Dobie

Each explorer required about nine pounds of meat per day for the difficult, straining tasks at hand, but many nights found the men abed with growling stomachs. Meat in the process of drying often was soaked by heavy rain; wretched heat ruined perishables; firewood could not be found; not every gunshot hit its mark; game, as always, found a way to hide. Food possibilities changed with the terrain, the seasons, and weather.

The party was overjoyed to find wild mushrooms, grapes, plums, seeds, pine nuts, and berries along the way. Sacagawea gathered edible, safe plants and roots (currants, wild onions) unfamiliar to the white men. Her husband Toussaint Charbonneau, mostly an incompetent team member, saved face somewhat by modifying the French sausage *boudin blanc* with a stuffing of buffalo intestine. The meat itself produced suet (fat) dumplings. From friendly Indians, the men purchased or traded for squash, beans, corn, wild licorice root, and wapato, a tuber.

In August of 1804, during a meeting with Shoshone chief Cameahwait, Captain Lewis found little food for entertaining a guest. A lot was at stake; the travelers were depending upon the purchase of Shoshone horses for portage over the Rockies as fall rapidly approached. Lewis delegated someone to cook wild berries and flour (perhaps with a little fat) in a skillet to accompany the small amount of pork meat that remained. What was called "a new fashion of pudding" impressed the chief, who deemed it the best thing he had eaten in a long time. We'd call it a "cobbler."

Over a long winter at Fort Clatsop on the West Coast, expedition members devised a process for extracting salt from ocean water. They boiled the water to the stage of evaporation, leaving a valuable supply of sodium for the remainder of the cold season and the upcoming return to St. Louis. Salt was valuable as a body nutrient, for flavoring, and, crucially, in the process of curing and preserving meat.

In company with most outdoor novices, the explorers drank liberally of water from rivers, creeks, and streams, with the usually-expected results of stomach cramps and worse. In the mountains, melted snow was a regular thirst-quencher.

Before and after the era of Lewis and Clark, solitary mountain men in the West found no ease in procuring food and water. Provisions having run short, they ate rattlesnake meat and munched crickets and handfuls of ants or roots. One group was so low on rations that they mixed flour with muddy river water. Jedediah Smith came upon Indians pounding grasshoppers with stones.

On better days, hunters found the usual wild animals – turkey, deer and elk, rabbits, bear, antelope, and bison. Like the explorers, trappers favored tough and fatty beaver tail, a readily-available fare.

Bison (commonly called "buffalo") was the staple food of Native Americans on the Great Plains. Though rich and wild of taste, bison meat seemed to rest easy on men's digestive systems. Too heavy to hang or turn over, the slaughtered beast lay on its stomach as hunters cut from neck to tail, pulled back the skin, and let each diner cut the pieces he preferred. Tongues were slowly roasted in the coals of a fire and livers dipped in body fluids. Humps, hump ribs, bones, marrow, and testicles required boiling. Innards were scorched over campfire flames.

From the buffalo's back came the most-favored fat, dried by the sun or by roasting. Pounded with meat, it produced the Natives' most-valuable staple, pemmican. Kidney lard ground with corn, if corn was grown or obtained in trade, made a similar product. A stew of meat, roots, herbs, or wild vegetables could be found simmering in every lodge. As cooks have done through the ages, Natives added to the soup almost anything edible that was brought through the door. Even underneath a heavy snowpack, tidbits usually could be found for the meat stew.

Over the Oregon Trail crept one of history's largest and longest land migrations. 1840s emigrants hunted and fished as they could, but the ox-drawn wagons heavy with household goods traveled very slowly and time could not be spared for much besides "moving on." Accordingly, most of the food required for many months was transported along with the load.

Milk cows in the wagon train were a dairy on the hoof. The rough wagon ride with its continuous motion wasn't so pleasant for a traveler, but the jolting motion efficiently churned butter through the day. Since most overland migration was undertaken in warm months, bread dough steadily rose, ready to be baked at the evening camp. Flour cooked with butter and wild berries made a fine, flaky pie.

Pressed to move forward as far as possible during daylight hours, emigrants assembled a simple breakfast and lunch of beans, pancakes, corn mush, and, perhaps, a slice of fried meat. Dried fruit brought from home made the snack a little sweeter. By nightfall, the glowing fireside was a welcome respite in anticipation of a more pleasant meal.

Randolph B. Marcy's handbook for overland travel recommended a good supply of fruits and vegetables, thinly sliced and dried in an oven prior to the journey, then rehydrated in boiling water at mealtime. Marcy mentioned horsemint or wild mint as a substitute for coffee. Cooking-by-place-and-season was his theme! Curiously, he suggested sprinkling gunpowder on a steak to be fried, much like salt and pepper. To say the least, the steak would be well-seared on the outside.

There's rarely a mention of ice in the weeks and months of migration. Had some type of insulated carrier been available, the extra weight would have been unacceptable. Burlap-wrapped barrels were as cool as anything on board; spring or river water offered a temporary chill.

Butter and meat safely soaked in salt brine – butter infinitely and meat for a short while, longer in winter. (The process was called "corning.") In warm weather, cow's milk was used right away unless it had been canned for the journey; raw eggs were perishable, but they could be boiled or pickled. There are anecdotes of snow mixed with sweet milk as an ice-cream treat – a small reward for difficulties in crossing the mountains.

Settled in their new homes, families planted vegetable gardens and raised farm animals and poultry. Outside the farmyard was the bounty of the wild, flush with meat from deer to duck, wilderness fruits, greens, mushrooms, and herbs for kitchen sideboards. "Sarvis" berries (serviceberries) were good for headache and nausea. A decent flour could be made from ground mesquite beans. Along with storage in root cellars, bottling in jars sufficed for preservation, as did "potting" (placing food under thick pastry or fat).

A barn and smokehouse were built early-on for a settler family and it was not unusual for several families to share a single smokehouse. Cold fall and winter days were the chosen time for butchering pigs and hogs, yielding hams, chops, and bacon. Warm salt was rubbed into the pork until no moisture was visible, and a little sugar was added, if handy. Then the meat was hung from the ceiling of the smokehouse for exposure to a corn-cob fire providing little flame but a lot of smoke. Neighbors using a friend's smokehouse typically left part of the meat as payment for the smoking. As villages grew closer together, goods and foods (eggs, meat, poultry, fish, antelope) were traded.

⁂ ⁂

By mid-century, miners packed their water buckets, forks and spoons, iron skillets, tin plates and cups, the ever-present coffee pot, and scooted headlong to whatever boom or bust awaited. Like their explorer and trapper predecessors, miners entered the wilderness carrying whatever food supplies they could muster ahead of time – salt pork, dried beef, beans, and rice. Coffee beans were purchased whole and pounded in a buckskin or canvas bag until they were ground fine enough for use. Brandy, likely homemade, was popular.

Feverishly searching for gold and silver, most men did not take time to hunt and cook. Though wild game and cold-river salmon and trout were abundant, many lived on little more than a mush of cheap flour and water. Scurvy was widespread in nutrient-poor diets; wild lettuce, orange marmalade, and potatoes soaked in vinegar helped prevent the scourge. Fresh fruits and vegetables were rarely found in the lofty bonanza mountains of the West, while large numbers of growers in California abandoned their lush produce fields to "get rich" in the mines.

The workers' primitive bread was no treat; "hardtack" was mostly a combo of flour, salt, and cream of tartar. Worse, miners were occasionally observed washing their grimy clothes in the water bucket or bread pan! Sourdough bread, said to have been introduced by the Boudin family of France, soon became a San Francisco staple. "Hangtown fry," an expensive omelet of eggs combined with bacon, oysters, or assorted other ingredients, satisfied those able to afford it. Successful miners "ate out" in hotels and restaurants before most Americans adopted the habit.

Commodities in mining communities were outrageously overpriced, with a single slice of bread or one egg selling for a dollar. In many cases, Chinese workers in the mines and on the railroad taught the "locals" a thing or two about wholesome food choices as they brought in fresh supplies of fish and vegetables from California's coast.

As cattle country developed, early roundups found each cowboy toting his own food – coffee, cold cornbread, biscuits – in a sack or saddle bag. On extended scouting campaigns, food supplies were carried by mule. Hardtack was softened somewhat by coffee, hot water, and bacon drippings. Dry kernels coated in oil and scattered in a hot skillet yielded parched corn.

Charles Goodnight, later a pioneer rancher in the Texas Panhandle, joined many a ranging party in his early days on the Plains, where meat was the main fare. Since most of the rabbits in the wild were eaten by wolves, prairie dog was the usual meat on a plate. Fat ones made an acceptable stew, he said, but it was not filling; the fellows were hungry again in a couple of hours.

Ignoring the guffaws of his men, Goodnight made a habit of collecting bacon skins from the first days of a trip on the range, when the bacon was still in good supply. When meat choices dwindled, he would broil the rinds for a meal, which the naysayers were eager to eat.

> "A command could be carried farther with a little flour soup and meat than anything else."
> Charles Goodnight

On the serious matter of lack of water, Mr. Goodnight offered counsel.

> "In case of dire thirst, a small pebble in the mouth will help, a bullet is better, a piece of copper, still better, and prickly pear is the best of all... cut off stickers and peel... put in mouth... keeps mouth moist indefinitely."

Once tinned vegetables and fruits became commonplace, his cowboys clamored for canned tomatoes, which they preferred in place of water. The acid, Goodnight observed, sated their thirst and provided a snack boost, as well.

After the Civil War, northern populations demanded Texas beef. Four-dollar-a-head cows went for $40 in large cities in the North and East. Large herds were driven from South Texas ranches over the open range to rail lines in Abilene and Dodge City, Kansas, or to fresh pastures in Montana and Wyoming.

Trail drivers sported Texas-sized appetites. In the early days of trailing, the cook had at his disposal only a cart or wagon, but later in the twenty-year span of the cattle-drive era the familiar chuck wagon appeared – an idea advanced by that notable cattleman, Mr. Goodnight.

Recognizing the importance of appealing and dependable meals for his cowhands, Goodnight started with a surplus iron-axle Army wagon; a wood craftsman added sturdy *bois d'arc* on the sides and a large pantry, or "chuck box," at the rear. The box's hinged lid laid flat for a work surface and collapsible legs made it a table. Shelves stored salt, cornmeal, dried beans, coffee beans, lard, and sourdough starter. Skillets and cooking pots hung below the wagon or rested in a box underneath, and a sling carried wood and cow chips (cut or gathered as the drive moved forward) for fuel. A tool box was mounted on one side and a water barrel on the other. Bedrolls, branding irons, and "war bags" (personal items of the crew) were stowed in the wagon's bed, easily covered in foul weather.

The chuck wagon became "home" for the hard-working cowhands.

For some it was their *only* home – a haven where they relaxed, talked, ate, and slept during six months a year.

In no uncertain terms, the cattle-trail cook was "king" and the chuck wagon was his "domain."

> "On the range the supply of cooks was always low and the demand keen."
>
> Ramon F. Adams

Second only to the trail boss, the cook enforced the rules of the trail and served as doctor, dentist, barber, banker, letter-writer, and, occasionally, referee. He saw to it that no horses preceded the chuck wagon or were tied to its wheels. Paid more than the cowhands, he also got the least amount of sleep, often rising at 3 a.m. to get breakfast underway.

Once the day's route was determined, "Cookie" drove the chuck wagon to the evening camp site in time to weave his magic in time for supper. Simmering the red beans dubbed "Pecos strawberries" or "Whistleberries" with dried salt pork, he'd prepare the meat course. Steak floured and fried in an iron skillet. Catfish, if anglers were lucky. Wild turkeys, deer, and migrating birds. Fragrant onions and crispy potatoes filled out the menu, and maybe there were pickles from a barrel.

When the beef supply ran low, a heifer or stray was killed, and the main dish for a few days was son-of-a-gun stew consisting of tongue, heart, and liver – parts that needed to be eaten quickly. The large slabs of meat were cooled, tightly wrapped, and stored in the wagon.

Cookie whipped up those tasty sourdough biscuits and, often, his one-of-a-kind cobblers. Dried raisins or apples and lucky finds of wild plums and pecans filled the crusts. Another treat was "duff [dough] pudding," featuring raisins, brandy, fruit, and flour. With sugar unavailable, sweetening was done with molasses. Even vinegar, admittedly with a good dose of molasses, made an oddly-pleasing pie. (On one of the few occasions sugar was on hand, a camp visitor was offered some for his coffee. Having never seen the granulated product, the stranger thought it was *salt*. "No thanks," he said.)

Coffee – hot and strong – was the opener for any meal. It was invariably Arbuckle's brand, the popular pre-roasted beans in one-pound bags and plenty of 'em. Basically, a handful of coffee was boiled in water for half an hour, yielding what some dubbed "six-shooter coffee" because it would float a pistol.

Cattle-trail cooks did not expect to have fresh eggs; some outfits carried new-fangled cans of evaporated milk. Now and then a farm family in the wilderness offered to swap some of these commodities for a portion of fresh beef. And, if the herd included cows, trail hands would gladly relieve them of any surplus milk, though it was understood that calves came first in the milk line. One happy day, cowboys came across some wild-turkey eggs and at once sought out a bit of milk for a custard pie.

Sourdough starter remains popular in our time. The old method called for flour, salt, and warm water to be placed in a barrel, set in the sun to ferment, and wrapped in cloth to sustain the warmth. On cold nights, it wasn't unusual for the camp cook to take the barrel to bed with him so the fermentation could continue uninterrupted. When a handful of starter was removed for making pastry, it was replaced by more flour, salt, and water. A batch of starter, if replenished and kept warm, can last for years.

The most essential piece of cooking equipment for early trappers, explorers, cowboys, and settlers was the Dutch oven, a pot similar to an iron skillet, but with high sides, a heavy lid, and a strong wire-bail handle. Stacked with others, buried in a bed of coals, hanging over a hot fire, or resting on a stove, the vessel roasts, fries, stews, and bakes with a steady, even heat. Sturdy, versatile, and indispensable.

"Come and get it!"

J. Frank Dobie cites use of coyote and wild panther as "dinner" in areas void of any other rations. Texas Rangers chasing Comanche raiders in 1874 found coyote preferable to starvation. Besides the usual bear, antelope, deer, and rabbits, Indians in Central Texas deemed rattlesnake a delicacy, and skunks and lizards might also have been devoured. Ben Drake spent several months in an Indian camp, eating dry-land terrapin and dog meat cooked together and was "glad to get it."

Military troops on the frontier endured the same dismal rations soldiers have experienced (and cursed) in any time and place. Though well-established military posts often attempted to cultivate gardens, the results were spotty, at best. It's been said that the general good health of the troops was more likely due to fresh air and vigorous activity than any nourishment provided them. Like the civilians, men in uniform often fulfilled their own food needs by hunting, fishing, and foraging in bountiful nature.

That innovative New York cannery in 1812 offered "sealed" fruits and vegetables, fish and meat. By mid-century, canned, packaged, and prepared foods were hauled across the country via stagecoach and, later, by a network of railroads. Civil-War soldiers required non-perishable rations; sacks and glass jars gave way to sealed tins. The earliest canned foods were tomatoes, soup, peaches, and beans, many of which went west to be opened with hammer and chisel.

Through decades, cans were smashed, punctured, or keyed open. At last, in 1870, William Lyman invented a wheel-driven opener, later serrated, that traveled around the rim of the can.

Ring that dinner bell.

The Comanche would sacrifice a valuable pony for food in an emergency, but refused to eat dog or coyote due to a sort of kinship with the creatures. Other tribes, however, savored canine meat.

Lewis and Clark did not re-hydrate their first batch of dried "portable" soup until September 14, 1805, deep into the expedition, when it was reported there were only 2-3 pheasants available to feed 30-plus explorers plus a few Indians. The hungry men "ditched" the gummy soup; they killed and roasted a horse, instead.

S. M. Buzzard of Colorado City, Texas, says it was not unusual to see the hind-end gate of a fellow's trousers labeled with XXXX Family Flour (a popular brand at the time). Flour-sack clothing was widespread during hard years when wool and cotton were very expensive or unavailable.

As pioneer Miriam Davis' husband hunted for food, she foraged along the river for roots and plants. In what must have been a last-choice solution, she tied her little children to chair legs to keep them safe as she searched for food. Hard, hard times.

Napoleon's assertion that "an army moves on its stomach" pushed forward the idea of food preservation by canning. By 1856, Gail Borden's condensed milk was available. In two John Wayne movies ("Three Godfathers" and "McLintock!") canned milk appears far out in the West.

Mountain folks say that serviceberries are so named because the plants bloomed in spring about the time circuit-riding preachers came through to perform weddings and funerals. *(Source: Southwest Parks and Monument Association, Tucson, Arizona)*

"The mountains have their ways."

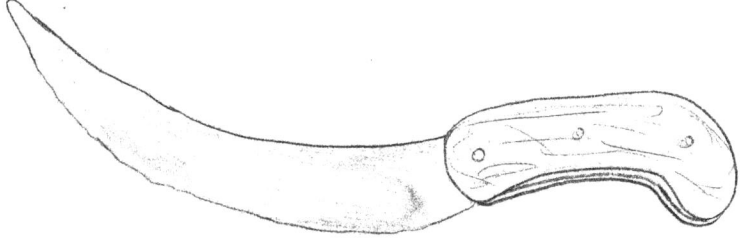

THE SAGA OF LIVER-EATING JOHNSON

True? Half-true? Totally false?

The re-burial of Mr. Johnson was much less complicated than the drama surrounding his life in the Old West.

Middle-school students in a California school were captivated by Johnson's name and story, as shared by their teacher. As the saga ended, they were dismayed to hear of the old man's burial, penniless, alongside a Pacific-Coast freeway.

With the zeal of youth, the kids embarked upon a campaign to move Johnson's remains to a peaceful resting place in Cody, Wyoming. They wrote letters to historians, legislators, and veterans' groups. Arguing that Johnson had died with no known relatives to make decisions about his welfare, students boldly suggested that the government designate *their entire class* as his next of kin.

After six months, and generous support from many, the grave transfer was approved. Mr. Johnson now lies in repose at Old Trail Town in Wyoming, near his last home.

The classroom discussion about Liver-Eating Johnson coincided with a movie which opened in autumn of 1972. "Jeremiah Johnson" starred Robert Redford in the role of John Garrison Johnson. The character "Jeremiah" in the film is loosely based on a real person who spent most of his life on the western frontier.

More than a century after his death, though, few hard-and-fast details exist about this enigmatic and colorful fellow.

The biographical facts are straightforward. Born "John Garrison" in New Jersey in 1824. Hardened by a mean and abusive father. Off to the sea as a young teen. Brief service in the U.S. Navy during the Mexican War. Disappearance after an attack upon a superior officer.

Ending up on the American frontier, John is said to have learned from an aged mountain man how to hunt and trap, then moved on through various interludes as a peddler, miner, whiskey-seller, builder, and woodhawk. Possessing enormous body strength, the young man developed a penchant for liquor and violence – and likely adopted the surname "Johnston" to cover past misdeeds and crimes. (Johnston's "t" disappeared later.)

The Old West was a wild and dangerous place. Survival required audacity, self-sufficiency, and not a little luck. Among the numerous true stories of toil and toughness, we can expect a fable now and then, especially when the tall tale grows up from the roots of family violence, rage, and drunkenness.

From that perspective, then, plunges the avalanche of liver-eating tales, starting with Johnson's assertion that his native Flathead wife and unborn child were murdered by Crow braves while he was away on a winter hunt. Over a period of two decades, the distraught Johnson claimed to have stalked and killed numerous Crow (sometimes exaggerated as hundreds) and eaten their livers raw, the final act of a revenge killing.

Another chapter finds Johnson ambushed by Blackfoot braves chasing a reward for his delivery to the vindictive Crow. Tightly bound in a tent, Liver-Eater chewed through the leather bindings, knifed his Blackfoot guard, cut off the slain brave's leg, and stole away, gnawing on the leg over 200 miles to a partner's cabin and safety. That is, after he used the leg *bone* to repel a mountain lion.

At some point in his long life, Johnson acknowledged that, indeed, the liver-eating fable had gotten out of hand.

Yes, he had knifed a brave (he claimed it was a Sioux) in self-defense and removed the weapon. A piece of liver being stuck to the blade, Johnson admitted he had merely brushed his lips with blood and *pretended* to consume it. Maybe he offered a "chaw" to his friends, and they began pointing fingers.

Johnson almost certainly distorted his reports of tangles with the Natives while savoring the reactions of listeners. Paradoxically, his occasional occupation as a woodhawk brought with it *genuine* peril.

"The roughest, meanest scum on the frontier," said David Crookes, for the West's woodhawks willingly undertook the risky work of providing cord wood for paddle steamers heading to Montana on the Missouri River.

The boats, loaded with passengers and freight, made routine stops to cut wood needed to fire the engine's boilers. Once they entered Indian territory, though, boat captains were hesitant to leave the safety of the ship. Frantic at the thought of being adrift without fuel in a hostile setting, they paid exorbitant amounts to the local woodhawks, who were equally at the mercy of Natives intolerant of white trespassers in their lands.

The only known first-hand report of Johnson in his boisterous years is a doozy. As he carried wood to the steamer *Huntsville* on the Missouri River, it was recorded that...

"([A] sight met her passengers which was certainly calculated to shock the nerves of any eastern tenderfoot. Along the brink of the river bank on both sides of the landing a row of stakes was planted, and each stake carried a white, grinning Indian skull...

"A little to one side, as if guarding them, stood a trapper, well-known throughout eastern Montana by the sobriquet of 'Liver-Eating' Johnson.'

"He was leaning on a crutch, with one leg bandaged and, the day being hot, his entire dress consisted of a scant, much-shrunken, red undershirt, reaching just below his hips. His matted hair and bushy beard fluttered in the breeze, and his giant frame and limbs, so freely exposed to view, formed an exceedingly impressive and characteristic picture."
Peter Koch, a *Huntsville* passenger

A photograph of the times reveals the same barbarous character; coupled with Johnson's lonely lifestyle, these images understandably may have led to the elaboration found in long-ago tales of strange and faraway places.

In later years, however, Johnson served honorably in the Civil War and as a peace-loving constable in Red Lodge, Montana, forging a brotherly friendship with his former foes, the Crow braves.

Liver-Eater or not, Johnson found a "family" of modern kids relishing the ridiculous adventures of a frontier villain while opening their minds to the cruelties and desolation of his entire life.

Then they opened their hearts to seek a serene rest for a forgotten soul.

"Real people with real foibles and follies. The mountain men weren't superheroes, but regular people living a hard and dangerous life."

John A. Roby

It was teacher Tri Robinson of Park View Middle School in Lancaster, California, who immersed his students in the real Old West, right out of the book Crow Killer: The Saga of Liver-Eating Johnson, by Raymond T. Thorpe and Robert Bunker.

Half of Mr. Robinson's class went to the disinterment of Mr. Johnson; the other half attended the reburial. Actor Robert Redford is said to have been there, too.

Robinson later entered the ministry as a pastor.

"When he shall die, take him and cut him out in the little stars, and he will make the face of heaven so fine that all the world will be in love with night and pay no worship to the garish sun."
William Shakespeare

JOHN, GALBA, AND BILLY

They were teenagers. Three of them. They died in the Alamo.

It was on March 6, 1836, that the old mission in San Antonio, Texas, fell to Santa Anna's Mexican army. All defenders were lost – William B. Travis, Davy Crockett, James Bowie, and...

John Gaston, Galba Fuqua, and William King.

John was 17. Galba was three days short of his 17th birthday. William, at 15, was the youngest victim of the savagery of Mexican troops that ruinous day.

All three belonged to the Immortal 32 – the only men in all of Texas to answer Travis' call for help as the brutal siege of the Alamo continued.

John Davis Gaston had aided the Texas Revolution from its very first day, stationed as a lookout on the Guadalupe River outside Gonzales the previous fall. The locals were expecting a Mexican force led by General Castaneda, because Mexico wanted its cannon back.

The little four-pounder had been given to the Gonzales settlement for protection against Indian raids. With tensions rising between Texians and the increasingly-oppressive Mexican government, possession of the cannon became an explosive affair.

With shouts of "Come and take it!" the Texians fired the ball, killing a single Mexican soldier and scattering the rest of the forces. It was rebellion, of course. With that shot, the Texas Revolution was underway. It was October 2, 1835.

By late February, 1836, Santa Anna and several thousand Mexican troops had laid siege to the Alamo. Trapped inside were approximately 150 Texian defenders led jointly by Travis and the ailing Bowie.

Messengers who slipped away delivered pleas for help to several locations, but the Gonzales Ranging Volunteers were the sole responders, with John Gaston accompanying his brother-in-law, John Benjamin Kellogg, Jr. The Immortals arrived in San Antonio at the first of March and entered the Alamo, bringing the total number of Texian protectors to about 186. All were massacred early on the morning of Santa Anna's attack.

There were some women and children in the old mission, as well, including Susanna Dickinson, whose husband Almeron was serving as captain of artillery, and their baby girl Angelina. In the heat of battle, **Galba Fuqua** rushed to the room where the women were hidden. He attempted to deliver a message to Susanna, possibly from her husband, but both of Galba's jaws had been shattered by a bullet and he was trying in vain to hold his face together in order to speak.

> "Susannah recalled that Galba, pale and suffering, stormed into the room, blood trickling from his mouth and through the fingers that were pressing his jaws together. His eyes were screaming, but there were no words."
>
> McAlister

The anguished young mother wrapped his cheeks with an improvised chin strap of cloth strips from Angelina's dress. Galba dashed back into the conflict and was killed.

Mrs. Dickinson's husband died, of course, but all the women were spared. Susanna and the baby made their way to Gonzales, where she described to Sam Houston the valiance of young Galba.

The young man's great-great-grandfather, William Fuqua, immigrated to Virginia in 1685 to escape religious persecution. Galba's father Silas brought his family to Texas, settling on the San Marcos River near Gonzales, and his uncle Benjamin married Nancy King, older sister of William King, the youngest Texian martyr.

William Phillip (Billy) King was a "private rifleman" whose father, John Gladden King, had joined the Gonzales Rangers. Because of their large family of nine children and some illnesses in the group, tall and thin young Billy begged to take his father's place on the march to San Antonio.

Reports say that the decision was made *in a moment* – just as the Immortal 32 were marching out of Gonzales and passing by the King family's property. Billy went.

Stunning.

Names of the three young men are inscribed on the Cenotaph outside the Alamo in San Antonio, Texas.

At ages 20, 22, and 24, brothers George, James, and Edward Taylor also perished in Santa Anna's onslaught at the Alamo. Taylor County in Texas is named in their honor. Farmers in the Liberty area, they joined the Texas Revolution after finishing the cotton harvest in fall,

1835, and arrived at the Alamo a few days before the final battle on March 6, 1836. (A few sources place the Taylor brothers at the Goliad Massacre, but a newspaper published their names as Alamo victims a full week before the Goliad tragedy.)

"I had holes in my jeans before it was fashionable."
Kenny Rogers

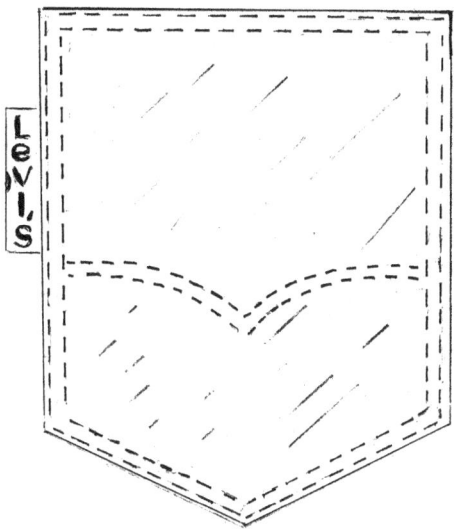

TIMELESS AND RIGHT

Oh, the joy.

Jeans for any occasion. Fit just so. Look good. Feel like home.

> "Why are blue jeans a classic? You just hit on something that happens to be *"timeless and right."*
> Diane von Furstenberg

Born in rough-and-tumble California during its gold-rush years and now grown to maturity, jeans trace parentage to a couple of 19th-century American immigrants.

Levi Strauss, born in Germany in 1829, was a child of six when his father died of tuberculosis. With his mother and sisters, Levi sailed to the United States to work for his two brothers in their wholesale dry-goods store, J. Strauss Brothers and Company, in New York City.

The young man peddled 100 pounds of blankets, kettles, and sewing supplies throughout the city, but returned to lower Manhattan each Saturday evening in observance of the Jewish Sabbath.

California's economic vigor coaxed the Strauss family to expand their trade to the West Coast. San Francisco was a roaring city of 70,000 with 117 dry-goods shops battling a continual shortage of stock due to the great distance from manufacturing centers in the East. The Golden State was starving for suppliers, and the Strauss family had the goods to sell. By 1853, Levi was in San Francisco, having sailed on a steamship around Cape Horn.

He launched a wholesale enterprise offering cloth, bedding, linens, and accessories like purses and handkerchiefs – all from his brothers' wholesale business in New York. Fabric was in great demand, and some of Strauss's best material was a rough canvas from Genoa, Italy. *Genes* fabric was used primarily for wagon covers, tents, and cots needed in mining and farming operations.

"...You should've brought pants [to sell.]"
A prospector

Right on, Mr. Prospector! Sturdy clothing was in short supply out West. The ordinary work pants of miners, teamsters, lumberjacks, and farmers were not up to the task; rugged conditions and the tendency of laborers to carry tools in their pockets turned flimsy garb into tatters.

Stay tuned. A winning team was soon to be assembled.

Jacob Youphres of Latvia immigrated to New York City about a year after the Strauss family's arrival there. Youphres operated a tailor shop in the city and Americanized his surname to "Davis." But then, he, too, moved to the West Coast, where he made wagon covers, cots, and tents with *Genes* canvas purchased at the Strauss store in San Francisco!

Davis may have heard the prospector's lament, but it's a fact he paid attention to the wife of a woodcutter whose thin work outfits required never-ending repair. Jacob laid aside his tents and repurposed the *Genes* cloth. Yippee! Sturdy trousers! In a light-bulb moment, he installed copper rivets on the pocket corners and front seams for heavy-duty wear.

> "The secret to them Pents is the Rivits that I put in those Pockets and I found the demand so large that I cannot make them up fast enough. My nabors are getting yealouse of these successes." [sic]
>
> Jacob Davis

Genes pants were snatched up as fast as they could be assembled. Wisely, Davis recognized the likelihood of product imitators, so he offered a partnership to Strauss if the latter would pay fees associated with patent application. On May 20, 1873, patent number 139,121 for "waist overalls" was issued to Strauss and Davis.

> "...I wish I had invented blue jeans. They have expression, modesty, sex appeal, simplicity – all I hope for in my clothes."
>
> Yves St. Laurent

For lasting strength, Davis' canvas pants retained their popularity, but the scratchy cloth caused uncomfortable chafing over a long workday.

Levi Strauss had his own moment of inspiration, for he replaced the troublesome *Genes* canvas with a twilled cotton cloth from Nimes, France. The fabric was known as *Serge de Nimes,* – soon Americanized into *Denim*.

Genes, of course, became *Jeans*.

Jeans from *Genoa*; *Denim* from *DeNimes*.

Levi's from *Levi's* store.

Customers promptly noticed that denim softened with wear and laundering without losing its durability. The comfort factor alone catapulted denim into immortality. Indigo, used for dying the fabric, does not totally penetrate the cloth; it rests outside each thread. (That's why classic jeans are white on the inside.) Denim's popular and unique coloring results from the chipping of its dye with aging and everyday use.

Mr. Strauss never married; he died at age 73 in 1902. As he had requested, his fortune was divided among his sisters, nephews, and various charitable institutions on the Pacific Coast. By 1907, Jacob Davis had sold his interest in the company, but stayed on as a supervisor until his death a year later.

Only five Fortune 500 companies remain from the 19th century; with a start-up date of 1853, Levi Strauss is the oldest.

Each generation has broadened the appeal of jeans. From western movies of the 1920s and '30s through World War II, when American soldiers wore the pants at leisure while out of uniform, the demand for jeans has grown exponentially. Born in the American West, Levi's were first sold outside that area in the 1940s.

Non-conformity, social protest, rock music, youthful rebellion, and casual living in the '50s and '60s were a natural "fit" for jeans. The banning of blue jeans in some schools naturally increased their popularity, leap-frogging the pants into standard wear and, eventually, into designer apparel.

> "...a closet full of clothes and nothing to wear. So I wear jeans."
>
> Cameron Diaz

By the late 20th century, however, Levi Strauss and Company was sandwiched between modern style trends from top fashion houses and traditional-look competition from trademarks like Wrangler and Lee. An old advertising slogan, "For Men Who Toil," reveals how the company may have lagged a bit in updating their winning product.

The twenty-first century, though, has seen the company blend current taste with respect for the brand, because, as *Harper's Bazaar* points out, "denim is basically our longest relationship."

"The little red tab means 'Levi's...'"

P.J. O'Rourke comments: "Jeans fit the mature male one of two ways, both dirigible in nature – either the Hindenburg or the Goodyear blimp." Sorry, guys.

Srauss Americanized his name "Leob" to "Levi" after arriving in New York.

Dungarees, also made from coarse cotton, appeared in the 17th century, worn by people in Dongri, India. (The Hindi name for cloth is "dungri.") The fabric was also useful in making tents and sails. Today's <u>Oxford English Dictionary</u> defines *dungarees* as "trousers with bibs," like overalls.

Speaking of overalls, Homer Campbell, a miner living in Constellation, Arizona, wrote the Levi Strauss Company several years ago, complaining that his latest Levi's overalls had failed following only three-years' wear (every day but Sunday). Said he: "I wish you would explain why they have gone to pieces. I have worn nothing but Levi's overalls for 30 years," and "I consider it my duty to help you every way I can" because "I know it is your aim to present a superior article on the market."

Levi's research lab claims that one pair of jeans requires 919 gallons of water in its "lifetime" – watering the cotton crop, after-dye washing for a softer look and feel, and routine laundering by the wearer (which, they say, consumes 50% of the total measure of water). Currently, there's a wide debate about *freezing* jeans for cleaning rather than *washing* them.

Jeans in the 1800's generally sported a single back pocket and a button fly. Men wore suspenders, so there were no belt loops.

Vintage jeans can command high prices; a 125-year-old pair of Levi's sold for nearly $100,000 in 2018. The 1893 owner was pioneer Arizona businessman Solomon Warner, wore the pants only a few times before his final illness.

"Are you men from California or do you come from heaven?"

Levinah Murphy

DOOM OF THE DONNERS

Their migration should have lasted five months. Tamsen Donner expected a quicker passage.

> "...this season we go to California to the bay of Francisco... a four-months' trip..."

Its last survivor reached safety one year and fifteen days after the journey began in Springfield, Illinois.

Responding to that trumpet-like call of the frontier, the Donner and Reed families closed out their Midwest farms, bid friends farewell, and joined a large caravan gathering in Independence, Missouri, the jump-off spot for westward travel.

A duo of advantages placed Independence at the forefront of westward passage. Its outfitters had 20 years' experience in preparing travelers for the long journey. There were ample stores of supplies – plows, harnesses, pans, shovels, and foodstuffs – while blacksmiths, farriers, and wheelwrights stood ready for last-minute repairs. For Independence and its upriver rival, St. Joseph, the local economy boomed each spring as emigrants camped for days or weeks till warm weather beckoned them across the Missouri River and onward to the West.

George Donner and his brother Jacob wanted one last big adventure. James Reed sought a fortune in California and a coastal climate for the health of his wife.

A late-spring departure in May, 1846, promised tall grass for the oxen, cows, and horses, pleasant travel through weeks of summer, and arrival in their new place of abode during a benign autumn. For a convoy two-and-a-half miles long, travel would be slow, but tolerable.

The first three months went smoothly for the company, moving along at a decidedly-relaxed pace. Lurking beneath the surface were the twin complications of frontier inexperience and the inevitable approach of winter.

Ahead were mountains higher and deserts deadlier than any in their experience. The farmers knew little about menacing Plains Indians or survival in a remote wilderness. Nevertheless, they could depend upon the Oregon Trail, which followed the Platte and Sweetwater Rivers to Fort Hall, where the California Trail branched off toward their final destination. It was a reliable and well-traveled route, used by more than half of California's settlers from the East.

But they didn't take that path.

At Fort Bridger, Wyoming Territory, George Donner and James Reed fell prey to the honeyed assurances of one Lansford Hastings about a "new and infallible trail," a shortcut sure to be quicker and easier, saving three weeks and 350 miles. A widely-distributed emigrant guidebook written by Hastings appeared to give credence to his dubious claims and, clearly, his "cutoff" spiel was directed toward the large group approaching from Independence.

In 1846, California was still part of Mexico. Hastings was a lifelong promoter; on this occasion, he was talking up a separate California republic free of foreign influences. His real goal, thinly disguised, was personal leadership of the new province, which would require many emigrants to populate and support his venture. The sooner they arrived, the better.

While the California Trail veered north of the Great Salt Lake, purposely (and wisely) avoiding Utah altogether, the Hastings Cutoff wound around the lake's south end and across the salt flats of Utah. Its promise of a minimized last leg of their journey naturally caught the attention of trail-weary emigrants.

In a disappointing turn of events, respected mountain man Jim Bridger echoed Hastings' praises for the supposed shortcut; Bridger coveted a flood of customers at his fledgling trading post on the "new trail." What's more, it's suspected that Bridger never delivered cautionary messages to the Donners from a traveler who'd endured the passage.

> "Mr. Bridger informed me that it is a fine, level road with plenty of water and grass. It is estimated that 700 miles will take us to Captain Sutter's fort, which we hope to make seven weeks from this day"
> James Reed, July 31, 1846

Hastings himself had ridden his trail once, maybe twice, on *horseback*. Burdened wagons, trudging oxen, and families were never meant to be in those deadly places. More troubling, Hastings did not meet the emigrants at Fort Bridger; he merely left orders for them to "follow along behind" and look for instructions posted on the wayside.

Stern words of warning for the Donners and Reeds came from an old friend and fellow sand-hiller from Illinois, James Clyman, a veteran of many years on the western scene as a frontier trapper. "Don't do it," he said. "You can't take wagons that way."

Leaders of the doomed party scoffed at Clyman's plea, but they were not alone in their ignorance. Many in the group greedily wished to reach California before other travelers in order to have a better choice of land.

On the other hand, Tamsen Donner, George's wife, was "gloomy, sad, and dispirited in view of the fact that her husband and others could think of leaving the old road and confide in the statement of a man of whom they knew nothing, but (who) was probably some selfish adventurer."

Her opinion didn't matter, either.

While most of the original caravan continued along the California Trail, the twenty wagons of what became the "Donner Party" broke away at Fort Bridger and headed across Utah the next day, August 1, toward the Wasatch Mountains and Great Salt Lake Desert.

The Hastings Cutoff had no beat-down trail, nor was it marked, save for a single note left on sagebrush. The travelers waited eight days for Hastings' appearance, only to receive a message that the trail ahead was impassable. In other words, the Donner Party was essentially on its own.

Precious time and energy were wasted, as well, on actually constructing a treading passage wide enough for the caravan. Men had to chop their way through thick cottonwoods and aspens; boulders were heaved aside and dirt mounds raised over streams. The laborers were easy prey for hostile Indians, who murdered at will and killed or captured horses, oxen, and cattle. With no draft animals to pull them, many of the wagons for which the trail had been hacked-through were simply left behind. The desert was 82 miles across, not the 40 miles mentioned by Hastings. Trackless alkali flats and glue-like muck formed by thin pools of water further wore down the party.

The Donner Party was exhausted by the time they rejoined the established trail. The Cutoff had eaten up three weeks and scattered their possessions and food. Paiute braves harangued the stragglers. Ahead were the rugged peaks of the Sierra Nevada, well into an early snow season by October. Five feet of snow. Sleet. Freezing rain. Another five feet of snow. Snowpack at 20 feet.

Most of the oxen and horses were gone. The party was stopped far short of the summit ridge. Deep snow and howling winds prevented forward progress, but they dared not retreat backward, where blood-thirsty Paiute awaited to pounce. Soon they were trapped in a wilderness of white. Patrick Breen's diary lamented that "nothing without wings could get about."

Men hastily put up flimsy shelters (some with only animal skins for roofs), lean-tos, brush sheds covered by wagon canvas, and tents. Drifts grew so high that different families could locate each other only by the smoke from their small fires. The flatlanders' clothing, shoes, and bedding offered little protection during the long season of frigid temperatures.

In December, a "forlorn hope" party of fifteen struggled toward California, but half of them perished. Unknown to the Donners, the Mexican-American War was underway, whisking away many able-bodied men who could have formed a rescue team. The first relief attempt in February faced the same unrelenting drifts – some thirty feet high – on the California side of the mountain.

Food supplies plummeted; people were forced to eat boiled bark, twigs, dogs, mice, string, shoes, and shoelaces. Ox hides were cooked into a gooey paste and bones boiled repeatedly for soup till only slivers remained. The daily search for food came down to poking holes in the snow in hopes of finding the carcasses of their lost and buried cattle.

No hunting was possible because the deer and elk had moved to lower ground for the winter, bears were in hibernation, and birds were long gone. No traps or snares had been brought along for capture of any smaller creatures that might have remained in the hills, and not a soul was skilled enough to catch mountain trout, even before winter came.

Was there cannibalism? Though scholars and scientists continually debate the issue, letters and conversations with survivors state the obvious facts. Without that decidedly despicable practice, far fewer would have survived. Tragically, the people involved were family members, children, and close friends. There was a silent pact for the starving not to ingest the flesh of their loved ones.

A dying Franklin Graves pleaded with his wife and daughters that "...his body be used to sustain the famishing... admonishing them to put aside their natural repugnance which stood between them and the possibility of life."

Mr. Graves' audacious comments made a lasting impression on little Eliza Donner, daughter of George Donner.

> "I, as a child scarcely four years of age, was too young to do more than watch and suffer with the other children...and with them survive because their fathers and mothers hungered in order that the children might live...days, weeks, and months of famine.
>
> My fondest affections must ever cling to the dear, quaint old pioneer men and women whose hand-clasps were warmth and whose givings were like milk and honey to my desolate childhood... "
>
> Eliza P. Donner Houghton

Donner himself would not live. He had suffered a severe cut in October while repairing a broken axle. Through the winter, gangrene set in and spread from hand to shoulder; he remained bedridden for months. When relief teams arrived, Tamsen Donner faced the unimaginable choice of staying beside her dying husband or attempting to lead their girls – ages 4, 5, and 6 – to safe haven.

At the moment of decision, Tamsen entrusted her daughters to rescuers and tarried at George's side until he succumbed in late March. Then, trying to catch up to the relief party, she died, probably of hypothermia, early into her escape. The orphaned children were taken in by a Swiss family in California.

Those "seven weeks" so confidently predicted by James Reed in July stretched agonizingly into months of insufferable trekking and wintry ruination before searchers rescued the final survivors, the last of which reached Sutter's Fort, California, on April 29, 1847. Of the 81 stranded on the mountain, thirty-six died and 45 survived.

The disastrous "shortcut" aside, other dreadful mistakes were made by the emigrants. The families had grossly over-packed for the long migration. Reed's wagon was outfitted with a two-story shelter of bunks and a heater for his 70-year-old blind and deaf mother-in-law, Sarah Keyes, who braved the trip to reunite with a son out west. She died early in the journey; aware of her fragile condition, she yet vowed to use her last energies moving toward her loved one, and the family did not deny her last wish.

As well, the travelers discounted the absolute necessity of moving forward without delay as the calendar marched on toward winter. With scant knowledge of western geography, they wasted precious days at rest or wandering about in search of lost livestock. In sum, they were farmers, not mountain men.

The Donner name identifies the worst disaster in American migration history. An isolated occurrence in a vast sea of westward movement, it will ever mirror human tenacity – the will to live and go forward as best one can.

> "More than the gleaming heroism or sullied villainy, the Donner Party is a story of hard decisions that were neither heroic nor villainous..."
>
> Ethan Rarick

The original party leaving Independence on May 1, 1846, consisted of 288 men, women, and children, but the group split several times and picked up a few more along the trail. Then there was the fateful parting at Ft. Bridger, Wyoming, when doomed travelers chose the Hastings Cutoff.

At the migration's start, the large group had 63 wagons and an astounding 58,484 pounds of breadstuffs (bread, flour, meal), 38,080 pounds of bacon, 850 horses and cattle.

After the Donner disaster, emigration to Utah and Oregon continued apace, but movement to California sharply declined in 1846-47, partly due to the Mexican War. The next year, the war's end and a discovery of gold flakes at Sutter's Mill in Coloma, California, opened the floodgates of travel again.

Readers of Swallowin' Sand Burrs may remember James Clyman, who endeavored to dissuade James Reed and George Donner from following the Hastings Cutoff. Two decades previously, Clyman had re-attached Jim Bridger's ear with needle and thread after a grizzly-bear attack.

Seemingly without remorse for his part in the Donner tragedy, Hastings persisted in self-aggrandizing schemes until the end of his life, including attempts to wrest California from the Union during the Civil War and, later, to set up a republic in Brazil with himself in charge, naturally.

Hastings' faulty judgment was budding when, as a first-time wagon-train captain en route to Oregon, he and a friend spent far too much time carving their artful autographs in sandstone at Independence Rock, Wyoming. The caravan had the good sense not to tarry, and the fools were captured by Indians who demanded a ransom. Food and some shiny trinkets bought their freedom.

"Are you men from California or do you come from heaven?" That's what rescuer Daniel Rhoads heard when, "at sunset we came to the spot where we had been told we should find the emigrants, but no living things were in sight. We raised a loud 'hello' and saw a woman [Mrs. Levinah Murphy] emerge from a hole in the snow. As we approached her, several others made their appearance, gaunt with famine, and I can never forget the ghastly sight they presented."

"Charming eccentricity"

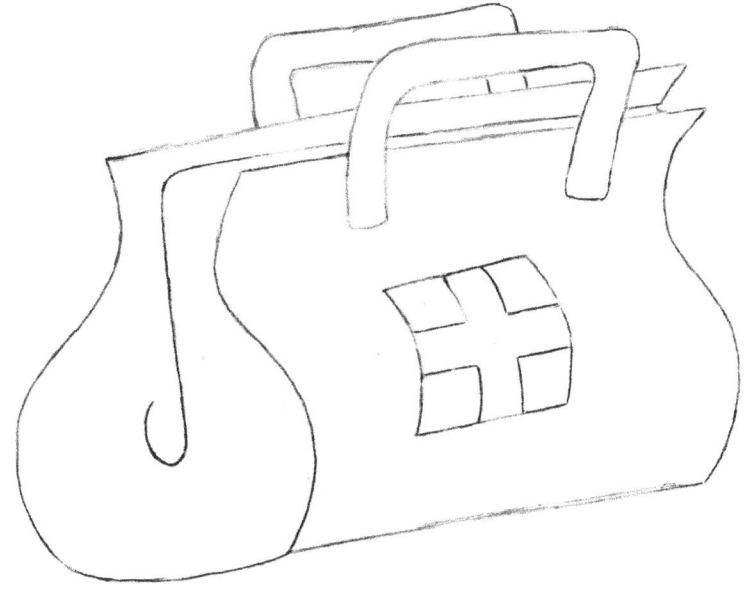

DR. SOFIE

One can understand why the fine ladies of Brazoria, Texas, tilted up their lovely chins and clicked, "tsk, tsk."

The new doctor in town was...unusual. Yes, *she* was.

Wore short hair topped by a man's hat. Proudly displayed her necklace of bullets. Rode horses and drove buggies. Hanging on for dear life, hitched rides on railroad handcars. Dressed in split skirts to avoid side-saddling a horse.

Maintained a rather exotic medical office decorated with snake skins, animal heads, antlers, a stuffed alligator, artwork, lace, a piano, a pharmacy, birds, a collection of books for lending, and jars of malformed body parts.

Suspended gunshot victims over a gurney.

Built an Episcopal church after the local Catholic priest rebuffed her polite suggestion that the parish cemetery needed cleaning.

Carried an alligator purse – with feet and claws still attached.

That Sofia Herzog – what a character!

Born into a large family of physicians in Vienna in 1846, Sofia Dalia, as a teen, was "married off" to a newly-certified physician, Dr. August Herzog. They moved to New York City where he became an administrator at the U.S. Naval Hospital.

Discovering the diminished status of female medical students in her adopted country, Sofia returned to Vienna for her own professional training. She bore 15 children, including three sets of twins.

August Herzog was never in good health in America, and he died in 1894. When her children were grown, Sofia left the medical practice she had established in New Jersey. A naturally-adventurous spirit drew her to Brazoria, Texas, where her youngest daughter was living. "Just a visit," she said.

And that's where the fun – and her legacy – began.

The "visit" became a permanent residence, as Sofie boldly opened a medical practice in the town she was growing to love. She purchased a small house; two rooms were utilized for her medical practice and a third was her bedroom.

The first female surgeon in Texas, she built a hefty clientele and was regularly summoned to treat injured workers on railway-construction crews in the booming area. After a time, Sofie's firm credentials and reputation gained her the position of chief surgeon of the St. Louis-Brownsville-Mexico Railway, but the job offer was rescinded once the "brass" in the main office discovered she was a woman.

"I'll keep this job as long as I give satisfaction!" exclaimed the lady. She did both, remaining on the railway's payroll till shortly before her death.

Dr. Sofie was credited with saving most of the gunshot victims she encountered in Texas' rough-and-tumble Southeast. Rather than digging around in a wound for bullets or shot, she chose to hang the victim with the entry hole pointed downward so gravity would "bring the offending bullet to me." And mostly, it did, within 24 hours, without the inevitable infection following a hand probe.

When she had recovered two dozen bullets, she persuaded a jeweler to fashion the unusual neckwear featuring slugs separated by gold beads.

A practical woman she was. Those split skirts enabled her to ride a horse more efficiently so she could reach patients sooner. Buggies were not her transport of choice; they could be expected to bog down on muddy roads or river bottoms during the rainy season, and that wouldn't do at all!

Sofie did her own taxidermy work and especially enjoyed skinning rattlesnakes. Unfortunately, she ignored warnings about being poisoned by a dead reptile – until she broke out in a mean, puffy, red rash over her body and around her mouth. For that, she was treated in Galveston and advised to cut back on messing with pit vipers.

For the office's "alligator" décor, Sofie hired a local man to find and deliver a nice specimen. It was an impressive seven-footer. She stepped over its latent form throughout the busy workday. Asleep in her adjacent bedroom late at night, she awoke to a dreadful noise.

The gator was very much alive.

She grabbed a poker from the fireplace and stood guard on her four-poster bed till daylight. Someone killed it; she stuffed it.

At age 65, Sofie married Col. Marion Huntington, a descendant of Stephen F. Austin's original settlers in Texas. They moved to his ranch outside Brazoria. The good doctor traveled back and forth to work driving her new Ford – the first automobile in the county. It figures.

Dr. Sofie remained active until her passing in 1925 and was buried wearing her "good-luck" bullet necklace.

Wisely, a granddaughter removed the curiosity jars from the office and interred them beneath the branches of a tree.

Though Vienna was a world-renowned center for studies in medicine, its universities did not offer actual medical degrees to women till 1897, so Sofie's initial certification in 1871 was probably in midwifery. She completed further training in the United States.

A thankfully-obscure list called the Directory of Deceased Physicians lists her type of medical practice as "eclectic."

Dr. Sofie was the first woman railroad surgeon (of a major railroad enterprise) in the world. The St. Louis-Brownsville-Mexico Railway, known as the Brownie, connected Texas towns for 200 miles along the Gulf Coast.

During an interview with the *Fort Worth Star Telegram* in 1960, Dr. Sofie listed 21 relatives in the medical profession.

"...with a star on his breast and Tolstoy in his pocket"
Edmond Morris

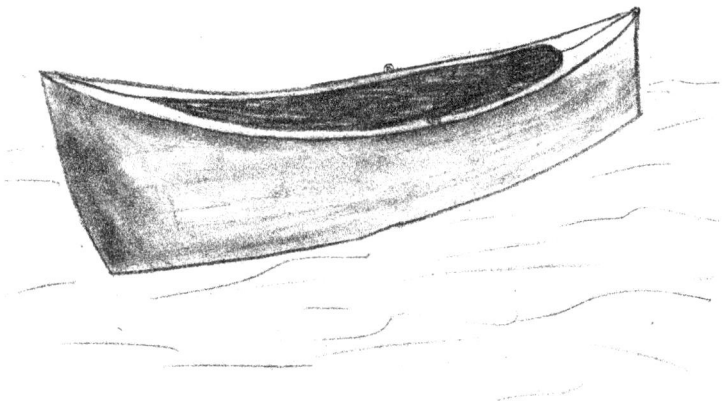

THE BOAT

"There is little amusement in combining the functions of a sheriff and those of an Arctic explorer."
Theodore Roosevelt

Armed and dangerous, they cut the rope mooring a small skiff and slipped away downstream. A zero-degree night in Dakota Territory. An icy river. The thieving trio needed to get away, and fast. Who'd go in pursuit of a dumpy little boat?

Theodore Roosevelt, that's who. His tiny tub, worth just $30, had been useful for ferrying ranch supplies and equipment from one side of the Little Missouri River to the other on his Elkhorn Ranch.

And Roosevelt was a deputy sheriff of Billings County, standing tall for law and order. The suspects? That was easy – well-known local hoodlums led by a ruffian named Finnigan, known for frequent thefts of horses and cattle, and likely on the run just ahead of a posse.

> "We had no doubt as to who had stolen it. They belonged to a class that always holds sway during the raw youth of a frontier community, and the putting down of which is the very first step toward decent government."
>
> Theodore Roosevelt

The 1886 blizzard had already killed 60% of the Elkhorn's cattle. The miscreants were convinced that pursuers would never risk a deadly chase over rugged, frozen terrain. And they were smugly aware that there was not another water craft for miles around. Their little thievery would go smoothly.

They misjudged Theodore Roosevelt by a country mile.

There *would be* another boat! The ever-ebullient deputy hastily rounded up a couple of ranch hands and set out to build a flat-bottomed scow – in three days' time. (Bill Seawall and Wilmot Dow were "tough, hardy, resolute fellows, quick as cats, strong as bears, and able to travel like bull moose.") They loaded up rifles, duck guns, paddles, oars, and iron-clad poles. Stowed bacon, flour, coffee, warm clothes and bedding, and a book. Confidently stashed a camera to record the eventual capture.

A hundred miles downstream, Roosevelt's party spotted the stolen skiff moored near a roaring campfire tended by a single thief. Shocked, to say the least, he was promptly handcuffed. Within an hour, along strolled Finnigan and the other. Captured.

> "The men we were after knew they had taken with them the only craft there was on the river and so felt perfectly secure; accordingly, we took them absolutely by surprise."
>
> Theodore Roosevelt

What next? Turning back upriver to the ranch would be deadly.

The Roosevelt trio, with its arrestees, continued poling downstream toward the nearest jail facility, all the while apprehensive about Teton Sioux in the area. Frigid weather, though, had brought all life to a standstill, and it was disappointing to find that the Natives had killed or driven off the wildlife that might have meant sustenance to the Roosevelt party.

Suddenly, the river became impassable due to a massive ice jam, and there was nothing to do but stop at once and wait for a sporadic thaw.

Eight days passed.

Roosevelt pulled out his copy of the Tolstoy classic, <u>Anna Karenina</u>, and read the book aloud from beginning to end, as the miserable captives huddled in bored and shivery frustration. Their own packs yielded dime novels and <u>History of the James Brothers</u> [that's Jesse and Frank], additional fodder for the deputy's unique and glacial read-a-thon.

Moving again, the party began running low on food supplies. Roosevelt opted to leave his companions with the boats while he headed overland alone with the culprits to the small town of Dickinson. He came upon a farm and rented a wagon, but its mares were too small and the mud too deep to pull four men. The prisoners, therefore, rode, while Roosevelt slogged forty-five miles through the slush and muck alongside the wagon – two days and a night without rest or sleep – his gun ever pointed at the boat-nappers.

A local physician described the party's arrival as "the queerest specimen of strangeness that had ever descended on Dickinson," led by "the most bedraggled figure" he had ever seen. It was Roosevelt, of course, limping, covered in mud, scratched and bruised, clothes in tatters, and "as determined as a bull dog."

After a harrowing eleven days on the river and another two afoot in an icy bog, Theodore Roosevelt at last delivered the conniving lowlifes to the local jail. He was reimbursed for travel expenses, plus three arrest bounties – a total of $50. (Deputies in the territory were paid only for expenses; their time was *gratis*.)

Throughout the ordeal, Theodore Roosevelt never wavered on his convictions about the principles of justice and a fair trial. (An observer asked why he didn't simply "hang or shoot the thieves, for heaven's sake.")

Truth is, while the "hard characters" were under capture, he refused to cuff their hands or tie their feet due to the likelihood of frostbite. Boots, however, were removed to thwart any ideas of escape. (That's "cold feet" any way you look at it.)

Within a year, Roosevelt received a letter from the Bismarck prison. Finnigan was inviting him to stop by the lockup for a visit.

"I should be glad to see you," wrote Finnigan.

"To submit tamely and meekly to theft or to any other injury is to invite almost certain repeat of the offense."
Theodore Roosevelt

Because those crooks were "on the radar" of local ranchers and facing the likelihood of a lynch mob, they took along their saddles in the purloined craft, possibly with a plan to steal horses downriver to continue their escape.

Theodore Roosevelt, born into a wealthy and prominent family, was sickly as a child and young man. An invigorating buffalo hunt in 1883 changed all that. A growing affection for pure air in wide-open spaces drew him repeatedly to North Dakota for his health, as well as solace after the deaths of his mother and his wife on the same day in 1884. Roosevelt's Elkhorn-Ranch experiences inspired his organization of the Rough Riders, recruited in New Mexico, Arizona, Texas, and Oklahoma, during the Spanish-American War.

The ranch was established in 1884 near Medora, North Dakota and managed for awhile by Wilmot Dow and Bill Sewall, who had accompanied Roosevelt on the "boat hunt." The property is now part of the Theodore Roosevelt National Park.

> "In American history, [Roosevelt] is still greatly admired for his untiring energy, his many writings, his foresight in conservation and defense, and because he was a President of the people in spite of his aristocratic beginnings."
>
> Patrick McSherry

"Maybe the law ain't perfect, but it's the only one we got and without it we got nuthin."

Bass Reeves

BASS REEVES

The three Brunter brothers were *mean*. When a tall deputy marshal presented the federal warrant, they laughed – they *guffawed*. As their eyes flickered a glance at the document, the lawman killed two and disarmed the third.

Bandit queen Belle Starr knew the marshal was armed with a warrant and looking for her. Without a word, she turned herself in at Fort Smith. It was the *only* time.

An abuser tried to set his fiancé on fire. Luckily, he didn't succeed, but he lay awake all night imagining what the marshal would do. Next morning, the offender showed up for arrest.

⚞⚞

Four desperadoes in a hideout nervously watched a ragged "farmer" approach their lair. His wagon appeared to have been damaged by a hidden tree stump. To keep the intruder at bay, they came forward with an offer to help. The "farmer" promptly helped *them* to jail.

⚞⚞

"Worn-out, starving, and hassled by a posse," whimpered the begging tramp with bullet holes in his hat and inching toward a little cabin. The lady of the house, mother of a pair of villains, invited the poor soul to rest in her cabin and maybe next day he could join her boys on their crime spree. "Tramp" cuffed the sleeping duo and marched them 20 miles to his wagon and off to jail. Shrieking mom followed.

⚞⚞

Curious folks came from 18 miles away to confirm the capture of Seminole renegade Greenleaf. The cold-blooded assassin had murdered three white farmers and four Seminoles, the last of which was shot 24 times at close range. (Greenleaf's victims had aided U.S. deputy marshals in Indian Territory.) The arrest went off without a hitch; the tall black lawman's posse caught Greenleaf asleep.

⚞⚞

Desperadoes had him right where they wanted him, having forced the deputy off his horse to face certain death. Rather unwisely, the gunmen asked if the unlucky captive had any last request. Yes, he did. "Can't read, you know. Would you read to me this letter from my wife?" The doomed man slowly slipped the envelope from his saddlebag and a killer reached for it. Quick as a flash, the deputy wrestled him from his horse and into chains. The partner was so startled he dropped his own gun and found himself bound up, as well.

Killer of eleven, Jim Webb weakly handed over his revolver to the deputy marshal and died in the street. Without his horse for escape, Webb had shot from 500 yards at the deputy four times. The first bullet scraped his saddle horn, the next shaved off a coat button, the next severed the bridle reins, and the last sliced his hat brim. Two shots from the marshal's rifle ended the damage.

This is the story of Bass Reeves.

Born a slave in Arkansas, he may have been propelled by his master into Civil-War action in that state or he may simply have slipped away to freedom. Either way, Reeves found refuge in Oklahoma's Indian Territory, seamlessly blending in with the Cherokee and other Natives of that wild and wooly no-man's land. There he learned five languages while acquiring skills in survival, tracking, hunting, and hiding. Some of those trusted Indian friends would eventually become his posse men.

White criminals, villains, and escapees also found refuge in Oklahoma. Most were wanted "dead or alive." Trouble was, the United States did not have jurisdiction – thus there was no law presence – in the 75,000 square miles of Indian Territory. Tribal law, while effective, applied only to Native Americans.

In 1875, President U.S. Grant pledged to tackle the lawless quagmire. Isaac C. Parker, the widely-respected "hanging judge" of the U.S. Federal Court in Fort Smith, Arkansas, was his man. Grant directed Judge Parker to sweep out crime and violence in Indian Territory – lickety-split and with a vengeance. In turn, Judge Parker commissioned U.S. Marshal James Fagan to find 200 deputies to arrest 'em and bring 'em in.

Luckily for law and order, James Fagan knew Bass Reeves.

Not a man was better-qualified for the job than this broad-shouldered, big-handed, 6-foot 2-inch, 180-pound quick-thinking friend of the Indians – a man who knew the sector "like a cook knows her own kitchen." Add a black hat, a thick, drooping mustache, and a massive gray horse. Throw in twin Colt .45 Peacemakers in quick-draw style across this ambidextrous man's chest, and you have a criminal's greatest adversary.

> "When you get as big as me, a small horse is as worthless as a preacher in a whiskey-joint fight. Just when you need him bad to help you out, he's got to stop and think about it a little bit."
>
> Bass Reeves

Like many slaves, Bass had never learn to read. (His mother had taught him Scripture verses; at times, he quoted appropriate passages to his prisoners.) As a deputy, Reeves memorized the contents of his arrest warrants, noting the letter-shapes of names, sometimes thirty or more. These he kept in proper order, and never arrested the wrong person.

Reeves traveled the long circuit with a wagon, a cook, and a posse man. The wagon was easily recognized and dreaded by miscreants. Heavy chains were attached for holding prisoners until the sweep ended and the fugitives, 12 or 16 at a time (once, 19), were delivered to Judge Parker's court in Fort Smith for trial.

> "My mom always said he was so tough he could spit on a brick and bust it."
> Willabelle Shultz, granddaughter of a fellow marshal

Agile, clever, and outdoors-smart, Reeves boldly crossed the "dead line." Beyond that point, marshals faced almost certain execution by criminals who, in a bizarre reversal of circumstances, brazenly posted "wanted" notices for any officer of the law, especially Bass Reeves. Undeterred, Bass carried several of the posters in his pocket as collectibles.

> "There was no Sunday west of St. Louis, no God west of Fort Smith."
>
> A saying of the time

Reeves was ready for anything. Along with the six-shooters pointed outward, he often brandished a rifle! Reeves carried a bag of costumes for disguise – ragged shirts and broken-down shoes for his tramp persona, suits for his preacher act, work-worn clothes suitable for a farmer. Behind his magnificent mount, he trailed a scruffy horse for use in completing his deceptions. From the Indians, he had learned how to sink his large frame low in the saddle, further refining the art of fakery.

> "Place a warrant for arrest in his hands and no circumstance can cause him to deviate."
>
> (News article)

Straight-forward and immune to corruption, Reeves brought his own son to justice after the young man murdered his unfaithful wife. (A model prisoner, he was released after ten years.) And when the preacher who had baptized Reeves was caught selling illegal liquor, Bass took *him* in, as well.

Oklahoma statehood in 1907 ended Bass Reeves' days as a deputy marshal. He had served 32 years, the only one of Judge Parker's hires to work from the original appointments until dissolution of Indian Territory. Reeves arrested 3000 felons and killed 14. Reeves himself was never shot.

> "He dropped, and when I picked him up, I found that my two bullets had hit within a half-inch of each other."
>
> Bass Reeves

Bass settled in Muskogee and joined its police department. He patrolled the streets of the city with a gun, a walking cane, and (some say) a pal toting a sack of pistols.

Few crimes were committed in downtown Muskogee.

WAS BASS REEVES A MODEL FOR THE LONE RANGER?

The popular character in books, comic strips, radio, television, and movie programs is believed by many to have been based on the career of Deputy Marshal Bass Reeves, though the usual attribution identifies the Lone Ranger as the sole survivor of a group of Texas Rangers.

The fictional loner rode a horse named "Silver" and traveled in company with a Native-American sidekick, Tonto. He distributed silver bullets, hid behind a black mask, and demonstrated supreme horsemanship.

Bass Reeves' horse was light gray. His posse men were Indian friends; one particular fellow, identity unknown, accompanied Reeves on many of his criminal roundups and could have been a model for the role of Tonto. Additionally, Reeves' trademark was a silver coin, and numerous costumes disguised his true mission. He was a master horseman and gunman.

Both the Lone Ranger and Bass Reeves exhibited a strict and consistent moral code.

What seems to clinch the connection is that a large number of the prisoners Reeves brought into Fort Smith ended up in a prison in Detroit – the city where the "Lone Ranger" radio shows were created on station WXYZ.

There's no definitive proof that Reeves and the Lone Ranger were (or were not) the same, but Art Burton's summary softens the controversy.

"He (Bass Reeves) was the closest in real life to have these characteristics...a combo of Superman, Sherlock Holmes, and the Lone Ranger."

Moreover, since Reeves' burial spot is unknown, Burton suggests "he's *still* in disguise!"

Deputy Marshal Reeves took his prisoners to "Hanging Judge" Isaac C. Parker's courtroom in Fort Smith, Arkansas. The upright, conservative judge presided 21 years in the U.S. Federal Court for the Western District of Arkansas; due to unsettled and lawless times, most of his trials were of the criminal variety. In over 13,000 cases, the judge sentenced 160 men to death, but only 79 were actually hanged – though, on two occasions, six were hanged at once.

Judge Parker never witnessed the executions, mainly for rape or murder, and made it a point to emphasize the vast difference between a legal mandate and a human opinion. "I do not desire to hang you men. It is the law." Overshadowed by sensationalism were the judge's efforts in improving the criminal justice system, rehabilitating criminals, and working for the benefit of the Indian Nation.

Bass Reeves may have suffered from dyslexia, which could explain his difficulties in reading. That his mother read to him indicates some education in the home.

"...a heavenly slice of American history..."

HARVEY GIRLS

They were tastefully dressed in black and white – dresses, hair ribbons, stockings and shoes, aprons, bow ties. Between 18 and 30 in age and well-spoken. Of good moral character, abiding by company rules, and agreeing not to marry for one year after starting the job.

Having left family homes rich and poor, yet timid to try large cities like New York or Philadelphia, the young women were yearning for a chance to see their country and earn a living, with some adventure on the side.

The "women who opened the West" actually *charmed* it with civility and good nature, while their work habits brought an unprecedented sense of propriety to the job of food server. Those were the Harvey Girls – 100,000 of them.

One can believe it was destiny for Frederick Henry Harvey. Fresh in America from Liverpool in 1850, the teenager scrubbed kitchen pots for $2 a day at McNeil's, a popular New York City restaurant. What he learned there from his fussy bosses – food-service priorities like quality ingredients, premium service, and honest business practices – served the young man well in years to come.

Working his way forward in the eatery business, Fred stayed awhile in New Orleans; then, with terrible timing, he and a partner started up a café in St. Louis. The day before their establishment's grand opening, the Civil War broke out and the associate "took the money and ran" to serve in the Confederacy. In the tumult of conflict and with finances shattered, the young entrepreneur watched customers and opportunity fade away.

A door of possibilities cracked open when Fred landed a job sorting mail at a railroad depot and was promoted to the position of freight agent. Fred's past restaurant experience sharpened his observation of the average train passenger's abysmal dining situation. Rail transportation was new and impressive, but customers' food needs were handled in a distinctly offhanded manner. Trains offered nothing in the way of food or drinks. Station lunchrooms, should they exist at all, were filthy and pricey.

Every 100 miles or so, a train would stop for an hour-long break. Hungry travelers left their seats and searched on foot through an unfamiliar town for a restaurant, often settling on a seedy saloon. They waited impatiently for their orders and bolted down the food when it finally made an appearance, or, worse, left the meal uneaten at the sound of the train whistle. Many a rider found himself stranded as the locomotive chugged off into the night.

Fred Harvey had an idea, and the superintendent of the Atchison, Topeka, and Santa Fe Railroad was interested – seriously interested.

Inside the train depot at Topeka, Kansas, Harvey's first lunch counter opened in 1876, featuring dining space, a kitchen, storeroom, and living quarters for cooks and waiters. Nicely-appointed and immaculate, with reasonably-priced good food, the eatery promptly became a training kitchen for future depot diners from Kansas to California, 84 in all. By 1880, there existed a Harvey facility – a simple lunch bar, coffee shop, or formal dining room – at every 100-mile point along the Santa Fe line. The eateries were placed inside the depots or in nearby remodeled structures. In Holbrook, Arizona, five boxcars near the tracks were decorated in an Indian motif, as elegant as the nicest Harvey café.

It was a bombshell idea. Travelers "ate it up," you might say, and the railroad folks were assured of a first-rate meal experience for their passengers, which in turn increased their customer load. "Meals by Fred Harvey" became the motto of the Santa Fe line.

For the timely serving of meals at the depot, a crew member would wire ahead the number of passengers aboard. A spotter alerted the diner's staff when the train neared the station. Two entrees, with the same side dishes for both, were offered, while servers efficiently handled glasses and coffee cups. Harvey's depot lunch counters and diners were prepared to serve eight trainloads of passengers per day.

From the start, Harvey had *carte blanc* in his business arrangement with Santa Fe; the company provided free rail transport for his workers, supplies, equipment, building materials, and food products. Before long, meal ingredients were delivered in refrigerated cars. The cordial relationship between the Harvey folks and Santa Fe remained virtually the same throughout their near-100-year association. Fred Harvey's name identified the enterprise, even after his death.

Harvey House was America's first chain-restaurant operation. In formal settings, meals were served on sparkling china placed on linen tablecloths adorned with fresh flowers and silver utensils. The clientele expected excellent cuisine, and they were rarely disappointed. Dressed in white coats, an all-male wait staff circulated through the dining rooms.

Even snappy jackets, however, failed to mask the rough quality of many of the servers. And, revealing the raw edges of frontier civilization, many of the travelers themselves lacked social refinement. It was an after-hours brawl among waiters in Raton, New Mexico, though, that led to a drastic change in service.

Harvey Girls.

Fred recruited his new wait-staff through newspaper ads and magazines in the East and Midwest. With wages offered at $17.50 monthly, free room and board, uniforms, and rail passes to their destinations, the gals who'd previously had been trapped in low-pay teaching positions and dull domestic jobs came running.

Harvey Girls worked out every bit as well as Fred had hoped. During the years it was said that there were "no ladies west of Dodge City and no women west of Albuquerque," the girls lifted waitressing from its low-end position. Their dignified behavior and professional appearance indicated that the "Wild West" was absolutely safe to enter.

In time, landmark hotels (with those fabulous dining rooms and, sometimes, a ballroom for community use) went up in resort areas throughout the Southwest, where Fred combined Spanish, Indian, and Mexican culture with his renowned hospitality.

Mr. Harvey had long-standing doubts, though, about gourmet meal preparation on a fast-moving transport. His design was to feed people *off* the trains! At last, Santa Fe rail bosses overcame Fred's hesitation and he reluctantly agreed to try in-transit dining on all routes out of Kansas City, insisting, of course, on his signature high standards. The "California Limited" was the first passenger train to offer Harvey meal service on board, where the entire group of travelers could be fed in less than an hour.

Cozy tables with lamps shining on elite menus featuring filet mignon and strawberry-topped ice cream made a lasting impression of elegant travel. Movie producers lapped up the memorable settings. Actors delivered their lines during a "meal;" they smoked, drank, flirted, and danced around tables and booths. Free and favorable publicity overshadowed the absolute lack of profit in dining cars.

The heyday years of the Harvey operation were traumatic times for many families, especially immigrants and homesteading farmers. Most Harvey Girls came from humble backgrounds, yet the young women became the company's most-recognized icon. The girls received valuable training for future jobs and those working at Houses in college towns were encouraged to attend classes; generous tips and service at special events helped pay for tuition and books.

Too young for work, underage daughters of widows nevertheless found refuge at Harvey's hotels during hard times. And, despite the contractual ban on dating and marriage, more than a few wedded couples confided that they, too, were given a place to live. "Family" is the word heard most often when employees recall their years with the Harvey group.

> "I learned about people, about hard work and responsibility, about discipline. And the people I worked for became my family. It was a very close group."
>
> Bernice Myers

Among the warm-hearted stories of former waitresses is that of Violet Bosetti, who felt that "all those Harvey Girls were just railroaders themselves at heart... all fascinated by the trains." At age 8, she and her 11-year-old sister pulled a wagon alongside the tracks every winter day to gather loose coal that had fallen off trains; they picked up discarded ice in the summer. Her father, a Kansas coal miner, had died, and the little family needed the coal for their stove and the ice to preserve food.

In the 1940s, Maxine Kellar of Cross Cut, Texas, shared a room with her sister upstairs in the Brownwood train depot. (Their room has been restored as part of the depot's museum.) The girls met a host of travelers as they waited tables, but Maxine herself had to wait a year for the job; she was only 15 when, with her father's permission, she left home for the big adventure.

Some 20,000 Harvey Girls are said to have married ranchers, miners, cowboys, railroad men, and perhaps 4000 had sons named "Fred," "Henry," or both. (The gals were free to marry after a year on the job.) Humorist Will Rogers suggested that the government issue a dime with Fred Harvey on one side and a Harvey Girl on the other, because Harvey "kept the West in food and wives."

The Harvey Girls, not highly educated or noteworthy, with no places or towns named for them, nonetheless became a part of the history of the West as they worked, raised families, and meshed together in communities.

> "If there is a moral to the history of the westward movement, it is this – the transcendent importance of small things and unimportant people."
>
> E.D. Branch

Under the guidance of Fred's son and son-in law after his death in 1901, the Harvey enterprise was set upon a course of dips and leaps through the 20th century. The end of World War I saw cars and improved roads diminish the lure of train travel. During the Great Depression, pleasure excursions all but disappeared.

Passenger and freight trains were on the move again in World War II, hauling troops, vehicles, and equipment, but the post-war boom of the Fifties with its interstate highways and airplane travel brought to a close the era of elegant rail cars and destination hotels.

Fred Harvey's enterprise ceased to exist in 1968, but two magnificent hotels and their signature dining rooms – El Tovar in Grand Canyon, Arizona, and La Fonda in Santa Fe, New Mexico – are still open in elegant style.

Thanks, Fred. It was quite a ride.

Fred Harvey defined "eating out" in America with his depot lunch counters, rail car diners, and fine restaurants and hotels. Charles F. Morse was the Santa Fe superintendent who decided to give depot eateries a try. With success, Morse deemed Harvey the "The Civilizer of the West." Harvey had initially approached Burlington Railroad; the company was not interested. A brief association with Kansas Pacific (now Union Pacific) was likewise unfruitful.

Even after his death, the enterprise kept the name "Fred Harvey."

The phrase, "No ladies west of Dodge City and no women west of Albuquerque," is credited to Harvey Girls author Lesley Poling Kempes.

A 1946 MGM musical, "The Harvey Girls," starred Angela Lansbury and Judy Garland. The movie introduced Harry Warren and Johnny Mercer's classic song, "On the Atchison, Topeka, and the Santa Fe."

Some Hispanic and a few Indian girls were hired as Harvey Girls, and many others were from immigrant families. Black ladies worked for the railroad as maids and cooks in the hotels and diners.

For his resorts in the Southwest, Fred commissioned renowned artists and architects so that his properties were styled authentically and in harmony with the regional background.

On his deathbed, Fred Harvey is said to have advised, "Cut the ham thinner, boys."

"We are friends; we must assist each other to bear our burdens."

Osage proverb

CHIEF BACON RIND

Wah-she-hah, "Star That Travels," was his Osage name. We remember him as Chief Bacon Rind.

Bacon Rind and newsman Pete Duffy, the mayor of El Reno, Oklahoma, met for an interview in 1913. The conversation may have been prompted by the mind-boggling fact that the Osage in those days were earning interest off $10,000,000 in oil revenues deposited in the federal treasury.

More about that in a minute.

So here was a conference of two chiefs. (Pete, as head of that state's editorial group, could be considered a chief, we suppose.)

The interview went like this, through an interpreter.

Bacon Rind: "No man is really happy who must work, and now that the Osage are rich, if any work is to be done, it is easy enough to hire a white man to do it."

Pete Duffy: "[I'd like to understand the] secret of your success, your 'recipe' for how the tribe live like kings while we work eighteen hours a day. Would the chief share his recipe with me, a brother chief?"

Bacon Rind: "Used to be, Indian, he take buzzard and, white man, he take turkey. [But now], Indian say he divide with Meester Duffy. He say he himself take *bacon* and give *rind* to Meester Duffy. He, big Chief, take *bacon* – yes."

Well, there you are. The Bacon and the Rind.

※※

The future tribal chief migrated to Indian Territory, Oklahoma, during the Osage removal from Kansas in the 1870s. A natural leader, he rose to the role of principal chief. Traditional in customs and costume, he nevertheless was a progressive executive protecting his people through the tumultuous development of oil and natural-gas resources on 1.5 million acres of reservation land.

Historically, the Osage were hunter-gatherers, but, as the cattle industry expanded in Oklahoma, grazing leases on their reservation north of Tulsa began to produce generous incomes. And then petroleum was discovered. (Oil deposits were well-known by Natives from early days; they used the petroleum for medicinal, water-proofing, and mosquito-deterrent purposes.)

The Osage nation's first producing oil well was drilled in 1897; by 1918, the reservation had 4000 active wells in the largest oil-producing area in America. That "underground reservation" produced more wealth than the California and Colorado gold rushes combined.

Official auctioneer for the Osage Nation was a lifelong friend of the Natives. Colonel Ellsworth Walters conducted sales encompassing millions of dollars in the shade of, yes, the Million-Dollar Elm on the grounds of the tribe's agency at Pawhuska. The largest bid taken by Colonel Walters in an Osage mineral rights auction was $1,990,000 in a lease of 160 acres by Josh Cosden.

Colonel Walters was hired by an Indian agent, J. George Wright, when the auctions began. While these go-between agents often were at the low end of respectability, Mr. Wright proved to be a gem, managing the tribe's auctions and financial considerations over two decades.

A 1906 tribal act called for the mineral income to be distributed annually to individual tribal members on a per-capita basis, or "headright." Each of the 2,229 individuals on that year's list held an equal share of the wealth. The original headrights have passed to descendants. $233 million was divided among the Osage between 1907 and 1929, when tribal mineral incomes were at their peak, making them the richest people per capita in the world.

As times and circumstances change, some of the headright arrangements and responsibilities have been modified; newer rules have tighter restrictions about inheritance and sale of headrights. Some of the income is placed in an account for all Indians' benefit and some is used for tribal government. Along with many other Native groups, the Osage gain additional profit from tribal casinos or other enterprises.

Four major oil companies have roots in Oklahoma, part of the Mid-Continent Oil and Gas Region. Cosden Oil and Gas was founded by Josh Cosden in Tulsa in 1917. The same year, Frank and L.E. Phillips started up Phillips Petroleum in Bartlesville. In 1919, William G. (Bill)

Skelly organized Skelly Oil Company. Continental Oil Company, or Conoco, originated in Ogden, Utah, but relocated to Ponca City in 1929; Conoco merged with Phillips in 2002.

One of the most-photographed of all Indian leaders, Chief Bacon Rind spent his later years as a delegate in Washington, D.C., speaking for his people. A "Bond of Friendship" statue at Skedee, OK, honors both Colonel Walters and Chief Bacon Rind. (The Skidi were a band of Pawnee.) The Osage gave Col. Walters a diamond badge and ring; Walters commissioned the statue in his home county, Pawnee.

As for the outdone Pete Duffy (who "got the rind," not the bacon) his reply was, "Huh! That old sport isn't an Indian, he's a *Kansan*."

Probably meant as a gentle insult, the statement rings true. Bacon Rind did come from Kansas. Remember the Osage removal?

The chief's "traditional" costume often showcased a Mexican blanket, beaded moccasins, and an otter-skin cap.

At the time of World War I, Osage men were not U.S. citizens; still, they honored the military draft with the highest percentage of any ethnic group in America. In World War II, they did the same.

The current population of the Osage tribe is about 15,000.

During a period called the Reign of Terror, a number of Osage were cheated or murdered for their oil wealth. The crimes ended and convictions occurred once the Federal Bureau of Investigation was formed. The Osage murders became the first large case handled by the F.B.I.

Colonel (his actual first name) Ellsworth Walters (1865-1946), though not a colonel himself, was named for Colonel Elmer Ephraim Ellsworth, the first Union Army casualty of the Civil War. E.E. Ellsworth was a friend of Abraham Lincoln and had worked in Lincoln's law office. On May 24, 1865, Union troops were in possession of Alexandria, Virginia, when Ellsworth spotted a Confederate flag atop the Marshall House Inn. He climbed to the roof, ripped down the flag, and was shot by the inn's proprietor, who, in turn was bayoneted by an Ellsworth aide.

Gladys Kitchen of the Pawnee Historical Society offers an example of a clever Indian nickname in her own family. As a little boy, Mrs. Kitchen's dad delivered groceries from his grandfather's market to the Pawnee roundhouse, a local community center. But the kid was usually covered in grease because his own dad worked in a machine shop. When the oily lad appeared at the roundhouse door, a good-natured Pawnee greeted him as "Nisada-skoo-hoots-a-keet-lashar." That's "little-dirty-chief-with-grease-on-face."

"We proceeded on..."

THE TRUSTED TRIO

Lewis and Clark's Corps of Discovery included an unusual triad – a dog, a black slave, and a young Shoshone woman. Each proved an asset of unexpected, yet immeasurable, proportion – together, an undisputed factor in the historic journey's overwhelming success.

SEAMAN

As Lewis departed Pittsburgh in preparation for the expedition westward, he purchased a black Newfoundland for a then-grand sum of $20. In no time, Seaman became "our dog." He romped, he rambled, he sniffed, and he hunted. Like a figurehead on the prow of the keelboat, he perched front and center. Those webbed, water-resistant feet and a sharp nose translated into many a supper for the crew and, providentially, as early warning against prowlers, charging buffalo, serpents, and vicious grizzly bears (a species never-before-seen by the adventurers).

The Natives took note of the pooch, as well. Some tried to strike a bargain for Seaman. Oregon Clatsop lured him away – briefly, as you might expect, given the affection of the explorers for "our dog."

YORK

York was not a servant; he and his slave parents were inherited by 15-year-old William Clark. York was devoted to his master, and Kentucky's forest environment encouraged a proficiency in outdoor skills. Nine Kentucky men were recruited by Clark for the Corps of Discovery, and York, having no choice, went along, as well.

Powerful in size, strength, and agility, York was the first African American to cross the continent of America north of Mexico. Excelled in hunting, scouting, rowing. Saved Clark in a flash flood and Lewis from a grizzly. Prepared meals. Doctored the sick and was an agile dancer. Fixed tents and sails. Bartered for food. Voted on expedition matters. Had his own rifle.

Not surprisingly, York was a "celebrity" with the Natives. Who knows how many clashes were averted by his distinctive, larger-than-life appearance? Oral history tells how "the [Mandan] chief took dirt to rub [the] black off and could not... The chief had respect that he was a man, strong and busy."

Sadly, York's exhilarating experiences on the westward expedition were not sustained at journey's end. The William Clark who was so admirable a leader and defender of York on the trail reverted to "master" afterwards. Almost all the post-1806 accounts elicit sympathy for York, for he received none of the rewards, accolades, or pay of the other travelers.

Clark at last manumitted his slave, though it was probably a decade later. Some believe York operated a freighting business, but it is likely to have failed. Possibly, he headed westward again to live in free and open country with Indian friends, though various accounts mention his death from cholera along the way.

SACAGAWEA

Forefront in the many fortuitous circumstances during the journey of the Corps stands the employment of a translator named Toussaint Charbonneau. The man turned out to be annoying and hapless as an expedition member. Ah, but Charbonneau had a wife, Sacagawea.

Recognized by most schoolchildren today, the young woman assisted the explorers every step of the great westward adventure. Her baby, Jean Baptiste ("Pomp"), brought smiles to men lonely for families back home. Sacagawea's cultural background made her an expert on edible and medicinal plants, preserving food in the wild, and repairing clothing broken down by continuous wear. Vital to the safety of the expedition's members was her keen observation of natural clues about the movement of the Natives in the area. In addition, her coolness under pressure once saved a number of valuable documents – expedition reports and scientific observations – when the party's pirogue came dangerously close to capsizing.

Sacagawea was a symbol of peace. The Corps of Discovery was in no way a war party, but Natives along the river and in the mountains might have deemed it so without the presence of a woman and child. What a saving grace she turned out to be – a silent, yet visible, symbol of non-aggression seated with her little boy in a boat.

The expedition traveled from St. Louis up the Missouri River to the base of the Rockies. Without a water link to the Columbia on the other side, and with no animals to portage over the mountains, the mission would have been forced, on the cusp of success, to turn back. It was Sacagawea's interaction with her people, the Shoshone, that resulted in the acquisition of horses and mules to bear the exploring party over the massive range to the headwaters of the Columbia, where they floated onward to the Pacific.

"Through Sacagawea, through York, through the lowliest privates, through the sergeants, up to the captains themselves, this was a family that had come together and formed a team for the exploration of the continent of North America. And they couldn't have done it if they hadn't become a family. And forged themselves into a team."

Stephen Ambrose

The votes of Sacagawea and York (on selecting a winter camp site) are recorded in expedition journals. The pair are the first known woman and African-American to have freely voted in our country, though, arguably, the ballot was not part of an official public election. Nevertheless, it's a testimony that each member of the Corps of Discovery was considered an equal partner in the endeavor.

The Lewis and Clark expedition ate an estimated 200 dogs over the course of their travels. "Our dog" Seaman, understandably, was off their menu (and more than once was rescued from some Native tribe's dinner plan).

In 2001, President Bill Clinton posthumously granted York the rank of sergeant in the U.S. Army. York Island is an archipelago in Broadwater County, Montana. Also, York is honored by a pair of statues – at Lewis and Clark College, Portland, Oregon, and at Riverfront Plaza/Belvedere, Louisville, Kentucky.

"There wasn't but seven Dimmycrats in Hinsdale County and you done et five of them."
    (Falsely-attributed to Judge Melville B. Gerry)

ALFERD PACKER

"Him too fat."

Such was the opinion of a Native American at the Los Pinos Indian Agency in April, 1874. Furthermore, there seemed to be an unusual amount of money drifting around little Saguache, Colorado.

Alferd Packer, a would-be miner and guide, had arrived at the agency with a tale beyond belief. He reported that he and five fellow prospectors had been stranded deep in a snow-filled valley near present-day Lake City, surrounded by towering peaks.

The previous November, Packer, who claimed to be an experienced mountaineer, recruited some eager would-be miners in Provo, Utah. The party, numbering about twenty, set out for Colorado and, almost immediately, became lost. Packer was unceremoniously dumped as escort, but the group managed to stumble into Chief Ouray's camp in the San Juan Range.

The benign Ute leader warned the men of winter's treachery in the high country and graciously invited them to remain in his village until spring. Fifteen settled in with the Utes, but the defiant Packer and a quintet of gold-mad fools trudged away from the warm and friendly lodges in February.

George Noon, James Humphrey, Israel Swan, Frank Miller, and Shannon Bell, along with Packer, were soon in deep trouble. Trapped and starving, they were reduced to eating pine gum and dead plants. Temperatures were unrelenting, the lake was frozen, and no hunting was possible in the depths of winter.

Sixty-five days later, Packer showed up well-fed at Los Pinos – alone and flush with cash and weapons. Whiskey was his request – not food. He told stories and more stories. Such erratic behavior brought forth plenty of questions about his previous whereabouts and actions.

In the eyes of law authorities, as well, Packer was under suspicion. Within a few days, he emerged with his first confession, but it was four months before the bodies of his comrades were located – in brutal condition – near Lake City. An artist for *Harper's Weekly* sketched the remains; his vivid drawings led Hinsdale County to convene a coroner's jury, which found sufficient evidence for prosecution. Self-deflected wounds of the victims plus de-fleshing of corpses almost certainly indicated murder followed by cannibalism. Money and rifles found in Packer's possession had been taken from the dead.

About that time, Packer mysteriously disappeared from his jail cell at Saguache and the case was at a standstill for nine years.

In 1883, Alferd Packer, living under a false name, was recognized in a Wyoming bar; his distinctive laugh was heard by Frenchy Corazon, an original member of the prospecting party.

A murder trial followed, in which Packer was convicted and sentenced to death by hanging. Judge Melville B. Gerry, reportedly convinced that the motive for the five deaths was robbery, is said to have spoken these words:

> "I hereby sentence you to be hung by the neck till you are dead, dead, dead."

That's the legend – and clever, at that. However, it's much more likely the learned and sober judge said:

> "Close your ears to the blandishments of hope. Listen not to the clattering promises of life, but prepare for the dread certainly of death."

Much more dignified.

The hanging never took place.

A "grandfather clause" in Colorado law protected Packer since the crimes had occurred while the Centennial State was yet a territory. By the time of his trial under murder statutes of the *state* of Colorado, the case was null and void.

In 1886, a second trial led to another conviction, this time for manslaughter, and a sentence of forty years in prison. Having served sixteen, Packer was paroled in 1903 for "senility, trouble, and worry." The old boy lived quietly, reportedly very friendly and kind to neighbors and children, until his death in 1907.

So – what actually happened? Through the years, Packer offered three assorted confessions. No living witnesses existed. Time and exposure to the elements had marred the campsite. It's hard to piece together the actual circumstances, but it could have been like this.

Half-frozen, starving, desperate men are not rational. A staggering series of mistakes may have occurred. Mr. Swan likely died first, probably of natural causes, and the others resorted to cannibalism for survival.

When that was consumed, Packer claimed, he was sent to look for meat; on his return he found three more bodies and Bell, obviously having killed the men, in a murderous rage. In self-defense Packer shot Bell, consumed some of his flesh, and took the rest along as he struck out for the Indian agency.

Disturbing was the evidence of violence at the scene. Victims seem to have been trying to defend themselves. An exhumation of remains was undertaken in 1985. The findings showed blunt-force blows, cuts, and nicks on the skeletons.

What's certain is that we will never know for certain.

Contrary to some accounts, Alferd Packer was not tried for cannibalism; there were no statues for that act.

Packer's first trial charged *murder* and the second, *manslaughter*. Concerning both this case and that of the Donner Party, an absorbing perspective has been offered by a specialist in forensic sciences.

> "I don't think there will ever be any way to scientifically demonstrate cannibalism. Cannibalism is, per se, the ingestion of human flesh. So you'd have to have a picture of the guy actually eating."
> James E. Starrs

After the exhumation of remains, the five victims were reburied in a wooden box on Cannibal Plateau near Lake City, Colorado, site of the calamity. Packer is interred in Littleton, Colorado.

In 1986, the University of Colorado at Boulder dubbed its dining facility, "Alferd Packer Memorial Grill." ("Have a friend for lunch" was its slogan.) After a tangle with the USDA and the GSA food service, the moniker at Boulder was dropped. But not lost. An eatery tent at the Philadelphia Folk Festival has its own Packer Memorial Grill, "serving humanity since 1874." Lake City, Colorado, as might be expected, sports a Cannibal Grill and Saloon. Packer fan clubs, movies, and songs abound, as well.

Alferd or Alfred? Gravestone says "Alfred" but his arm tattoo read "Alferd." It's reported that the ink artist couldn't spell precisely and that Packer liked the disarrangement of letters. He was known to spell it both ways himself!

Some have observed that, since the alleged murders took place on Ute reservation lands, any trial for Packer should have been held in a federal court.

Who exclaimed, "Him too fat"? It can't be proven, but some think it might've have been Chief Ouray himself, while visiting the Los Pinos Indian Agency after the snow melted in the San Juans. Could the chief have recalled his earlier encounter with the foolhardy Packer?

Alone among the states, Idaho banned cannibalism in a 1990 statute, with an exception for "extreme life-threatening conditions as the only apparent method of survival." (Code 18-5003 was still on the books in 2016.) The lawmakers' concern was the possible use of the practice in ritualistic ceremonies. Cannibalism *per se* isn't a crime elsewhere, but actions associated with it might violate laws against murder or corpse desecration.

A posthumous pardon for Alferd Packer was denied in 1981.

"The Pathfinder" John C. Fremont described Colorado's San Juan range as "the highest, most rugged, most impracticable and inaccessible" of the Rocky Mountains. He should know; his "Fatal Fourth" expedition resulted in the deaths of ten men.

"...simply exasperating...I never got a shot."
                                    Theodore Roosevelt

TEDDY'S BEAR

Miles of timber and briars, and not a bear to be found.

Theodore Roosevelt, as a young man, had been astounded by the grandeur of the West's soaring peaks, high adventure, and healing climate. It was there he latched onto an outdoor lifestyle that endured.

Early in his Presidency, Roosevelt traveled by train to Mississippi for a grand bear hunt in the South, a region not very friendly to this particular leader of the nation. Wary of hecklers, he'd emerged furtively from the train car. Dressed in leather, flannel, and corduroy, with a hunting knife tucked into his belt, he toted his custom-made Winchester rifle, its walnut butt marred by cougar bites.

The sporting party rode horseback into a remote forest near the Little Sunflower River, their supplies hauled in by mule. After the meticulous preparation, it was embarrassing that no quarry was sighted on the initial day's foray. 'Round the campfire that first evening, the President regaled his comrades with anecdotes of his years in the Wild West, where he had put a fine point on his zeal for boundless vistas and thrilling buffalo hunts.

And then Roosevelt was in his second day afield without a speck of hunter's luck. In his rambunctious way, he was growing impatient. The scouting team returned to the woods alone with their search dogs after lunch, resolute about not disappointing their distinguished guest.

The guides spotted a bear – an old black one, but small, about 235 pounds. Chased by the dogs and exhausted, the animal dived into a watering hole and struck out with his paw, breaking the spine of one of the canines. As the other dogs stood growling, a guide tied the bear to an oak tree, cracked its skull with the butt of his gun, and bugled that the President should hurry in for the kill.

Enraged at the sight of the pitiful animal, Roosevelt boomed, *"Put it out of its misery!"*

The dreary excursion lasted three more days in the humidity of southern-woodland mists. There would be no trophy kills on this hunt. As expected in the news business, every move by the President had been recorded and reported. By the time the entourage returned to the White House, the nation was nodding its approval of the Chief Executive's adherence to the sportsman's code.

Political cartoonist Clifford Berryman printed a now-iconic illustration of the hunting scenario with the caption, "Drawing the Line in Mississippi." In the picture, the irate President stands up for a cowering little bear. The image would initiate the most enduring of all the Teddy Roosevelt legends.

Seeing the cartoon in the New York papers, a Russian-born immigrant in the city asked his wife to make a toy bear. Morris and Rose Michtom operated a candy store; to make ends meet, Rose often stitched up dolls at night and sold them to customers.

Her bear of plush velvet featured black shoe-button eyes and was tagged "Teddy's Bear." Placed in the front window of their shop in Brooklyn, the little cuddler with a famous name was immediately in demand.

Right away, Morris and Rose sent Mr. Roosevelt one of the bears and asked his permission to attach his name to the toy. Teddy replied, "I don't know what my name may mean to the bear business, but you're welcome to use it."

The Michtoms couldn't keep up with orders for the little furries, so they left the candy business to focus on that "bear business," forming the Ideal Toy and Novelty Company (now Ideal Toy Company).

About that time, totally unrelated to happenings in New York, Richard Steiff of Germany exhibited a toy bear with movable arms at the Leipzig Trade Fair of 1903. Steiff and his Aunt Margaret, a seamstress who had founded the company in 1880, were almost certainly unaware of "Teddy's Bear." Steiff is reported to have observed bears performing upright at a circus, latched onto the idea of a "standing" toy bear, then visited the Stuttgart Zoo to sketch cubs.

The German bear's name was "Petsy" ("bear" or "bruin"). Europeans didn't express much interest in the toy animals, so Steiff exported many of them to America, particularly to F.A.O. Schwarz of New York City.

"Teddy's Bear," though, was the American original and remains the most popular toy bear of all time. *Plaything Magazine,* October, 1906, changed the name slightly to "Teddy Bear" and thus it has remained. Roosevelt always called the toy "Berryman's Bear," while Clifford Berryman titled it "Roosevelt's Bear."

In 1963, the Michtoms' grandson Benjamin presented the original bear to Theodore Roosevelt's grandson Kermit and his family. One month later, the Roosevelts donated "Teddy" to the Smithsonian Institution.

The gallant Mr. Berryman never sought compensation for all the sales, uses, and images of the cub he created. He would simply smile and say, "I have made thousands of children happy. That's enough for me."

The 100th anniversary of the teddy bear was celebrated in 2002.

"...from wet and angry to soft and cuddly"
                                                Gilbert King

Some argued that the "Drawing the line in Mississippi" caption on Clifford Berryman's cartoon had a double meaning. The picture shows President Roosevelt refusing to cross a line into unsportsmanlike conduct. Cynics, however, insisted that the President was in Mississippi at the invitation of Governor Andrew H. Longino to help settle a dispute between that state and Louisiana over the *boundary line* between the two. Oh, balderdash. The cartoon very plainly featured a frightened bear and a bold President.

President Roosevelt used "his" bear in the successful re-election campaign of 1904. In the 1908 Presidential race, another toy company introduced a pet for nominee William Howard Taft – a plush opossum named "Billy Possum," with the absurd slogan, "Goodbye, Teddy Bear – Hello, Billy Possum." What a flop. Taft liked to <u>eat</u> the possum he hunted, but he won the election anyhow, defeating Wm. J. Bryan.

The German bear had a long snout, and all the original toy bears had beady eyes.

In modern times, the eyes are larger (and securely attached), and the noses are smaller. As of 1905, the Steiff bears have a trademarked button in one ear.

Clothes for bears have remained popular for kids who like to dress them. *Ladies' Home Journal* sold patterns for bear clothes early on, and today's pattern books offer guides for almost any type of doll or toy animal.

Berryman's newspaper cartoon inspiring the Michtoms appeared November 14, 1902, and it's said that Rose placed their new little bear in the store window that very day. It was probably early 1903 when the Steiffs' bear made its public debut.

"At my age I suppose I should be knitting. But I would rather play poker with five or six experts than eat."
                                               Poker Alice Tubbs

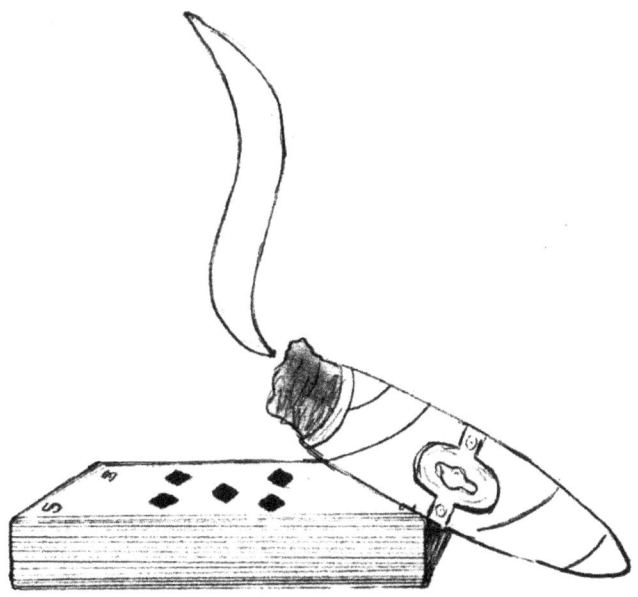

POKER ALICE

It was a long way from the refined Virginia lifestyle of a schoolmaster's daughter to the rough-and-tumble mines of Leadville, Colorado.

The song of silver enticed Alice Ivers' family to pull up stakes and move westward, settling in the chilly, high-altitude town. At age 20, Alice married mining engineer Frank Duffield, who was, at heart, a gambler. His young wife watched distractedly as he played, but her interest peaked as she discovered her own proficiency at poker and faro.

Alice had no means of support after Frank was killed in a mine explosion. Teaching was out of the question; there was no school in

Leadville. Boldly, Alice went into action. She would make her living by gambling, and she already had the "chops" to do so, in high demand as a player and dealer.

Alice looked lovely at the tables – petite stature, blue eyes, and lustrous brown hair. Attired in fashionable clothing, the lady traveled from camp to camp in search of favorable winnings. Oddly, she took to puffing on a large black cigar while maintaining an expressionless "poker face." She carried a .38 revolver (as did all serious gamesmen) and refused to work on Sundays. Always drawing customers and onlookers, Poker Alice was welcome in the gaming halls whenever she chose to appear.

> "Praise the Lord and place your bets. I'll take your money with no regrets."
>
> Poker Alice Tubbs

The popular lady gambled in Colorado, New Mexico, and South Dakota, sometimes winning as much as $6000 in a single evening at the tables. Her gaming stints were periodically interrupted by rollicking trips to New York City for more frilly outfits.

In South Dakota, Alice found her permanent home. She married Warren G. Tubbs, a housepainter (and dealer/gambler, naturally), and they had seven kids. Time to settle down, live the ranch life, and raise the children.

But Warren died of pneumonia. Legend has it that Alice loaded him into their horse-drawn wagon and drove him to town for burial, pawning her wedding band for funeral expenses. And so...she returned to the parlor to win back her money.

The peace and quiet of the country satisfied Alice, but she was widowed a third time when the ranch-hand husband she had wed because "I owe him so much in back wages I figured it would be cheaper to marry than pay him off" fell ill and died.

At age 60, the widow entered the entertainment business with a saloon, gambling parlor, and bordello. She bought an old house and secured a two-year loan to add some rooms for "her girls."

The banker was astounded when Alice paid off the note in less than a year. Alice herself was taken aback at her quick profits at the "baudy house," but only momentarily so.

"Well, it was this way," said Alice. "I knew the *Grand Army of the Republic* was having an encampment here.

And I knew that the *Elks'* convention would be here, too.

"But I plumb forgot about all the *Methodist preachers* coming to town for a conference!"

In old age, Alice's fashionable outfits gave way to a faded skirt, a man's droopy shirt, and a battered hat. Sadly, the years of heavy smoking finally degraded her health.

She claimed to have won $250,000 in a lifetime at the gaming table and proudly asserted that she never cheated a soul. Poker Alice Tubbs died at age 79 and is buried in Sturgis, South Dakota.

"Nature's Perfect Food"

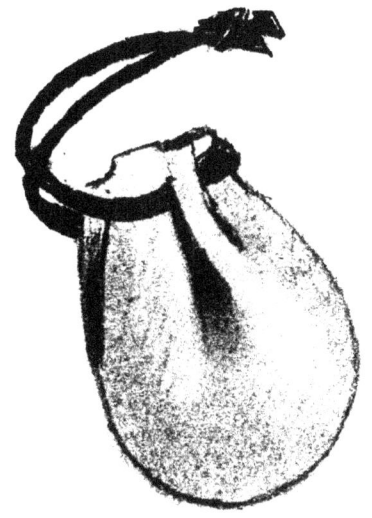

PEMMICAN

Created by Natives of North America. Embraced as a mainstay of the Plains Indians' diet.

A Cree word, *pimikin* or *pimihkan* specifies lean parts of meat dried in the sun, pounded into powder, and mixed with melted fat. Buffalo, elk, deer, moose, and caribou meat all make first-rate pemmican.

Fish pemmican was common, as well, in the Hudson Bay area and in the Northwest, where Natives pounded dried fish and mixed it with sturgeon or seal oil. Nature itself may have offered the original pemmican – an animal caught under a fallen tree, a morsel of meal clinging to a gobbled-up carcass, or a dead fish washed ashore.

Similar to jerky, pemmican nevertheless boasts several advantages over the dried slabs of jerked meat.

Pemmican's covering of melted fat renders it less difficult to chew; it proved more satisfying for humans whose teeth were not as well-treated as ours. The fat makes pemmican waterproof, resistant to mold, and well-preserved for up to 30 years, according to some reports. Unlike jerky's awkward strips, the pulverized dried meat of pemmican was easily packed and carried by nomadic people, and it was an important trade item among Native societies.

It was a more efficient product, as well. "Jerked" meat must be separated from connective tissue and tendons. Up to 1000 pounds of beef are required to yield just 90 pounds of jerky – considerably more costly than pemmican in terms of time, labor, and reduced output.

Natives made pemmican in all seasons, but their best-quality goods may have been put together during long summer days that afforded time for careful preparation, starting with the removal of bone bits and gristle from edible flesh. Then the meat was thoroughly dried, perhaps on mats high off the ground on a framework of poles. With stones, it was pulverized into a powder, placed in bags, and coated with sun-melted suet (fat). The bag was sewn shut, completing a packing operation that provided a long-lasting snack eaten raw or cooked.

Extra-special to pemmican was the twang of sweet and tart berries, in season. Favorites in the wild were cherries, cranberries, blueberries, June berries, and Saskatoon berries (serviceberries).

Winter's frosty bitterness, fortunately, was not prohibitive in making this commodity. Wind dried the meat naturally, and cold weather safeguarded it. Flies would not annoy, and, with much-reduced travel during frigid months, preparation and stashing of pemmican was not a burden. During rainy spells, the process of dehydration took place over a fire, in a tent, or under the shelter of trees.

Like jerky, pemmican's appeal did not fade as time marched onward. A Canadian Mountie, on field duty in 1874, shunned eating the product raw, but pronounced it quite tasty cooked with flour and water in a stew called "rababou" or "robbiboe." It was equally good fried in a hot skillet. Potatoes and dried onions, he said, dressed it up considerably.

Expeditionary parties, such as those bound for the Arctic and Antarctic, relied on the lightweight concentrate of fat and protein during long and arduous journeys. Robert Peary carried pemmican on his three treks to the North Pole.

> "Too much cannot be said of the importance of pemmican to a polar expedition; it is absolutely *sine qua non*. Without it a sledge party cannot compact its supplies within a limit of weight to make a serious polar journey successful."
>
> Robert Peary

Today, "paleo food" has squirmed into a prominent niche in the realm of high adventure and online blogging. Once the mainstay of old-time Natives, hunters, trappers, soldiers, and explorers, pemmican in current trendy times may incorporate rump roast, London broil, grass-fed beef, and honey.

> "Before granola became a mainstay, pemmican was the ultimate portable snack food."
>
> Greg Parham

In 1851, Gail Borden produced "meat biscuits," a dehydrated beef product similar to pemmican. Successful at the 1852 London World's Fair, he must have missed the mark at home, because the U.S. Army refused to contract the biscuits for its soldiers.

Returning by sea from London, Borden was horrified at many deaths of children on the ship due to contaminated milk from onboard cows. He swiftly turned his attention from meat to the production of canned condensed milk. As well, Mr. Borden's urge to preserve milk in tin cans may have reflected his deep sadness over the recent starvation deaths of families in the Donner Party, some of whom might have been saved by the product, had it been available.

Adventure-writer Brad Rohdenburg's trendy version of pemmican mixes equal parts powdered jerky, fruit, nuts, and raisins, all combined with peanut butter and honey. For a sweet-and hot flavor, add a dash of cayenne pepper. Skip the rawhide sacks and store in plastic zip-bags.

Pemmican for the modern world.

Brad Rohdenburg scoffs at MREs (the Army's familiar "meals-ready-to-eat") because the food requires preparation, using pans, utensils, and heaters – completely undoing the "ready" feature. He sticks with the time-honored quartet of pemmican, jerky, hardtack, and parched corn.

If you're interested in hardtack, think again. The name says it all – salt plus flour plus water. Parched corn – ditto; it's merely corn kernels dried in an oiled skillet.

Must you? Well, dip the hardtack or parched corn in bacon grease, hot water, or coffee and you have primitive gourmet cookin'.

"Don't get out; I never bother the passengers."
                                            Black Bart

GENTLEMAN ROBBER

He was afraid of horses.

His armed heists of Wells Fargo gold shipments were carried out on foot.

Wrote poetry, leaving it as a souvenir after the thefts.

Never fired a shot in 8 years and 28 robberies.

"Please throw down the strongbox."

"No, ma'am. I'm only after Wells Fargo."

"Sure hope you have a lot of gold. I'm nearly out of money."

※※ ※※

British-born Charles E. Boles ventured to California to prospect for gold, without success, then married in Illinois and served honorably in Union forces during the Civil War, seriously wounded at the Battle of Vicksburg.

A restless Boles found himself in the West again, never returning to his wife, but writing her about a grievance with Wells Fargo, the banking and rapid-express delivery company. In his anger, Boles must have recalled that...

Wells Fargo carried gold – in strongboxes.

In December, 1875, a stagecoach in Calaveras County, California, was accosted by a most uncommon robber. A flour sack with holes for eyes covered his head; two more bags covered his boots. He wore a long linen duster coat, carried a double-barreled shotgun, and spoke in a deep, resonant voice, ever polite and spouting no foul language. A heavy "imperial" mustache shadowed the face.

One of the dime novels popular in Gold-Rush days presented a grimy dark-haired, black-bearded character named Bartholomew Graham, or "Black Bart." Mild-mannered Charles E. Boles therein found his new identity. With a twist. The "new" Black Bart wrote poetry.

> "Here I lay me down to sleep
> To wait the coming morrow.
> Perhaps success, perhaps defeat
> And everlasting sorrow.
>
> "Let come what may. I'll try it on.
> My condition can't be worse.
> And if there's money in that box
> 'Tis 'munny' in my purse."
>
> Black Bart, PO 8

The next year, a Yerba County coach was robbed by "four men," one of whom did the fancy talking. Afterwards, it was discovered that the "three accomplices in the bushes with rifles" were cleverly-placed sticks. The scheme worked on that occasion, but thereafter the bandit operated in true solo form.

Over eight years, Black Bart continued hauling in about $6000 per year, according to his later statements. Always a gentleman, he refused to place a driver or passenger in real danger, yet no lawman could catch the elusive holdup man.

Until 1883.

Stage driver R. E. McConnell was on his usual run. Having exited a ferry boat on a mild afternoon, McConnell decided to offer his coach's "shotgun seat" to the teenage son of the ferry captain. The kid, Jimmy Rolleri, would be good company and could hunt small game along the way.

As the Wells Fargo wagon inched up a steep hill, Jimmy hopped off and walked along a creek bank, expecting to meet the coach on the other side. But the stage had been stopped on the hilltop by Black Bart.

The robber's smooth pattern was disrupted by Jimmy's abrupt approach and the unforeseen situation of a strongbox bolted to the floor. "Bart" ran for the brush, scattering this and that and taking a shot to the hand. It wasn't long before investigators found a derby hat, snacks, field glasses, flour sacks, and a man's large handkerchief with the laundry mark F.X.0.7.

A check of ninety-one laundries in San Francisco narrowed the search to a local "mining engineer" whose out-of-town trips seemed exquisitely timed to the past few years' string of roadside robberies.

Bart's unsophisticated criminal style never wavered in the end. When apprehended, he calmly confessed, "Gentlemen, I'm done."

Boles, polite and cooperative, was sentenced to six years and served four, saying at the end of his jail term, "I am through with crime."

He vanished in 1888.

An "imperial" is a mustache, typically waxed and upturned, above the upper lip and across the face.

Hiding and walking in the outdoors suited Boles, his stamina having developed during long marches in the Civil War.

"PO 8" (po-eight) was probably Black Bart's humorous stab at the word "poet." He surely was aware that the rhyming lines were silly, but he was enjoying his reckless behavior. Less likely, "PO 8" is a reference to "pieces of eight" in Spanish currency.

What was Boles' beef with Wells Fargo? No one knows for certain, but there may be something to the story that, at an earlier time, the company owned land adjacent to his property and cut off his water supply.

Boles' self-ban on profanity slipped a little in his sentiments about Wells Fargo.

> "I've labored long and hard for bread,
> For honor and for riches,
> But on my corns too long you've tread,
> You fine-haired sons of b_ _ _ _ _ _."
>
> Black Bart, PO 8

"[We] proceeded on..."

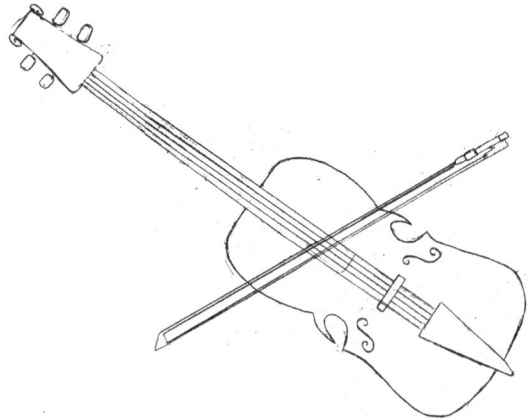

PLEASANT PIERRE

Pierre Cruzatte was a nice fellow to have around.

It didn't matter, really, that he was blind in one eye and near-sighted in the other.

An 8000-mile round trip into unknown wilderness. Rivers and mountains. Boats and horses. Add a couple of fierce winters, a garden variety of adventures and misadventures, and some real hardships. Top it off with breathtaking vistas and ultimate triumph. That was the Corps of Discovery expedition under the dual leadership of Meriwether Lewis and William Clark.

President Thomas Jefferson authorized the trip in 1804 to ascertain what America had gained in its 1803 Louisiana Purchase from France. The transaction had doubled the size of the country, stretching it westward to the Rocky Mountains. Not well-broadcast was Jefferson's mandate for the explorers to push *beyond* the Continental Divide to the Pacific Ocean.

Many questions required answers gained solely from a first-hand view. What geographical features graced the territory? Would there be possibilities for hunting, fishing, mining, forestry, agricultural use, and trapping? Was trade feasible with unknown Native Americans?

Of foremost gravity, America needed to stake a firm claim to the West Coast.

It was a good day when, late in the recruitment period for the Corps, Pierre joined the company as a private. No confirmed date of birth is available, but "Old Peter" had the measured judgment and wide experience indicative of maturity; most likely, he was the senior member of the group.

Having a French father and an Omaha mother gifted Cruzatte with proficiency in both tongues and a boldness in sign language, of utmost value in communicating with Natives. A jolly soul, he became the face of good will among the indigenous population, and his calm, reliable behavior in scary wilderness locales offered a measure of comfort for the novice explorers.

Cruzatte was the group's most-experienced boatman for the exploratory mission; travel was mostly by water, the greater part of which was totally unknown. Slim, but sturdy, and of small stature, he possessed the ideal physique for maneuvering the pirogues and canoes many months through wicked river currents.

Once the group reached the Rockies, Pierre's experience in creating proper caches enabled the travelers to store their goods and watercraft safely for the return trip. They crossed the mountains on horses and mules acquired from the Shoshone. On the western side, the explorers fashioned rough dugout canoes with the help of friendly Nez Perce.

With no maps or prior experience in the Northwest, the "Pilot of the Boats" used a sharp eye to guide the little sloops down the Clearwater and Snake Rivers; at last, his skillful navigation through the Columbia's Great Chute and Cascades propelled the Corps to the Pacific.

Pierre Cruzatte played the fiddle. "Extreemly well," wrote Lewis, who spelled poorly, but was most appreciative. Consider the relaxation and camaraderie engendered by lively entertainment around the campfire at night. A little touch of civilization in a far-flung back-country. Of consequence, Cruzatte's musical exhilaration in song and dance was reported on several occasions to have soothed shaky interfaces with restless Natives.

And he knew mushrooms. Enough said.

Expedition members catalogued over 300 animals and plants. Animals "new" to them include American bison, wolverine, coyote, elk, mule deer, badger, pronghorn antelope, mountain goat, prairie dog, mountain lion, golden eagle, and...grizzly bear.

Cruzatte seems to have been the principal hunter in the group. Providing meat to the hard-working explorers was a serious business.

As for grizzlies, Cruzatte killed the first one of the behemoths, identified by his comrades as "white bears." Lewis simply deemed them "turrible." Natives indicated to the expeditioners that they themselves would not hunt the animals with fewer than 8 or 10 marksmen in a group. At first, Lewis attributed the Natives' caution to their simple bows and arrows. He soon changed his mind!

Yes, Cruzatte's hunting prowess was notable.

Until the very *end*, that is.

As the trip neared St. Louis and home, Pierre's eye handicap caused him to mistake Captain Meriwether Lewis for an *elk*. The shot went through Lewis' left thigh and right buttock.

Thick willows, brown buckskin clothing, compromised vision – perfectly explainable.

Lewis recovered painfully, but rapidly, lying front-side down in his boat for a few days. His initial anger at Cruzatte's error eventually subsided, possibly upon reflection that his injury, annoying as it was, amazingly turned out to be the most serious of the entire crew on the expedition of two years and four months.

> "This Crusat [sic] is near-sighted and has the use of but one eye. He is an attentive, industrious man... (in) whom we both have placed the greatest trust during the whole route."
> William Clark, August 12, 1806

Pierre Cruzatte is said to have returned to the wilderness as a trapper and hunter and died around 1825, possibly killed by Blackfeet.

Corps of Discovery crewmen often tagged Pierre Cruzatte "St. Peter," as a sign of admiration and confidence.

Although Cruzatte was less adept with the language of the Teton Sioux, he managed to communicate skillfully enough to ease the explorers past the contentious Natives.

Pierre Cruzatte is not known to have married or had children.

As with any group with a task to accomplish, there is set of skills to be utilized. Lewis, Clark, and their fellow explorers demonstrated a unified effort (and the enhancement of their chances of survival) made possible by a variety of talents and experiences. Chief among the attributes of the 33 adults was the ability and willingness to "get along." Their support of each other and their general good nature proved not only enjoyable, but crucial to the success of the massive undertaking.

"a hearty man of God..."

THE SNOWSHOE ITINERANT

"I had made up my mind to see Pike's Peak; that was, if I could see it at all."

Father John Lewis Dyer believed he might lose his eyesight before viewing the West's majestic mountains. Having surrendered to preach in middle age, John was doing the work of a Methodist-Episcopal circuit-riding minister in the Midwest. He resolved to continue this style of service in the mountains.

In 1861, Dyer completed the trip from Minnesota to Denver in just under two months, having started out on a good horse with a saddle and bridle and toting a carpet bag containing his Bible, a hymnal, and a change of linen shirts.

It wasn't a smooth journey. In Iowa, the horse foundered when a careless landlord left it in a stall full of corn. Dyer was forced to exchange the ailing creature for a gun, an old watch, and fifteen dollars.

With no other transportation options, he joined a wagon train in Omaha as a walk-along traveler. A friendly soul in the caravan agreed to provide food for Dyer and haul his gun and carpet sack. Though it was a 600-mile journey, mostly on foot, Father used the opportunity to preach as he went – at remote chapels, in prairie homes, even in hovels of ill repute.

> "I found that a man of 47, getting fat, could walk, work, and preach off all the fat."

In Colorado, the preacher gazed upon his long-sought Pike's Peak, then headed straightaway into the mountains. Based in the tiny hamlet of Buckskin Joe, he began a ministry among miners and settlers in the territory's highest-altitude towns. As his vision improved, Dyer conducted the first religious services held in a church on the western slope.

> "I decided to stand the storms and leave the events with God to do the best I can to build up the church of God in this wilderness country."

Following the example of John Wesley in England a hundred years before, Father Dyer vowed to take the message to the people rather than wait for the people to come to him. He shared the Scriptures in barns, gambling halls, stores, drafty cabins, and outdoors. There was no "putting on airs" with the rough miners who listened somewhat patiently to his hour-long sermons. As ministers do, the reverend married, buried, and doctored folks; occasionally, he was forced to wallop a disrespectful listener. His messages formed the only spiritual guidance many had ever encountered; for each lonely man, the services were a reminder of home.

Whenever the pastor's pants grew threadbare, he hoped for a lift in offerings to buy a new pair. While disappointed in the meager collections, he nevertheless was keenly aware of the workers' harsh existence – miserable labor with low pay, few benefits, stuck at the bottom of the scale of wealth, but always willing to divide what they had. Dyer was as poor as the miners. If a trip to Denver was necessary for supplies or business, he walked the 100 miles, because the stage fare was a steep ten dollars.

History's sharpest recollection of Father John Dyer, however, is his identity as "The Snowshoe Itinerant."

Lack of reliable communication was a major drawback of settlement in the Old West. Stagecoaches and young Pony Express riders were transporting mail back and forth across the country, but in rough mountain areas, the job was done by equally strong and determined men. Mail was hauled as far as trains could go, whereupon pack mules and wagons went the rest of the way most of the year. Severe winter conditions, though, left the task of postal delivery to individual human carriers wearing "snowshoes," an early version of today's skis.

To improve his financial situation, Father Dyer carried the U.S. Mail to inaccessible locales several times weekly for almost three decades. For his work, primarily on Indian trails over 13,000-foot Mosquito Pass, Father Dyer earned about $18 a month. Danger aside, the job seemed perfect. He wouldn't be required to work on Sundays and could preach as he went about his deliveries. Fully trustworthy, he earned a little more cash as an express man for gold dust; the job required carrying the sacks to assay houses away from the mines.

His Norwegian-style skis were cut from split pine logs boiled and turned up at the tips. A twenty-foot pole helped the skier keep his balance, propel himself, brake efficiently, and gauge a terrain covered in snow anywhere from three to twenty feet thick. Strapped across his body was a 25-pound mail sack. Dyer often chose to tackle the slopes at night to avoid the daytime thaw of snow and ice that would not bear his weight, even in snowshoes. Not many thieves or rebels were encountered in the darkness, but the solitary nature of the journey and an occasional menacing animal jarred the nerves.

Over the years, there were enough close calls in the forbidding heights to sap the courage of ordinary folk. In his memoirs, Father Dyer described one particular storm in which he, at age 78, waded through waist-deep snow for six hours, periodically leaning up against a tree to rest. He made it through, but had calmly resolved in those difficult hours to keep moving until he could go no more. At that point, he planned to hang his mail-sack on a pine-tree limb and find a smooth spot on the trunk to write his epitaph: Look for Me in Heaven.

Intriguing stories describe the adventures of stalwart mail-service contractors in the West. In the Silverton area, especially if local mines remained open year-round, citizens expected postal service on a regular basis, so, at great risk, the carriers forged onward. In 1876, T. G. Andrews sidestepped seven snow slides, only to be swept downhill and buried by an eighth avalanche. He managed to dig himself out and return to work; in a later storm, his ears, hands, and feet were frozen. He survived that one, too.

Two sad outcomes found Jack Grinnell "in a white sea and solitude," dead with the mail pouch safe in his hands and Swan Nilson carried away by avalanche, the bag of Christmas mail still upon his back.

Father Dyer bought a rough cabin in Frenchman's Gulch, cutting his own wood for an old-fashioned fireplace beside a bed of fir-tree branches on a hay-tick mattress.

> "How glad to get back, stand up my snowshoes against the house, strike up a fire and warm a little...take flour, baking powder, and make a delicious cake baked in a

frying pan. [With] the meat fried and coffee boiled and a can of fruit or diced apples, I was ready to thank God and eat."

Late in life, John bought property near the county courthouse in Breckenridge, Colorado, and built a 50' x 25' chapel with a sixteen-foot ceiling – largely with his own hands and his own funds.

A bell tower erected in 1890 was dynamited within a year by miners protesting the closure of saloons on Sundays. The Father Dyer sanctuary, with part of its original structure intact, was moved to another location in 1977. Renovations were completed in 2003.

The white-frame chapel where worshippers have congregated over 135 years is known today as the Father Dyer United Methodist Church. "Father" is an affectionate title only, for the Methodist church does not utilize the term for its ministers. In Breckenridge, though, the historic place of worship graciously retains its descriptive name.

After 40 years of mountain-itinerant ministry, 29 of which were coupled with high-altitude mail service, Father John Dyer died in 1901 and is buried on Mosquito Pass. A beloved character in Colorado history, he is acknowledged as one of sixteen major founders of the state.

Father Dyer's son, Judge Elias F. Dyer, died in Granite, Colorado, at age 39, victim of a murderous mob who disagreed with one of his court rulings. "I die for law, order, and principles," he said.

Father Dyer and John B. Stetson both went west "before it was too late." Dyer feared losing his vision before he could view the great mountains, and the future hat-maker's battle with killer tuberculosis led him to purer, drier air. Thankfully, both men survived and thrived. Similarly, Theodore Roosevelt's time at his Elkhorn Ranch encouraged the good health and vigorous lifestyle he had always sought.

Look for Me in Heaven, Mark Feister's biography of Father John Dyer, took its title from Dyer's near-death experience in deep snow.

"Remember, boys, nothing on God's earth must stop the United States mail."

John Butterfield

BUTTERFIELD

"California is no longer a colony of the East," exulted *Harper's Weekly* upon the opening of John Butterfield's Overland Mail.

Colony, indeed!

Three events in as many years centered California on the nation's stage. The Mexican Cession in 1848 added parts of seven current states, including California, to America's West. Almost simultaneously, gold was unearthed at Sutter's Mill, whereupon eager Forty-Niners hurried their pace to the new territory. It wasn't a mere territory very long. California entered the Union as the thirty-first state in 1850. At last, America had that "bookend" state on its western extreme.

The place was exploding with commerce, population, and a general excitement. Euphoric optimism, though, could not compensate for excruciatingly-slow communication across America's broad expanse. Consequently, the emerging West enjoyed little participation in the economy and government of Eastern states.

Personal mail, business letters, packages, legal papers, newspapers and magazines, merchandise, and freight crept back and forth. The West's growing dependence on Eastern manufacturing centers was hamstrung by slow delivery via clippers and steamers rounding Cape Horn or a railroad pushing through Panama. Cargoes were subject to piracy, storm delays, and shipwreck, while their crews fended off mosquito-borne diseases, seasickness, and injuries. Shipments headed eastward faced the same obstacles in reverse.

Short-run pack trains, regional coaches, and John Studebaker's 20-mule freight wagons crept along, carrying supplies and mail. Delivery by steamboats and random enterprises, where drivers traveled by day and camped at night, bumped up costs to unmanageable levels.

That new and unabashed state-to-be-reckoned-with cried out for a dependable, affordable, and permanent tie to the rest of the country. In 1858, they got it.

John Butterfield of New York began driving stagecoaches at age 19. In an age of rapidly-expanding commerce unblessed by reliable transportation, he realized, early on, the business potential for mail and freight service by long-haul coach.

Similarly, Henry Wells and William Fargo established a freighting enterprise in California at the height of the Gold Rush and added banking services to their company. Minerals, postal goods, and passengers were carried by the popular new Concord coaches, conveyances which traveled back and forth among the mining camps so frequently that their trails sometimes had to be watered to settle the dust.

In 1850, Butterfield joined with Wells and Fargo to form American

Express, which, in competition with three other private companies, operated various short runs across America.

Meanwhile, the U.S. Congress was developing plans for a massive overland stage route to satisfy demands for a standard continental system of transport and communication. With the support of President James Buchanan, Postmaster General Aaron Brown authorized a plan for direct mail delivery from St. Louis to San Francisco. Receiving the contract was the most-experienced stagecoach manager in the nation.

That man was John Butterfield.

The competing bidders were invited to join the new public enterprise, which took the name Overland Mail Company. Half of Butterfield's eight associates were experts in the operation of stages; the other four excelled in finance. Wells Fargo was a backer of the overland express as its primary lender. In 1857, work began.

One year was allotted for preparation of the route.

Would it be a northern, central, or southern course?

Without hesitation, a northern trail was discounted due to construction difficulties and long, severe mountain winters. Many supported a central route running in a fairly straight line across the middle portion of the country, but reports of late-season deep snow packs in western ranges discounted that choice. It fell to the Postmaster General to make the final selection, and Brown chose the southern path, perhaps due to his roots in Tennessee. As likely, his decision was based upon the absolute necessity for year-round use of the Overland.

The Great Oxbow Route was 600 miles farther than the shortest northern or central plan, but its selection started the project in earnest.

It was divided into eastern and western halves, each with a superintendent.

The curious pike, like a "U" horseshoe, led southwest from the Mississippi River through Arkansas and a corner of Indian Territory (now Oklahoma). In Texas, the trace swung west from the Red River to Franklin (now El Paso) on the Rio Grande, the halfway point. (One historian suggested that Overland-route planners were fooled by a generously-wet spring in Texas, unaware of that state's climate extremes.)

The route's latter half trailed northwest through New Mexico and Arizona Territories to San Francisco. Communities along the Oxbow craved the stage stations, even as towns in later years fought for a rail line and, in modern times, an interstate highway.

A Chickasaw Indian named Benjamin Franklin Colbert operated a ferry for the Overland across the Red River between Texas and Indian Territory. Farther west, the burg of Franklin also benefited nicely from the enterprise. Jobs were created for blacksmiths, harness-makers, cooks, and guards; repair shops and restaurants opened for business.

It would be the world's longest stage line. Roads and fording places were graded, to some degree. Plank bridges and stables were constructed, rocks removed, and wells dug. Relay ("way") stations and supply depots were built or fashioned from existing buildings. Along some rivers, stations were equipped with ferries or rafts for poling a vehicle to the other side. At night, in calm waters, the stage was guided by a man carrying a lantern on horseback. Employees numbering 1500 were hired; 34 Concord coaches, 66 Celerity wagons, and hundreds of horses and mules were purchased.

The relay stations, 139 in all, were situated at intervals for an exchange of drivers, conductors, equipment, and animals. Mail and freight were dropped off or picked up at each stop. In daytime, passengers stepped off the stage briefly for a meal (if available) at their own cost; often, the repast was no more than tough meat, dry bread, and weak tea. Upon approach to a station, the coach's conductor blew a horn so transfers could be made quickly.

One eastbound stage and one westbound stage departed on Mondays and Thursdays at 8:00 a.m. for a 25-day-or-less trip to the "other side." The western terminus was San Francisco, California, and the main eastern point was St. Louis, Missouri, though cargo was transferred to a train at Tipton, Missouri, for the last 160 miles to St. Louis.

The first eastbound stagecoach left San Francisco on September 15, 1858, and arrived in St. Louis 24 days and 18 hours later.

The initial westward run of the Overland departed from St. Louis on September 16, 1858. John Butterfield, Sr. carried two sacks of mail and was accompanied by Waterman L. Ormsby, a special correspondent for the *New York Herald*. The two rode the train to Tipton, where Ormsby boarded the Overland stagecoach and headed to San Francisco.

Ormsby, the only passenger on the westward swing, detailed his journey of 23 days and 23 hours in dispatches sent to the newspaper from various stops on the overland stretch. Mincing no words about the rigors of the passage, he also offered generous perspectives – exquisite descriptions of the ever-changing terrain, anecdotes about agents and drivers, and, always, an emphasis on the necessity of speed in delivery of the mail and goods aboard.

While passenger travel was not a priority of the Overland, riders were welcomed aboard; their $200 fares boosted the company's finances. Traveler *safety* was important; comfort, not so much. "Guests" were jammed together, sharing space with mail and cargo. In motion night and day, up to nine passengers shared three seats, some of which reclined for sleeping.

> "I can remember no night of horror equal to the first night's travel on the Overland Express."
>
> Edmund Hope Verney

A wild and wicked ride it was. Writer Ormsby recalled getting off the stage during a delay in the middle of nowhere and actually feeling reluctant to climb aboard again.

The company stuck to its time limit for the 2812-mile trip. (Some treks were completed in as little as 22 days.) To thwart hold-ups, gold, silver, valuable jewelry, and payroll bags were not carried on Overland coaches. An armed conductor rode beside each driver. The passengers, mail, and express were in his charge, but he was not allowed to shoot unless lives were in danger. Riders themselves often carried personal weapons. Though harassed by bandits and Indians, no traveler or driver was killed during the 2½ years of operation, though a conductor suffered a leg wound in an Indian attack at Apache Pass.

> "Now I know what hell is like. I've just had 24 days of it."
> Waterman L. Ormsby

Both horses and mules were used to pull the coaches and wagons, but mules were preferred for surer footing on rough ground and steep grades, especially in areas swarming with Indians intent on stealing horses. The beasts were undoubtedly sturdier, but their obstinate nature caused many a mishap. "The mules," said Ormsby, "reared, pitched, twisted, whirled, wheeled, ran, stood still, and cut up all sorts of capers," resulting in jumbles and delays.

> "If I had any property, I certainly should have made a hasty will."
> Waterman L. Ormsby

Sheer desolation, unbearable distances of untamed territory, and perennially-choppy trails overshadowed some remarkably well-planned details of the project. Each driver had his own course, a stretch of about 60 miles; he drove the same path back and forth and rested at each end. The journey became as expeditious and secure as possible, since the captain knew every inch of his assignment, even on dark, narrow mountain ledges, through stormy weather, or with murderous savages about.

Only a small portion of the trail accommodated the familiar Concord stagecoaches. The Overland's Southern Route was so grinding that sturdier Celerity wagons, equipped with canvas tops, low sides, smaller wheels, and leather-strap support, carried passengers and the mail 70% (about 2100 miles) of the way. Both Concord and Celerity vehicles displayed "Overland Mail Company," never Butterfield's name, on their sides.

Like the Pony Express that followed, Butterfield's overland line lost money and John ultimately was forced to return the business to Wells and Fargo. The last Oxbow run was on March 21, 1861, three weeks before the first shots of the Civil War. Wells Fargo moved the route northward for a stint of service; the company continued scattered deliveries around the country for years to come, using many trails.

A few Butterfield stage stops remain in Arkansas, California, and Texas. Railways and highways were built along the old trails, and the line's water wells held out for many years.

In 1958, American Airlines erected a six-foot stainless-steel trylon "pilot memorial" on Guadalupe Peak, the highest point in Texas, in commemoration of the delivery of both transcontinental overland and air mail. The occasion was the 100th anniversary of the Overland Stage and Mail. Studies are underway for a national historical trail following the old route.

Butterfield's Overland Mail Company, our nation's first transcontinental mail service (1858-1861) was followed by the brief and memorable period of Pony-Express delivery (1860-1861). Soon, two transcontinental giants, the telegraph (1861) and railroad (1869) rendered "wagon" mail, long-route shipping-by-sea, and stagecoach travel obsolete. Undeniably, the great four-horse coaches crisscrossing the country were a novelty in their time, a giant stepping-stone toward a continent linked as one in transport and communication.

There is a bit of confusion about the eastern terminus of the Overland Mail.

Officially, it was St. Louis, but a 160-mile rail line between that city and Tipton, Missouri to the west, gave much faster service. Tipton, then, was the stopping point for a coach headed *east* toward St. Louis and the starting point for a coach headed *west* from St. Louis.

Some coaches terminated at Memphis, Tennessee, as mail and packages from the Overland were handled there, as well. The separate branches of St. Louis and Memphis – like a two-tined fork – merged at Fort Smith, Arkansas, and from that city westward there was a single trail. Overland mileage from San Francisco to both St. Louis and Memphis was almost identical.

Butterfield actually preferred the Central Route at the 35th parallel of latitude, but acquiesced to the choice of a Southern Route.

For forty years, the Overland Stage Building was the largest structure in El Paso.

At journey's end, the worn-out news writer Waterman Ormsby traveled home from San Francisco to New York by *steamer*. William Tallack agreed. "Not one in 100 travelers go...by the Overland on account of its risks and discomforts."

"...young, skinny, wiry fellows, not over 18. Must be expert riders, willing to risk death daily. Orphans preferred. Wages $25 a week."
                Advertisement for Pony Express riders, 1860

POSTMEN OF THE PLAINS AND PRAIRIES

"The mail must go through."
                Motto of the Pony Express

Slipping off his horse in a blinding snowstorm, Billy Fisher sheltered under a tree. As he drifted off to sleep, something licked his face.

Startled awake and somewhat annoyed, the young rider scared away the little rabbit. On second thought, he deemed the furry nuzzle an act of Providence to save him from freezing.

Robert "Pony Bob" Haslam rode 380 miles in 36 hours during a Paiute uprising in Nevada since no other rider was willing or able to relieve him.

That's not all. In March, 1861, Haslam's route again crossed Paiute-heavy Nevada. Armed guards stood ready at relay stations, but the open trail was a solo adventure for the Pony rider. Bob suffered a broken jaw and the loss of five teeth in an attack, but continued to shoot with both hands till an arrow penetrated his left shoulder. "Fetch me a clean rag to hold in my mouth; I'm going through," he shouted at the next station. Indeed he did – 120 miles in 8 hours and two minutes, aboard 12 different ponies. His precious package: a script of President Lincoln's inaugural address on its way to eager readers in the West.

On the initial run of 185 miles over the Sierra Nevada on trails 30 feet deep in snow, naysayers in California gloated, "They'll never make it!" Dead wrong. The run was completed in 15 hours and 20 minutes.

The *doughnut* may have been "invented" when Johnny Fry's girlfriend poked a holed in a pastry so her sweetheart could catch it with the barrel of his gun as he dashed by the Troy (Kansas) Station on his assigned ride.

The Pony Express lasted only 18 months. It didn't earn a cent. The developers went bankrupt. Begun as a private enterprise, the firm never received the government support necessary to keep it running.

Even so, the Pony, like the overland stages, filled that niche of time between western settlement and the coming of the telegraph and rail service – tying our tenderfoot nation together across its vast, empty mid-section.

The Butterfield Overland Mail's 25-day service from St. Louis to San Francisco had been in operation a couple of years when the approaching Civil War increased unease about the political leanings of California. Though it had entered the family of states as "free," many in Washington feared a reversal of loyalties in favor of the southern cause. Frankly, California's staggering wealth was considered vital to the Union.

Faster, much faster, communication (days, not weeks) was deemed an absolute necessity. The Golden State must not be "hung out to dry."

A contract for speedy cross-country mail service was awarded to the freight-and-stage firm of three entrepreneurs named Russell, Majors, and Waddell. To keep up with obligations, the company had borrowed heavily for their freight enterprise; they hoped the express contract would lift them out of debt.

The partners came up with a bold scheme. There would be no wagons, stagecoaches, or ox-drawn carts in the new endeavor. Instead, "men and swift saddle horses in short relays" were slated to form "a line of flesh and blood between the muddy Mississippi and the bright Pacific."

Two months later, on April 3, 1860, the Pony Express sent out its initial riders, believed to be Johnny Fry riding Sylph west from St. Joseph, Missouri, and Sam (Billy) Hamilton headed east from Sacramento, California. The mail arrived at each terminus in ten days. Ten days! Less than *half* of the overland stage's time.

On that first run, East and West are said to have sent 50-70 missives each. The letters, documents, and telegrams were written on tissue paper, since the cost of delivery was five dollars per half-ounce. In today's economy, that would be the steep price of $75 for a typical letter, but much of the mail was business-oriented, and commercial establishments were willing to pay for speedy communications. Frontier citizens receiving newspapers and magazines with reports concerning the growing tensions between North and South likewise bore hefty postal costs. Once Pony mail was established, its rates were lowered somewhat, except for packages.

Mail was carried in a *mochila*, a soft sheepskin-leather cover draped over the horse's regular saddle. Slits were cut in the cover to accommodate the saddle horn and cantle, and the rider actually sat on the pouch. Four hard leather pockets fitted with locks held the mail securely.

The lightweight nature of the *mochila* (one-third the weight of a standard saddle bag) allowed the rider to transfer it to a fresh horse in two minutes, though most were back on the trail in 30 seconds. Time was everything. Once the mail pack left the point of origin, it was not to stop moving for any reason. Should a horse be lost or killed, the rider was mandated to carry the *mochila* on his back to the next station. Missing a rider, the horse would proceed onward.

The "ponies" of the Express were small, fast horses – not young colts, for which the repeated dashes across the country would have been much too arduous. Initially, ponies covered 25-mile stretches, but they proved better-suited to half that distance, about ten or twelve miles at a time.

"Young, skinny, wiry fellows...expert riders...willing to risk death daily" were recruited and paid a princely salary of $100 per month, plus expenses. At start-up, each rider carried a revolver, a rifle, a Bowie knife, and a Bible, but excess weight soon reduced the load; most settled on toting only the guns. The young men were encouraged not to fight, but to rely on the speed of their horses as their best defense.

Each week, one relay headed east and the other went west; at any one time, about 80 riders were active.

An enthusiastic spurt put the first riders in sporty red shirts and blue pants; before long, practicality dictated buckskin duds. Each employee signed a pledge to "conduct myself honestly, faithful to duties and actions," including abstinence from alcohol, fighting, and profanity. One writer notes that some of the lads, being on the rough side, may have neglected reading the Good Book, but not a single occurrence proved them less than totally loyal and devoted to duty. (Even though the famous recruiting ad suggested a preference for orphans, there's no evidence the subject ever came up. Furthermore, the average age seems to have been around 19, and one record cites a rider over age 40.)

Day and night and in all seasons, a fellow rode his pony to a *relay station* (*swing station*), leaped onto a waiting steed, and continued his journey in a flash. Stations were located 5-20 miles apart, depending on terrain; ideally, the distance was 10-12 miles, in favor of the ponies. Each rider covered 75-100 miles per day, rested at a *home station*, and then started a shift going back the other direction.

Now and then, a rider such as "Pony Bob Haslam" pushed forward without an exchange if his relief man was unavailable or the relay station was in ruins due to Indian depredation.

184 stations, 1900 miles. In total, 400 ponies, 200 or more riders. No expense was spared in procuring the ponies, which may have cost up to $200 apiece. In the West, California-stock horses and half-breeds of native-origin Plains horses such as mustangs and pintos were preferred. From the East, thoroughbreds and Morgans came largely out of cavalry units.

Riders were expected to move along in a steady lope, but a 10-mile-per-hour gallop was allowed in an emergency. Wagon trains kept the stations supplied with necessities, hay and grain for the animals being a top priority. Food caches contained cured meat, dried fruits, beans, bread, corn meal, pickles, molasses, and coffee. Hunting would have been an option, but the young men and station caretakers found little time to spare.

The Pony route encompassed the nation's most-challenging terrain, Indian raids, vicious storms, horse thieves, bandits, boiler-plate heat in summer, and the worst Mother Nature could dish out in winter. Stationmasters, alone in isolated huts, were an easy target of bloodthirsty Natives, and several were slain, but it's believed that only one Pony rider perished, as those devil-may-care young men and their ponies could outrun almost any danger.

Express historian Raymond Settle has patched together figures for the 78 weeks (about 18 months) of overland mail service; the service was halted for a short time during the Paiute war. Settle estimates there were 308 runs *each way*, for a total of 616,000 miles and 34,753 pieces of mail carried. That's 24 circumnavigations of the globe. (Others calculate 330 trips each way at 650,000 miles.) A single bag of mail was lost; perhaps it was two. The Pony Express National Museum in St. Joseph, Missouri, has compiled a list of 228 names of young men who rode the circuit.

Settle opines that the Pony Express failed in only one way; it was a total financial flop. Central Overland California and Pike's Peak Express was its official title, and the company's erratic financial condition led some employees to consider that COC and PP meant "Clean Out of Cash and Poor Pay."

Yet the Pony retains its unique place in Americana. Christopher Corbett jests, "There are so many people out there with ancestors who 'rode for the Pony' that Russell, Majors, and Waddell would not have needed to buy expensive horses, but could have lined up all those "riders" so that the mail passed hand-to-hand all the way from St. Joseph to Sacramento!"

By late October of 1861, the Pony Express enterprise had ended. A transcontinental telegraph line connected America's coasts, at once solving the nation's communication gap. Eight years later, rail service completed the ground link.

Mark Twain spotlighted the mystique of the Pony Express. Anxious to see the Pony in action, he arranged to view a rider on his route. Twain watched in dismay as "all that passed us... managed to streak by us in the night, and so we heard only a whiz and a hail, and the swift phantom of the desert was gone before we could get our heads out of the windows."

Greatest cheering section of the overland mail, naturally, was U.S. state #31. In alliterative fashion, the *California Pacific* exulted that the Pony Express proved "a faithful friend to our far-off state."

> "You came to us with tidings that made your feet beautiful on the tops of the mountains... We have looked for you as those who wait for the morning, and how seldom did you fail us!
>
> "When days were months and hours [were] weeks, how you thrilled us out of our pain and suspense – to know the best or know the worst. You have served us well!"

Facts and figures about the Pony vary widely. The Civil War promptly drew attention away from the overland-mail experiment. Years later, when the nation's interest returned to the captivating stories, the young men had become old and many had died. That said, scattered descriptive passages survive.

British explorer Captain Sir Richard Burton went down the actual Pony line in the summer and fall of 1860, observing and taking credible notes. Horace Greeley described stage stops that became stations for the Express.

What the National Park Service calls "a rollicking yarn that helped create the lasting legend of the Pony Express" was penned by Colonel William Lightfoot Visscher in 1908, long after riders and horses were off the trail. Visscher, in fact, was not a colonel, did not compose factual accounts, worked on the bulk of his "research" at a bar, and drank a quart of gin daily most of his life.

Not long before World War I, Mabel Loving personally interviewed surviving riders (of whom there were a scant few) and shared their stories in a little book, The Pony Express Rides On. Not a polished work, it nevertheless was, like her surname, *lovingly* and sincerely prepared.

There are few Express business records available, partly because the owners operated in the red from start to finish and partly because the Pony's financial arrangements were mixed in with the company's stagecoach and freight accounts. Not only did the express-mail enterprise turn out badly for the three partners, none of them succeeded in any financial endeavor afterwards. Once the Civil War got underway, disrupting the nation's economy, they were essentially broke.

Pony historian Raymond Settle, attempting to understand the firm's financial tangle, came to believe the company was bankrupt at least three years *before* the Pony Express made its first ride. Majors' son said his father had spent the equivalent of one-half million dollars outfitting the project. Russell and Waddell never wrote about the enterprise; Majors didn't record his sentiments until late in life.

In colonial days, mail had been delivered by mounted couriers; a century later, ambitious individuals attempted to duplicate the process in remote mining areas.

Out West, private mail-haulers rode from one camp to another, distributing and collecting letters and packages; they were paid in ounces of gold dust. If a mule was the beast of burden, the process was tagged "Jackass Mail." Camels also carried mail while hauling goods in the Southwest.

Christopher Corbett, a researcher and writer, attends many National Pony Express Re-Rides, held annually in June and timed with a full moon so riders will have light on the overnight shifts. Riders carry a *mochila* and alternate yearly east-to-west and west-to-east.

William ("Buffalo Bill") Cody, said to have ridden for the Pony, most likely did not, though he was a local messenger boy for Russell and Majors, two eventual partners in the endeavor. Cody was almost certainly in school in Leavenworth, Kansas, during the era of the rides, but he centered the legend of the Pony Express in his astoundingly-popular Wild West Show for many years. Even better, William Cody was a true gentleman and a fair and benevolent employer, offering equal opportunity and compensation to women, Blacks, and Natives.

James Butler ("Wild Bill") Hickok worked as a relay-station stock tender, but was older and too heavy to ride on the Express.

Mochila derives from the Spanish *mochil*, meaning "delivery boy." A *mochila* mysteriously arrived in New York City on May 3, 1862, possibly retrieved from a pony that had escaped an Indian attack. It was said that the Natives did not destroy wayward parcels because they revered something that made the riders travel so fast.

Astronaut William Fisher is the great-great-grandson of Billy Fisher, the youthful rider saved by a rabbit's twitch.

"Broncho Charlie" Miller, at 82, claimed to be the last of the Pony riders. If so, he'd have been riding over the Sierra Nevada at age 10 or 11. Outrageous claims aside, the public adored his rascally charm and flashy garb.

"Pony Bob" Haslam *was* authentic, however. He later drove for Wells Fargo and appeared in Buffalo Bill's Wild West Show.

Ralph Moody is credited for the phrase, "the greatest ride in American history."

"Our little friend, the Pony, is no more."

TWO OCEANS UNITED

"I announce to you that the telegraph to California this day has been completed. May it be a bond of perpetuity between the states of the Atlantic and those of the Pacific."

Message to President Abraham Lincoln,
October 24, 1861

TRANSCONTINENTAL TELEGRAPH

By mid-century of the 1800s, overland mail by stagecoach took three long weeks. Replies added another three weeks. The Pony Express cut the time to ten days each way.

Not fast enough. The Old West was hankering for the original "instant-messaging."

Once Samuel F. B. Morse perfected his electromagnetic telegraph in 1844, Eastern cities enjoyed reasonably fast and reliable contact with each other. A separate system in California connected municipalities in that state. But there remained a great silence across the broad expanse of mid-nation.

Congress' Pacific Telegraph Act of 1860 approved construction of a line to California and awarded the contract to Western Union Telegraph Company. Crews would start eastward from Sacramento, California, and westward from St. Joseph, Missouri, meeting in Salt Lake City, Utah. A superior agent, Edward Creighton, was put in charge, and he immediately hired two able sub-contractors. Work began on both ends on July 4, 1861.

In an ambitious display of committed effort, the telegraph line of 1150 miles across plains, prairies, and high places was strung in only 113 days. The goal of eight miles' completion per day, with about 25 poles per mile, was daunting. The remote parts of the country were shy of vegetation and drinkable water; all supplies, including tree trunks for poles, were hauled in from the outside.

For all that, the job was swiftly finished. The crew from St. Joseph arrived in Utah on October 18. James Gamble's men from the west, having built over the Sierra Nevada and Rocky Mountains, reached the meeting point on October 24.

Though the telegraph was sure to put the Pony Express out of business, the energetic Pony riders cheerfully cooperated with the project, passing information down the line from crew to crew as they carried their last deliveries of mail from one side of the country to the other. Even better, their proven overland mail routes were judged advantageous for the new telegraph lines, sparing the enormous struggle of time and expense to find a separate route.

Some of the problems *then* seem humorous *now*. Buffalo found the telegraph poles handy for a rub, their massive bodies often toppling the staffs. The Cheyenne were curious, as well, but Superintendent Creighton solved that problem by having a few Indians hold a live wire. Thinking lightning ran down the wire, the Natives dubbed

Creighton "Big Medicine Man" and meddled no more. A party of Sioux absconded with some wire to make bracelets, but a chieftain's warning about "bad medicine" ended that type of foray.

"Our little friend, the Pony" would ride no more. Yet the innovative experiment of whisking overland mail by rider and pony, and the high-spirited exuberance of those young fellows who joined the endeavor, have never lost their charm.

Veteran Pony rider William Campbell's perspective, at age 94, is both gracious and intriguing.

"[The telegraph was] the greatest of all inventions to me, because it affected me directly. In the two minutes we used to be allowed to change horses at a station, Western Union now sends a message to New York or even London. The telegraph today does in a second what it took 80 young men and hundreds of horses 8 days to do when I was a rider in the Pony Express."

TRANSCONTINENTAL RAILROAD

In 1869, America's transcontinental railroad, a project predicted by naysayers to be a century away (if ever!), became reality.

Completed four years after Abraham Lincoln's death, the coast-to-coast rail line, known as the Overland Route, begat our familiar time zones. Similar to Butterfield's Overland Mail and Stage, the Pony Express, and the transcontinental telegraph, the railroad's task was to complete the link from East to West, starting at the Mississippi River. In the case of the rail line, the final leg picked up mid-continent at Council Bluffs, Iowa, and terminated in Sacramento, California.

Two Pacific Railway Acts (1862 and 1864) had been passed by a U.S. Congress without its Southern members, who had seceded in association with the Civil War. Naturally, the Union was anxious to bind California to its side; a nation-spanning rail line would fortify that connection.

Confronted with the same geographical barriers as those before them, planners settled on two possible courses. The Central Route roughly followed the old Oregon Trail. A Southern Route, reminiscent of Butterfield's trail, wound through Texas, New Mexico, and Arizona to avoid weather and construction obstacles in the mountains. Lewis and Clark's path could have become a Northern Route, but that option was abandoned yet again due to long months of wintry conditions.

Anticipating the Southern route, the United States in 1853 had paid Mexico $10 million for the Gadsden Purchase, the extreme southern portions of what later became the states of Arizona and New Mexico. The extended parcel of land was necessary for the construction project; in addition, it would establish firmly the border with Mexico in that particular area.

By the time Congress authorized the construction, the Southern route was abruptly axed, because Texas had joined the Confederacy. With further consideration, project engineers came to believe that the Pony-Express riders' year-round success proved the Central course very workable.

It was a good choice; the professionals were able to expedite the route by straightening the old migrant-trail veers toward grass and water. Grazing, vital to the pioneers, was no longer necessary, and temporary water wells could be drilled as needed.

The Union Pacific (east-to-west) and Central Pacific (west-to-east), both independent companies, were given land grants (ten sections per completed mile) by Congress. Once rail service was established, the rail companies could sell plots to pioneers who wished to settle in towns or on farms and ranches near the line.

> "The railroad [was] really going to be the conduit of civilization that pulled settlers in record numbers westward."
>
> Walter Borneman

For working capital, Congress issued loans that paid for each mile built. Easy grades earned $16,000 per mile, high plains, $32,000, and mountainous terrain, $48,000. Construction would begin from each direction and meet at a place to be determined.

On the eastern side, laborers were mostly Irish immigrants and Civil-War veterans, some of whom were West-Point-trained construction engineers who had gained experience in building and repairing rail lines during the War. In Utah, the company added Mormon workers.

Beef, bread, and black coffee rounded out a dull menu. The company provided a moving herd of cows for food, and buffalo-hunting was encouraged. Water-borne illness was a continual problem. Indian threats and attacks kept the Easterners, unaccustomed to Plains culture, on edge. Portable bunkhouses or tents provided shelter, but hygiene wasn't a high priority and the men were "troubled by cooties."

Initially, on the western end, the labor force was heavily Irish, with some British and Canadian workers. By 1868, 80% of the crews were Chinese, of whom contractor Charles Crocker said, "Wherever we put them, we found them good." The oriental cuisine enjoyed by the Chinese was much more palatable, featuring vegetables and dried fish from San Francisco, live pigs and chickens for weekend meals, lukewarm tea, and no whiskey. Washing their bodies and clothes regularly and avoiding tainted water, the Chinese sidestepped maladies like dysentery that plagued the average worker.

When a foreman declined to use the Asian-immigrant workers on a difficult mountain summit, Mr. Crocker shot back, "Did they not build the Chinese Wall?"

East and West, one-fourth of railroad crews consisted of tracklayers, including hammer-and-spike men, gaugers, levelers, fillers, and bolters. Others were blacksmiths, engineers, stonemasons, teamsters, telegraphers, cooks, waiters, clerks, and carpenters. Tent cities sprang up with food shacks, gambling houses, and, occasionally, a laundry.

Construction began on both ends in 1863. Hard to believe, but most of the work was done by simple manual labor, using shovels, pickaxes, wheelbarrows, carts, scrapers, and ropes. Black powder blasted solid rock into tunnels, some requiring almost a year to complete. Toward the end of the project, a new chemical, the hazardous "touchy" nitroglycerin, was used on a summit tunnel, the longest of the project. (Alfred Nobel's stabilized nitro appeared too late for this undertaking.)

The transport of building materials to the site was an ongoing logistical headache. At that time, America's major factories were located in East-Coast cities. To supply the Union Pacific builders, manufactured products were delivered to the site by wagon train and on flatcars as track was completed. Horse-drawn carts accompanied the moving assembly line laying crossties and rails.

As always, delivery to builders in the West was a costly and delay-prone issue. Everything the Central Pacific needed, from bolts to bridge materials, traveled 18,000 miles around the southern tip of South America or, at greater expense, across the Isthmus of Panama.

Right-of-way along the line was 400 feet wide, with additional space for sidings, rail yards, stations, maintenance buildings, and, as it turned out, telegraph lines. New wire setups were erected overhead as track was laid. Eventually, the original 1861 telegraph companies merged their lines with those along the route, where they were easier to supply, maintain, and protect.

Railroad ties, 3249 per mile, were hardwood, preferably oak and hickory, treated with creosote. Iron rails were used prior to the Bessemer-processed steel that was developed later in the century. Crushed stone was used as ballast, or underlay, for several purposes: drainage, elevation to avoid flooding, stabilization of cross ties and rails, and prevention of fires caused by sparks.

As human nature goes, there was considerable waste and inefficiency in the government-subsidized project. The two companies vigorously competed, often carelessly, in miles of track laid in order to collect as much money as possible. Toward the end, the Central Pacific and Union Pacific actually made separate right-of-ways parallel to each other for 200 wasted miles. Sometimes builders used wood instead of rock for bridges and culverts. Another irresponsible act involved track laid in haste over ice in the Rockies; it had to be redone when the ice melted.

The runaway project finally met its end when Congress was forced to set a stopping point at Promontory Summit, Utah. On May 10, 1869, a final spike of sturdy iron secured the last piece of track. The ceremonial "golden spike," too soft to be driven, was gently dropped into a pre-drilled hole; it now rests in a museum at Stanford University. A fancy laurel-wood crosstie, replaced afterward with durable pine, was moved to secure storage in San Francisco; it burned during the earthquake of 1906. The sound of the final spike at Promontory Summit was scheduled to be carried by telegraph across the country. Due to technical difficulties, the "blows" were actually struck by the telegraph operator.

Present at Promontory Summit's last-spike gala was Dr. Hartwell Carver, who, in 1832, had advocated a Lake-Michigan-to-Oregon rail line. In 1847, he submitted a proposal for a transcontinental line to Congress, to no avail. He'd planted a seed, though, and twenty-two years later, he was alive to witness his grand idea become reality.

Route mileage from Council Bluffs to Promontory was 690 miles.

From Sacramento, the figure was 1087 miles – a total of 1777 miles. The rail line was extended across the river from Council Bluffs to Omaha four years later, following construction of the Upper Missouri River Bridge, and, in the west, track was laid from Sacramento to Oakland on the bay. Only then was the project truly complete.

Soon east-west travel was reduced in time to one week. With both a transcontinental telegraph and a transcontinental railroad, our country was at last the *United* States of America.

In 1942, Southern Pacific, which had absorbed the Central Pacific, tore up the entire Promontory line and donated the iron scraps to the war effort. When the rail was disassembled at Promontory Summit, a small group gathered to witness the "undriving" of the last spike, which had been placed in 1869. Among the guests was Mary Ipsen, age 85. Seventy-three years previously, as a twelve-year-old, Mary worked in the food car of a work train building the Union Pacific-Central Pacific line.

America's first railroads connected cities in the East, the earliest being the Baltimore and Ohio. The South soon had a scattering of rail lines, but the western terminus was at Omaha, Nebraska, and Council Bluffs, Iowa, sister cities on either side of the Missouri River. The job remaining for the Central Pacific and Union Pacific was to begin at that western terminus and complete the transcontinental route to California.

Early on in the operation of the railroad, the line was re-routed to avoid the troublesome steep grade at Promontory Summit. That high spot seemed a poor choice for a grade in the first place, but Congress was in a rush to establish a stopping point for the mad-dash construction, and the summit may have been selected as a nice spot for the ceremony.

The two largest cities in the Great American Desert, Denver and Salt Lake City, were bypassed by the original transcontinental line, but feeder lines were laid to those cities.

Considering the financial failure of Butterfield's Overland Stage and Mail and the Pony Express, it is unlikely any company would have undertaken the completion of the transcontinental railroad without government assistance.

"...the driving is like Jehu, the son of Nimshi, for he drives furiously."

II Kings 9:20

CHARLEY PARKHURST

When Charley Parkhurst at last escaped from the orphanage, he was taken in by Ebenezer Birch, owner of the local livery stable in Providence, Rhode Island. The young stable boy cleaned stalls, fed and groomed horses, and scrubbed floors in the barn.

Seeing extraordinary talent in the lad, Birch taught him to drive a coach – one horse, then four. Wasn't long before Charley was a genuine whip on a six-up. (That's a *driver* of a *team of six*.)

Stagecoach operators were in great in demand once the California Gold Rush ramped up, and Charley turned his eyes to the West. About 1851, his six-months' journey cut through Panama to a ship bound for the land of the Mother Lode, where Charley began driving stages during the mining-boom days.

The reins were not so easily taken in the boisterous West, with ruts for roads, wicked weather, and washed-out bridges. In those days before the transcontinental railroad, coaches handled passenger transportation, mail service, and delivery of valuables along the treacherous trails of the High Sierras. Having lone drivers rendered stages a mighty tempting target for bandits in the wild.

But Charley had a "feel" for the road and soon learned not to mess with hoodlums. A nasty desperado known as "Sugarfoot" stole the strongbox the first time he stopped Charley's coach. The second time, Charley was packing a .44 pistol and shot Sugarfoot dead.

Charley built his reputation as one of the West's best whips in handling a team of horses and, in good fun, using his strap to slice paper or cut a cigar out of a man's mouth at fifteen paces. Reportedly, he could drive speedily over a silver dollar with both front and rear wheels. When a mule kicked him in the face and ruined an eye, he simply added a patch and never missed a delivery. "One-Eyed Charley" delighted his passengers, the Wells Fargo bosses, his peers, and little children who reached for the candy in his pockets.

Parkhurst chewed tobacco, drank with the guys, smoked cigars, and spoke in a rough tone of voice. He usually slept in a stable with his best friends, the horses.

Twenty years as a driver, and then railroads began to suck business from the stage companies. Rheumatism from years of bouncing rides convinced Charley to hang up the whip and raise chickens on his small farm.

When Charley died, his neighbors came, according to custom, to prepare the body for burial. They made a shocking discovery.

"Charley" actually was "Charlotte."

Yes, indeed.

Birth and census records prove Charlotte's existence, but no peers or kin have been able to identify her. Local scuttlebutt indicated her father may have left his little girl at the orphanage after her mother's death.

Perhaps she left the institution dressed as a messenger boy; typically, those were urchins who did errands for a coin or two, coming and going without notice. The girl-to-boy concealment was easy enough because poor foundlings all wore the same simple shirts, pants, and short hair that was easier to keep clean and vermin-free.

Why did Charlotte Darkey Parkhurst live in disguise? Possibly, she sensed that men had a better chance at a working life. She might have been a tomboy at heart; it's evident she scrambled to gain the professional skills for a job she loved. In California, Charley observed that stage drivers were typically unkempt and standoffish; they tended, overall, to be loners. Outfits of long duster coats, floppy hats, buckskin gloves, and tall leather boots enabled her long-time deception.

If she wanted to be "Charley," she'd have to dress that way throughout her life. She did.

> "On Sunday last there died a person known as Charley Parkhurst, aged 67, who was well-known to old residents as a stage driver. He was in early days accounted one of the most expert manipulators of the reins who ever sat in the box of a coach. It was discovered when friendly hands were preparing him for his final rest that Charley Parkhurst was unmistakably a well-developed woman."
>
> Obituary in *Sacramento Daily Bee*

Charlotte died in Watsonville, California, on December 28, 1879. The cause of death was tongue cancer.

California claims her as their first woman voter. In the Presidential election of 1868, Charley registered as a man, of course, 52 years before women gained suffrage in that state. Actually, her voter *registration* is recorded, but there's no proof she actually voted. California thinks she did. Good enough.

The popular Concord stagecoaches that Charley drove were built in Concord, New Hampshire. State-of-the-art vehicles, the coaches were lightweight and durable, with braces and a free-swinging motion that replaced the jolting discomfort of a spring suspension. It was said that the Concords wore out before breaking down. Mark Twain deemed them "cradles on wheels."

"No man in the wrong can stand up against a fellow that's in the right and keeps a-comin'"
Bill McDonald

TEXAS RANGERS

On the back of a land document dated August 4, 1823, Stephen F. Austin penned a summons for ten men to act as "rangers for the common defense at $15 per month payable in property...[They need] a good, sufficient horse...with 100 rounds of powder and ball."

Austin had fulfilled his father's contract with Mexico to bring Anglo settlers to Texas. Under Mexican law, an empresario was authorized to form a militia for protection of his charges. The rangers were an additional force, though history does not record their names or details of service, as they stepped up when needed to protect the greenhorn colony from rampaging Karankawa, Lipan Apache, and Comanche raiders. When not "ranging" settlement environs, the men were in the pastures or shops of their occupations.

These recruits of the "Father of Texas," sturdy and seasoned though they were, bore scant resemblance those identified as Texas Rangers in years to come.

Controversial, triumphant, thrilling, and breakthrough events weave the story fabric of the Texas Rangers, but, overall, the characters have stood behind the star for law, order, justice, and peace. Nowhere is the legend of the Texas Rangers better portrayed than in the men who *made* it legendary.

> "Charged with the mission of operating beyond the boundaries of civilization and with minimal support or communication from higher authority, they lived and often died by the motto, 'Order first, then law will follow.'"
>
> Thomas W. Knowles

Since the days of Stephen Austin, Texas Rangers have dealt with Mexican invasions, border chaos and banditry, the Ku Klux Klan, out-of-control boom towns, world-war intrigue, sabotage, mob rule, oilfield violence, secret terror societies, illegal fights, spying, integration unrest, arson, family and neighborhood feuds. They've faced Indian marauders, bank and train robbers, cattle rustlers, fence-cutters, rioters, vigilantes, bootleggers, merciless murderers, kidnappers, smugglers, gamblers, and escapees. Often outnumbered 50-1, the officers might carry several pistols, a rifle, and knives.

Early Rangers did not wear badges or uniforms. (They were lucky to be reimbursed for their horses and ammunition.) The first badges probably were made by the men themselves; Ira Aten made one in the 1880s for self-identification in dangerous situations. The current badge came into use in 1962, when Ranger Hardy L. Purvis and his mother donated rare cinco-pesos in honor of Purvis' father, Ranger Hardy B. Purvis.

Each star-in-a-wheel badge is actually a silver star in a cut-out five-peso coin. Mike Cox points out that the peso is a reminder of "Texas sovereignty over former oppressors." The central star comes from the Great Seal of Texas, as do the oak leaves on the left ("strength") and the olive branch on the right ("peace").

> "...men who knew how to ride, shoot, and tell the truth."
> J. Frank Dobie

The Texas Rangers frame the oldest state law-enforcement agency in North America, and they come from varied social and ethnic groups. Currently operating as the investigative arm of the Texas Department of Public Safety, Rangers continue to use "all reasonable means to take lawbreakers into custody, commit justifiable homicide to prevent crime on Texas soil, 'stand their ground,' and fight."

"One riot, one Ranger"

BILL McDONALD

Halloween, 1895. The mayor of Dallas was nervous. An illegal fight, a boxing match portending violence, was about to be staged in the city. A call to the Texas Rangers yielded only Bill McDonald, who casually stepped off the train and met the skepticism of local officials by drawling, "Hell, ain't I enough? There's only one prize fight." One riot, one Ranger, indeed.

On another occasion, a rowdy mob pressed forward, intent on hanging two prisoners in McDonald's custody. "March out of here and get away from this jail or I'll fill this yard with dead men," warned McDonald. The troublemakers left the scene.

"Bravo too much"

JOHN COFFEE "JACK" HAYS

Fall of 1841 found Jack Hays atop Enchanted Rock in Central Texas in defiance of troublesome Comanche who were harassing surveyors and Rangers in what the Indians deemed their sacred area. Hays' three-hour stand on the granite dome resulted in the deaths of 20 attackers and the swift retreat of all the others.

Hays had a "secret weapon" – two Colt 5-shooters.

When Samuel Colt came to Texas a couple of years previously with his revolutionary weapons, he found little local interest in the new repeating pistols. Ranger Jack Hays, however, instantly recognized the guns' potential against the always-proficient Indian attacks upon white men forced to dismount in order to reload their black-powder weapons.

Galvanized into action, Hays (as tough an outdoorsman as they come) distributed Colts and practiced at an intense pace with his scouts and horsemen – shooting at posts, standing, sitting, kneeling, stretching under the necks of their horses – employing the same tricks as their native adversaries.

And then they were ready.

"Whip them and then talk of treaties."

JOHN S. "RIP" FORD

"Rip" got his nickname in the Mexican War. Assigned to make a list of the dead, Ford respectfully added "Rest in Peace" at the end of each record and on the notes he penned to families of the deceased. As the lists lengthened, he sadly had time to write only R.I.P. in sympathy.

Active for decades in Texas, Ford was a writer, politician, lawyer, surveyor, doctor, explorer, soldier, and Ranger leader. He fought Mexican bandits and Indians along the Rio Grande and in the Nueces Strip.

Of his fellow Rangers, Rip Ford said this (and said it very well):

> "A large proportion...were unmarried. A few of them drank intoxicating liquors. Still, it was a company of sober and brave men. They knew their duty and they did it. While in a town they made no braggadocio demonstration. They did not gallop through the streets, shooting and yelling. They had a specie of moral discipline which developed moral courage. They did right because it was right. You might kill them, but you could not conquer them."

> "Their enemies were pretty good. The rangers had to be better."
>
> Walter Prescott Webb

SAMUEL WALKER

Walker lived only till age 32, but he assisted Ranger Jack Hays against Indians and doggedly challenged Mexican invasions of Texas. He worked with Samuel Colt to improve Colt's revolver, that innovative pistol allowing multiple shots before reloading. Together, they produced a newer model known as the Walker Colt. The heaviest black-powder revolver Colt ever produced, Walker's

1847 six-shooter held six charges of black powder behind six bullets of .44 caliber lead balls.

❋ ❋

"They did right because it was right."

MANUEL GONZAULLAS

"El Lobo Solo – The Lone Wolf." Manuel Gonzaullas served Texas from its oil fields to the international border. Alone, he pursued bootleggers, gamblers, and drug runners, his bent trigger finger "geared to that .45 of his."

When the East Texas oil boom of the 1930s made Kilgore the most lawless town in the state, Gonzaullas was sent to clean up corruption and keep the peace. As drifters, opportunists, swindlers, and the like flocked to the area, Gonzaullas grew suspicious of anyone without the rough hands of an oil-field worker. On one occasion, he chained a long line of suspects to a steel cable, checked identification papers, and said they could go if they'd leave town within four hours. Most were gone within 10 minutes.

> "Crime may expect no quarter in Kilgore. Gambling houses, slot machines, whiskey rings, and dope peddlers might as well save the trouble of opening because they will not be tolerated in any degree. Drifters and transients have a choice of three things: engaging in a legitimate business, getting out of town, or going to jail."
>
> "Lone Wolf" Gonzaullas

Understandably traumatized at age 15 by the murder of his only two brothers and the wounding of his parents by home-raiding bandits, Gonzaullas dedicated his life to law and order. "Medium height, scarred face, no sense of humor, a very serious fellow," said

Watson Wise, a local oilman. Rode a black horse and carried a pair of pearl-handled pistols. Yet he was soft-spoken, polite, and fair.

> "Give us more Rangers of the caliber of Lone Wolf Gonzaullas and the crime wave we are going through will not be of long duration."
> Evan Smith, *Dallas Morning News*, 1934

⁂

> "A Ranger is an officer who is able to handle any given situation without definite instructions from his commanding officer or higher authority."
> Capt. Bob Crowder

ROBERT A. "BOB" CROWDER

In 1955, 81 inmates of the Rusk State Hospital for the Criminally Insane initiated a riot and took several hostages. With a Colt .45 on each hip, Bob Crowder walked unaccompanied into the building to seek surrender from the leader of the disturbance.

Before he took his first steps inside, however, Crowder addressed the felon via the jail phone:

> "I'm not comin' in unarmed 'cause you already got three people over there as hostages and I don't want to be the fourth one – and I'm not gonna be. I just want to tell you this. If something goes amiss, I know who's gonna fall first."

The standoff ended peacefully.

"They were men who would not be stampeded."
                                        Col. Homer Garrison

JOHN BARCLAY ARMSTRONG

Texas' most notorious killer, John Wesley Hardin, was apprehended on a train in Pensacola, Florida, by Ranger Armstrong and other lawmen. Hardin is said to have exclaimed, "Texans, by God." The prisoner was brought by rail to Austin, then transferred by wagon overland to stand trial for the murder of Brown County Deputy Charles Webb three years earlier. The nerve-wracking trip to Comanche, Texas, was a four-day ordeal with a heavily-bound prisoner and curiosity-seekers lining the road.

"Go get your man. Get him alive if you can, dead if you can't, but don't come back till you get him."
                                        a Ranger slogan

FRANK HAMER

As a young ranch hand, Hamer single-handedly caught a horse thief, a brave action that caught the attention of the Texas Rangers. During his long career, he shifted from a horse to a car. Then, as a special investigator for the Texas Prison System, he undertook the task of locating and capturing the crime duo of Bonnie Parker and Clyde Barrow in 1934. That gun-happy pair had murdered more than a dozen officers and unarmed citizens in a multi-state, multi-year crime spree. Within three months, Hamer and his crew had ambushed and killed the outlaws in Gibsland, Louisiana.

BEN McCULLOCH followed his friend Davy Crockett to Texas in 1835, but a case of measles kept McCulloch out of the Alamo. He aided Sam Houston at San Jacinto, battled Indians as a Texas Ranger in Jack Hays' unit, fought in the Mexican War, and died in combat during the Civil War.

What a character! Folk hero WILLIAM "BIG FOOT" WALLACE, at 6-foot-4 and 240 pounds, was a giant of a man for his time. The massacre of his brother and a cousin at Goliad propelled Wallace to Texas, where he gave valuable service as a Ranger, particularly during the Civil War, by staying behind and guarding the frontier against bandits, murderers, and Indians taking advantage of vulnerable civilians whose men had gone off to battle. "Big Foot Wallace" took his nickname in stride, joking that "Lying Wallace" or "Thieving Wallace" would be much worse. He could afford a generous spirit; he was a descendant of the Scottish hero, William "Braveheart" Wallace.

The post-Civil War and Reconstruction years were chaotic in Texas. A key figure in the newly-established Frontier Battalion was its commander, Texas Ranger JOHN B. JONES. Jones was "all business." His strategies fended off Mexicans and Indians in frontier areas until local law enforcement was securely in place, and he helped mold the Rangers into a modern force for law and order.

JOAQUIN JACKSON, a modern-Ranger icon, stood straight as an arrow at 6'5" and was an imposing symbol of strength and resolve. During his 27 years of service, Jackson looked to the simple hobby of hunting arrowheads to settle his mind when the job was overwhelming. Jackson maintained that everyone must be treated the same and "the goal of a Ranger is the protection of life and property and the preservation of the peace."

Devoted to their leader, his men called themselves "Little McNellys." Early in life, LEANDER McNELLY developed tuberculosis;

it killed him at age 33. As a Ranger, he joined Rip Ford in taming the infamous and frothing-with-violence Nueces Strip between that river and the Rio Grande. His methods often were questionable and possibly illegal, but in those desperate times McNelly considered his fellow lawmen "not as men of vengeance... but as men of law... and justice."

※ ※

Official reports filed by Texas Rangers often were short and to-the-point.

Ranger James D. Dunaway, hit 17 times while attempting to manage a violent wet-dry election, sent a telegram to the Governor: "Shot all to pieces, but not serious." (He recovered.)

※ ※

An unnamed Ranger described a transport: "Left to escort prisoner to Austin. Norther hit right after we had crossed the Pecos. That night [the prisoner] kicked his blanket off and froze to death."

※ ※

Telegram from Ranger Jeff Milton: "Send two coffins and a doctor."

※ ※

"Why do you carry a .45 pistol?" asked a reporter. The Ranger replied, "Because they don't make a .46"

※ ※

Ranger Kiowa Jones, taking on Big Nose Smith, a prisoner: "Mean as hell. Had to kill him."

Anonymous Ranger report: "We had a little shooting match and they lost."

The "stand-their-ground" quote is credited to Harold J. Weiss.

Texas Rangers are recruited from within the ranks of the Texas Department of Public Safety. The first full-time female officers were commissioned in 1993.

Field Headquarters Offices are located in 7 cities of Texas, with general headquarters in Austin. Today's average Ranger is in his 40s, and there are 150 or so serving at any one time.

The unusual spelling of Manuel Gonzaullas' surname is explained by his family's origin in Spain. The pronunciation is about the same as the more-familiar "Gonzales." Added to his many contributions to law enforcement in Texas was prior service in the U.S. Treasury Department. In retirement, he was a technical consultant for motion pictures and radio/television shows presenting the story of the Rangers. Particularly popular was the TV series, "Tales of the Texas Rangers." As well, he created a crime lab for the D.P.S. second only to that of the F.B.I.

Ranger Bill McDonald's quote has become the Texas Ranger creed: "No man in the wrong can stand up against a fellow that's in the right and keeps a-comin.' "

"I do not disdain my red brethren because their skin is darker and I do not think more of the white people because their skin is lighter."

John O. Meusebach

THE UNBROKEN TREATY

An unlikely quartet. A superlative pact.

Three Comanche chiefs and a German baron.

Former baron, to be exact. Ottfried Hans Freiherr Von Meusebach sidelined his title to salvage the shattered plans of hundreds of German immigrants in the rocky Hill Country of Central Texas.

The man became, simply, John O. Meusebach.

Meusebach arrived in Texas in 1845 to find the affairs of the Adelsverein in a jumble. A protective society for Germans, the Verein had purchased almost four million acres, the Fisher-Miller land grant, for the settlement of families seeking escape from political unrest and overpopulation in their home country. By 1844, the first wave of exhausted immigrants was moving inland.

Not so admirably, Verein authorities concealed their aim to establish a German feudal state in what they viewed as a militarily-weak Republic of Texas.

Dominated by noblemen in the Old Country, the Verein had no experience in conservative finance, commerce, or the settlement of farm families. *Money and power,* they understood. The company's designated leader, Prince Carl of Solms-Braunfels, was an aristocratic rogue with intrigue of his own. To keep the German immigrants from interacting with Americans, he purchased a site on mosquito-plagued Matagorda Bay as a "private" port of entry, then led the travelers along a remote route toward the grant.

At the Guadalupe River, about halfway between the coast and the tract, Texas Ranger Jack Hays advised the immigrants not to proceed onward due to the onset of winter. Prince Carl at once acquired two leagues of local property for the settlement he named "New Braunfels," a nod to his home castle. Within weeks of the town's completion in March, 1845, the prince left for Germany and never returned.

John Meusebach donned the mantle of leadership, paid off Prince Carl's massive debts, stabilized the community at New Braunfels, and founded several other villages, including Fredericksburg, also outside the grant, but near its southern edge. By late 1845, Texas had become a state, thus ending the threat of a German province.

1846, though, was a troublesome year for the kindly new commissioner-general. A second wave of Germans, perhaps 4000, arrived on the Texas coast, bound for the large tract belonging to the Verein. Meanwhile, the Mexican-American War got underway, diverting to the border most oxcarts and wagons essential for the delivery of colonists and their goods to Central Texas. Drenching rains flooded creeks and rivers; a cholera epidemic followed.

Because Prince Carl had abandoned his post before actually reaching the premises, two conditions for settlement in the grant had not been met. The contract required both a professional survey and a peaceful-occupation agreement with its inhabitants, the Penateka Comanche. The deadline for settlers to be in place was just months away. Failure to comply would mean forfeiture of the transaction.

The Fisher-Miller grant, located between the Llano and Colorado Rivers, had been sold by Henry Miller and Burchard Fisher to the Germans without disclosure that the property was in the Comancheria. The Verein, ignorant or unconcerned about Native tribes and lifestyles (and, it seems, basic legal and real-estate principles), had accepted the land deal without question.

Who in his right mind would enter the Penateka Comanche domain? How would one tell a war party that white settlers would soon follow, overrunning traditional Native hunting grounds? No help could be expected from the federal government, whose surveyors flatly refused to risk their lives without military escorts, none of whom were available due to the war with Mexico.

John Meusebach was willing.

He formed a private mounted company to protect his own surveyors and, in February, 1847, Meusebach himself met with Penateka chief Katemcy. At the outset, the chief was amused by the German's flaming red hair and beard; of greater consequence, he was reassured by the man's calm, respectful demeanor and, notably, the non-threatening farm activities which had been observed by Comanches spying on Fredericksburg. The two parleyed, then agreed on a meeting a month hence.

With moms and kids in Fredericksburg shaking in their boots, Meusebach and town leaders strode out to a council with Buffalo Hump, Old Owl, Santa Anna (Santana), and some lesser chiefs. The white men disarmed their weapons as a sign of non-aggression.

Meusebach calmly walked into the group of Natives and donned a buffalo robe. He pointed out the value of both red skin and white skin and commented that the new immigrants were neither Texans nor Mexicans, both of whom the Paneteka had reason to be wary.

Then he revealed his most-unusual plan for peace, a contract completely unlike any other between disparate peoples.

Comanche and white men extended to each other the freedom of movement in the broad land between the two rivers. The Comanche agreed to share their hunting grounds; the whites invited their Native friends to "go where they pleased" around the settlements.

It was a non-capitulation contract – an equal balance for each party. Neither side would be debased to an inferior position. Each pledged to recognize the dignity of the other, acting as friends and allies. The partisans vowed to keep an open line of communication, speaking candidly to each other in case of trouble or wrong-doing.

The treaty was completed March 2, 1847. Meusebach offered gifts and supplies. And then whites and Natives shared a meal and a campsite.

There was peace, beautiful peace.

In American history, the Meusebach-Comanche treaty remains the sole covenant between a Plains tribe and a body of citizens acting privately. To the relief of weary German immigrants, three million acres of land were opened to settlement. Government officials rightfully recognized the pact, but had no part in its composition or application.

While negotiations were underway about 70 miles north, Comanche scouts stationed themselves on the hills ringing Fredericksburg and built large signal fires to keep each other apprised of activity both in town and at the parley site.

The little German boys and girls, already apprehensive due to the tension around them, were terrified by the overhanging bonfires. When news was transmitted to the scouts that a treaty had been signed, the flames may have been stoked to leap higher in celebration. Even scarier for the town tykes!

Resourceful mothers to the rescue! Knowing their kids were familiar with the numerous jackrabbits in the wild, these Fredericksburg moms hatched a clever plan.

"It's spring," they said. "Look! The Easter Bunny is making campfires! He needs hot water to dye his eggs, you know. Then he'll add bunches of spring flowers for their pretty colors."

Strictly speaking, the treaty was created on March 2, but Easter that year occurred on April 4 and the pact was ratified in May. It seems the good people of Fredericksburg rushed the old-world bunny tale forward just a bit for their children's sake!

Exhilaration burst forth like spring blossoms in little towns suddenly secure from uncertainty and depredation.

The treaty remained UNBROKEN.

And that's what Fredericksburg celebrates today.

Fredericksburg, Texas, continues to commemorate the unbroken treaty. Off and on since 1948, townsfolk have turned out in costume ("bunnies" being the most-popular get-up, they say) for the Easter Fires Pageant.

Interpreter for Meusebach is believed to have been a former captive of the Comanche, Lorenzo de Rojas.

Castell, Texas, is the only town remaining of the five established in the Fisher-Miller land grant. Many of the immigrants preferred living in the country.

Comanche chief Santa Anna should not be confused with Mexican dictator Santa Anna. A Penateka Comanche, his name is often spelled "Santana." Six chiefs signed the treaty (written on March 2) on May 9, 1847, outside Fredericksburg.

John Meusebach settled over 5000 Germans in Texas between 1845 and 1847.

The treaty document was returned to Texas from Europe by Meusebach's grand-daughters Cornelia Marschall Smith and Irene Marschall King and presented to the Texas State Library in 1972.

"Each teacher will bring a bucket of water and a scuttle of coal for the daily session."

1872

SCHOOLS AND GOLDEN RULES

It darkened Winifred Shipman's day to discover that her school in tiny Philmont, Montana, was an empty chicken house. The shack had one door and one window, a rough board for seating, and a blackboard without chalk.

Winifred, however, was not to be outdone.

Not finding a single book, she copied stories onto brown paper for her students to read. She scratched out maps on the dirt floor and shooed the kids outdoors to observe birds, plants, weather, rocks, and stars. At night, this doggedly-determined educator prepared her lessons under the dim light of a rag wick over a simmering cup of hog grease.

Our nation's schools hardened the backbone of American society. On the frontier, despite formidable challenges, those lively centers of learning forged traditions binding "readin' and writin' and 'rithmetic" together like a sturdy, well-worn book.

Whose picture was hanging on the front wall of an old-time schoolroom? What was unusual about the shoes worn to school? Name the first published reader for first-graders. What handy classroom item slapped the knuckles of mischief-making kids?

In frontier settlements, there were home chores before and after school. Students entered the classroom about age 6; after grade 8, schooling ended for most, though, occasionally, adults dropped in for some learning. Boys left their classes to work on the farm or get a job; girls helped with younger children at home, cared for aging family members, or, in some cases, trained six to twelve months to become teachers themselves.

Bare feet were common at school; shoes were worn in winter and passed down to younger siblings. In the early 1800s, most shoes were not constructed as "left" and "right." They were made on a straight *last*, a foot-shaped model, and expected to conform to the wearer's feet over time. One technique called for switching shoes from one foot to the other each day to even out the wear. Two widths existed: slim and wide.

A one-room school was like a factory in motion. Boys and girls sat on opposite sides of the classroom. Teachers started the day with beginners; while these "abecedarians" worked on assignments, the instructor went on up the grades, each level helping the ones below. Rarely were there enough desks for all. It wasn't unusual for students to sit on benches or three-legged stools and do their writing or drawing on shelves nailed to the wall. Class sessions of ten to fifteen minutes each were allotted for reading, spelling, arithmetic, history, and geography, mostly taught by rote, oral drill, and recitation. Eighth-graders had heard those repetitions over and over; surely they retained some of it!

In primal situations, charcoal was used for writing on pieces of smooth wood. Blackboards started out as walls or planks painted black. Slate became the preferred material for the boards, paired with chalk of soft soapstone (talc) and cloth or sheepskin erasers. Slate boards were sturdy and long-lasting, and individual small ones, "slates," enabled students to work on their own. Frequent cleaning was required for all the writing surfaces.

Paper, rare and expensive, could be hand-bound into writing booklets. Sharpened goose quills or wood pieces served adequately as pens, with ink made of maple bark and copperas.

Lunch at school was plain, perhaps a sugar-sprinkled bacon-grease sandwich or a cold sweet potato from the night before; often the food froze while stored in an unheated cloakroom on icy mornings.

In pleasant weather, the midday meal was eaten outside under a tree and games such as "Cat and Rat" or "Blindman's Bluff" were played. Winter found students huddled around a pot-bellied stove in the center of the room, with younger children seated nearest the warmth. Teachers arrived early to tend the stove, and students often were asked to bring a stick of firewood to class each day.

Lads carried water from the outside pump or well and poured it into the classroom barrel. A dipper or cup (perhaps shared by all) served the water. Students swept floors, gathered trash, and cleaned slates and blackboards. Older boys chopped and stacked wood and made many trips to the timber pile.

Music was not part of the regular curriculum, but a talented teacher might give lessons in singing or violin. Almost any instructor could lead "She'll Be Coming 'Round the Mountain," "My Darling Clementine," or "America, the Beautiful."

Rural and frontier schools swung with the seasons. Since whole families helped with spring planting and fall harvest, school terms were adjusted accordingly and ran Monday through Saturday. Ironically, the optimum time for classes often was in shivery winter weather, when outdoor work was mostly at a standstill. When buildings served students within a four-to-five mile radius, kids arrived on foot or in tandem with two or three on a pony.

Along with the local center of worship, a schoolhouse was founded early-on in a pioneer community. Structures ranged widely in style – borrowed space above a store, an abandoned shed, barn, sod cabin, dugout, or, perhaps, a room in a private home or shared space in the church. As soon as possible, a dedicated building took shape in one of those memorable "raisings" by local citizens. Popularly located at a village crossroads, the school served as a social center and the setting for many a party, picnic, Christmas play, dramatic production, and political debate.

A rudimentary hut would offer only dirt floors; windows were covered with oiled paper or cloth. Stuffing of some sort was required to fill wide cracks on the walls and between logs. Insects, birds, and unwelcome critters were shooed away. Teacher Anna Johnson recalled setting mousetraps in her desk drawer, but that was a mild nuisance compared to the abundance of snakes in crevices, walls, and under raised floors. Soddies, while surprisingly warm in biting Plains winters, were notorious for all types of creepy crawlers.

> "No record of pioneer days would be complete if snakes were left out."
>
> Genevieve Giddings

The portrait up front? George Washington, of course, probably the popular, but unfinished, work by artist Gilbert Stuart, showing a white "cloud" beneath the President's shoulders. Perched in a small tower on the roof or held firmly in the teacher's hand, the school bell brought happiness at least once a day!

Often, the only books available were a single dictionary or two and whatever a child might bring from home, usually a Bible. Sometimes an entire class was forced to study from different books. What a wonderful boost it was when McGuffey Readers were published in 1836! The first, and most popular of a series of six, was a primer using everyday terms for rural youngsters: "A is for ax, B is for box, C is for cat," and so on. Stories portrayed children doing chores and activities familiar to them.

Schoolteachers could expect modest salaries and uncompensated work as janitors, record-keepers, counselors, and babysitters. (Future President Lyndon Johnson recited his lessons in a teacher's lap at age 4.)

"Per head, per day" described the payment structure in many areas; that system meant instructors were compensated only for students in attendance, even if their absences were due to illness, a farm emergency, or impassable roads. Teachers welcomed longer school terms, which translated into decent earnings for the year.

Good health was a challenge for all pioneers, and teachers were on the front lines of disease. Think about it! They were in close quarters all day with sniffling, sneezing, and feverish kids who bathed infrequently, drank from the same dipper, and washed in a common basin of water at school. Don't overlook a drafty building, travel to and fro in all weather conditions, and, markedly, the absolute void of disinfectants, vaccines, and antibiotics.

Nevertheless, many teachers chose country classrooms! Motivated by a sense of independence and, one must admit, adventure, they were drawn westward, anticipating a career of their own and financial independence. Many who felt "born to teach" were daughters of the country's first literate parents, whose zeal for education was motivational and contagious.

Historian John Unruh categorizes the urgency to teach in the West as a set of "push" and "pull" factors – the strong *pull* of a desire to spread education and a *push* for personal economic stability. Equally noteworthy was an unshakeable devotion of teachers toward their students.

In 1853, another writer noted that "a competent number of women have been found to give up the comforts of home for the benefit of the barbarous West." By the 1870s, over 25% of white women born in America had taught at some time.

Family histories spoke of women who "went out West" to teach, and a significant number of Western folk claim descent from a grandmother or great-grandmother who relocated there as a "schoolmarm."

> "I decided to go teach school in the West. My home was in Missouri, with five brothers and a sister. All mother and I did was wait on the menfolk. A schoolmarm in the West would not have to work any harder than we did at home. Besides, there were many eager men in the West."
>
> Unknown

Do tell. Spinsterhood was all but unknown "out there." Still, some single women saved money to purchase their own homesteads. A nagging problem for school administrators was job turnover. In most cases, women were barred from teaching after marriage; they were expected to keep the home fires burning and tend to their own children.

Male teachers expected and received salaries one-third to one-half larger than ladies in the same job. In colonial times and early in the 19th century, schoolmasters almost invariably had been men, but many used the educational profession as a stepping stone for higher aspirations, such as politics or service in the church. Out West, however, women greatly outnumbered men in the classroom, though some men taught in an off-season period away from farming or surveying. Industry, mining, agricultural work, and construction attracted the large majority of men to an abundance of full-time jobs in the growing West.

Housing was scarce for frontier teachers; they sometimes found it necessary to "board around," that is, stay with students' families on a rotating basis. (Oh, the horror.) And it was not unheard-of to ban teachers from drinking, smoking, riding bicycles, and visiting pool halls, dance halls, and barber shops. One particular district recommended that, at the end of a ten-hour school day, teachers spend time at home reading the Bible.

Such arbitrary suggestions might be expected from the all-male, locally-elected school board, which, along with setting school-tax rates, also hired and supervised its employees. When a teacher in Washington (state) complained about the lack of a restroom, even an outhouse, at her school, the directors observed, "Now you see what comes of hiring someone from the outside. We never had any trouble before and there are plenty of trees to get behind."

> "If there were no restrooms of any kind, boys walked *up* the hill and girls walked *down* the hill."
> A teacher

In far-removed settings, the board also took on the task of certifying teachers, but some instructors seeking credentials attended seasonal institutes or received training assignments by mail. As time progressed, most teachers earned their diplomas from "normal" schools, so named because the emphasis was on "norms" or models for a successful classroom. Many normal schools later became state universities.

The old notion that only *men* could control unruly youngsters was rapidly debunked. Rulers and hickory sticks slapped punishment onto misbehaving kids.

> "Whenever it shall become necessary for teachers to resort to corporal punishment, the same shall not be inflicted upon the head or hands of the pupil."
>
> School directive

Loss of recess privileges, being seated among the opposite sex, or the burden of extra chores probably did the trick most of the time.

Stories of pure Americana emerge from the days of frontier schools, which, hand-in-hand with educational facilities across the country, were striding boldly toward an educated populace.

In rural Concord, Pennsylvania, a horse was trained to pull a buggy farm-to-farm to pick up students each morning; the trip was repeated in reverse at the end of the school day.

The Berg children in North Dakota traveled to school and back in an open wagon a total of six hours daily, even in sub-zero temperatures. When gale-force winds and blinding snow raised drifts, the girls spent entire weeks camped out in their remote schoolhouse – and classes continued.

Wyoming's first schools were established at Fort Laramie (1852) and Fort Bridger (1860) for the children of soldiers and traders at the posts. Laramie soldiers who could read and write were forced to teach. Most hated the assignment and began showing up drunk, which cost them time in the brig and a $10 fine out of their $11 monthly wages.

In the boomtown of Virginia City, Montana, Sarah Raymond's exam for teacher certification (1866) cost her a fee of six dollars in gold dust. Otero, Arizona Territory's T. Lillie Mercer earned $30 in 1876, teaching 30 students in one end of a general store that sold liquor, groceries, and dry goods at the *other* end.

At Waldene, in Hamilton County, Texas, teacher Ann Whitney was murdered by Comanche savages as she spread her sweeping skirt to cover cracks in the floorboards under which terrified students were hiding.

The early-1900s backcountry-Alaska schoolroom of Hannah Breece was the hamlet's only public place besides a saloon and was used seven days a week for everything from Sunday school to sewing and cooking classes for the primitive people there. 100 pupils eager for schooling were divided into 50 younger ones in the morning and 50 older kids in the afternoon. Miss Breece was the only teacher.

At age 16, Mabel Steele began teaching ranchers' children in a log schoolroom at 9,836' elevation in the Upper Rio Grande Valley of Colorado. Most years, classes were held only from May through September.

Maude Frazier's discovery of her grandfather's papers chronicling his migration to the Northwest Territory inspired the young woman to leave Wisconsin for tiny Genoa, Nevada, a mining community losing most of its teachers to lovelorn bachelors. Nevada was definitely a challenge. Floods, fires, Indian raids, snakes, coyotes, classroom scorpions, cattle stampedes, runaway horses, drunk cowboys, lack of heat in winter and lack of books most times, sandstorms, pencils falling through floor cracks. She discovered that her job description included "janitor." Even worse, it was *non de rigueur* for teachers to ride bikes.

> "There was nothing to compare to janitor work to let off steam."
>
> Maude Frazier

But her students rarely missed school, and Maude herself stayed on.

Elevated to the Nevada Department of Education, Maude traveled alone over a 40,000-square-mile territory in an old Dodge named "Teddy;" it was a "rough-rider," you see. There were no road signs (and, sometimes, no roads); she located her destinations via crude maps drawn by garage mechanics. In "Teddy" she toted a shovel, an ax, tow ropes, a tire pump, water, gas, oil, a flashlight – and a deck of cards. Strangers assisted with car repairs and offered shelter in storms.

Concerned over the paltry choices of higher education for Nevada students, she was instrumental in the founding of Southern Nevada University, now The University of Nevada at Las Vegas (UNLV).

Arkansas, then in Missouri Territory, may claim the most unusual early schoolhouse – a cave in the easternmost Ozark Mountains. The three R's were taught, along with Bible lessons, two decades before statehood. With a moderate temperature year-round, School Cave attracted students – even though panthers and bears often chased their horses on the way to class.

Having left behind families and old friendships, settlers nurtured close relationships in community schools and churches. A popular quip explained that rural folk "had little else to spend, so they spent the day."

"Do unto others as you would have others do unto you" was a guiding principle in pioneer classrooms, along with honesty, hard work, and patriotism. With the simplest of teaching tools, fundamental subjects were mastered. Business, political, educational, and family leaders were products of the little frontier schools with big dreams.

> "The charcoal frescoes on its wall,
> Its door's worn sill betraying
> The feet that, creeping slow to school,
> Went storming out to playing."
>
> John Greenleaf Whittier

    Historical societies across the nation are restoring long-abandoned schoolhouses in projects reminiscent of community "school-raisings" of the past.

    Genevieve Giddings, who described the abundance of snakes in schools, was a school superintendent in Keith County, Nebraska.

    The most-popular portrait of George Washington is the unfinished work of Gilbert Stuart in 1896.

    A 1907 nostalgic song, "School Days," by Will Cobb and Gus Evans, inspired the title of this story. The original Golden Rule suggests, "Do unto others as you would have them do unto you." Good advice anytime.

    Maude Frazier believed in attics! (That's where her own adventure began.) "Modern homes never have them, with the result that young people live only in their own generation, feeling no intimate connection with the past. Their roots will grow deeper if their homes have attics." Rare finds in forgotten attics (once popularly known as "garrets") often end up in one of the museums of the Smithsonian Institution (fondly known as "The Nation's Attic") in Washington, D.C.

"Tombstone has two dance halls, a dozen gambling places, and more than twenty saloons. Still, there is hope, for I know of two Bibles in town."

Judge Wells Spicer, 1881

30 CENTS
(THE STORY OF TOMBSTONE)

"The only stone you'll find out there is your tombstone."

Friends sternly warned Edward Schieffelin about those outings in the wild. They added, only half in jest, "You'd better take your coffin."

Ed was an Army scout on assignment to monitor Chiricahua Apache in Arizona Territory. He relished the colors of the desert landscape where purple mountains hugged the San Pedro Valley and whispering cottonwoods lined its river under a cobalt sky. Accompanied by Beck, his mule ("better than a dog"), Ed took to wandering at will, picking up unusual rocks and feeling safe enough by not building campfires.

Though silver play was waning at the famed Comstock Lode in neighboring Nevada and other mines were marginal, Schieffelin would not be swayed from his excursions. He was right. In 1877, Ed found random pieces of silver ore in a dry creek bed and doggedly located the source, a rich vein of silver. "Tombstone," he named it, perhaps as a gentle stab to the doubters. Laughter aside, what Ed needed was a grubstake – money and provisions to develop his mine

Thirty cents short of flat broke, wearing clothing and a hat that were mostly patches, he sacked up some of the ore rocks and set out to locate his brother Al, working in the northern part of the territory. Ed's pennies were spent on tobacco, so he labored in mines along the 400-mile trek to keep from starving – and to buy "shoes" for Beck. More than a few "experts" during those months pronounced his specimens worthless. In frustration, Ed tossed most of his precious rocks out the front door of Al's cabin one day, but then relented and kept three samples. Good thing!

In a turnaround of circumstances, respected assayer Richard Gird, astounded by what he saw, confirmed the value of Ed's pieces and asked to be taken to the site. Ed and Al garnered little attention, but Gird's exuberant and hasty departure raised eyebrows. For a few tense weeks, it appeared to be a race of hopefuls heading to Ed's silver strike, but our guys won and went on to develop not only "Tombstone," but also "Lucky Cuss" (Ed's moniker) and "Tough Nut" (harder-to-find) silver strikes. The honest Mr. Gird joined a handshake partnership, informal and enduring, with the Schieffelin brothers.

The Schieffelin mines yielded "horn silver" of the purest class and good enough to quash the idea that Arizona wasn't mine-rich. That said, of 3000 mines in the San Pedro Valley's broad band of silver, only 13 were fully worked – better odds than in most other places. Through the next decade, almost $40 million in silver deposits was extracted from the region.

A community sprang up, settling itself on Goose Flats near the mines and taking on the name "Tombstone."

Ranchers, gamblers, gunmen, lawmen, businessmen, fancy ladies, and land speculators came to the fastest-growing town between St. Louis and San Francisco. Businesses were open 24 hours a day; round-the-clock miners needed services provided by banks, mercantile stores, blacksmith shops, and restaurants.

Families and homesteaders arrived, as well, and, remarkably, there always seemed to be room for refined living, after a fashion.

Still, the world remembers Tombstone for its disorder and violence. Two massive fires decimated the town, the first having started when a cigar ignited whiskey in a saloon!

Colorful names, such as O.K. Corral, festoon the community. A local newspaper, *The Tombstone Epitaph*, is still published monthly. Also notable is Boot Hill, final resting place for scores of unfortunates who died suddenly, violently, and with their boots on. The cemetery, for all its gloom, has some clever gravestone inscriptions – veritable or not.

HERE LIES
LESTER MOORE
4 SLUGS FROM a .44
NO "LES," NO MORE

The Bird Cage Theatre, named for balcony-seating boxes, was a place for raucous entertainment, including what's described as the longest poker game in history, almost 8½ years of continual playing (1881-1889). Supposedly, $10 million exchanged hands during the "Cage of Hands."

By 1879, Tombstone's population had grown from 100 or so miners living in tents to 7000 citizens. But the town was increasingly plagued by a carnival of crime led by a large group of outlaws, the Cochise County Cowboys, whom the *Epitaph* denounced as "a band of thieves and cutthroats with no difficulty evading the law."

Cowboys generally are widely-respected for their range skills and courtly manners. ("Howdy, Ma'am," with tip of hat.) However, the Cochise County ruffians, numbering about 300, sullied an honorable name and grew into a murderous band of rustlers and extortionists.

Legitimate ranchers at that time were identified as cowmen, stockmen, drovers, and cowhands. With profitable enterprises, these men were prime targets for an organized-crime spree led by the Cowboys.

Before the Earps arrived, their rampages went unchecked.

Mid-afternoon on October 26, 1881, the Wild West's most-recognized shootout occurred in downtown Tombstone, Arizona Territory.

Marshal Virgil Earp, his deputized brothers Morgan and Wyatt, and policeman Doc Holliday attempted to disarm the Cowboys near the O.K. Corral. (Actually, it was on Fremont Street six doors down.)

Thirty shots were fired in thirty seconds.

Three were killed – outlaws Billy Clanton, Tom McLaury, and Frank McLaury. Three were injured – Virgil Earp, Morgan Earp, and Doc Holliday. Two Cowboys, Billy Claiborne and Ike Clanton, ran away from the fight.

The Earps and Holliday were no angels, but in that raucous setting they represented the law in a thin and tenuous line of authority attempting to hold back desperadoes in the wild and wide-open stretches of the Old West. On numerous occasions, the quartet had been threatened by the raging hoodlums.

While the O.K. Corral fight undoubtedly initiated the downfall of their crime racket, the Cowboys continued their evil deeds, including a "payback" maiming of Virgil Earp with three shotgun blasts and the outright murder of Morgan Earp. Lack of evidence and crooked officials hamstrung justice in many cases, but the violent deaths of many of the gang's members and the threat of military intervention by President Chester A. Arthur brought the era of the Cowboys to a simpering close.

Though the Earp brothers and Holliday were cleared of criminal charges relating to the Corral shootout, disagreement surfaced about the legality of their violent behavior in disarming the bandits. Virgil Earp argued, correctly, that the Cowboys knew Arizona as "the only place left for them to operate, resisting official interference with the greatest desperation."

It may have come down to this: "If we don't get them, they will surely get us."

Doc Holliday died of tuberculosis. Wyatt and Virgil moved away from Tombstone.

The silver boom that had launched Tombstone lasted little more than a decade. Once the mines were dug so deeply that they reached the water table, the end was near. The nose-dive of silver prices in 1890 sent "boom" careening at last into "bust."

Tombstone settled into a quiet oblivion until Stuart Lake's not-so-factual biography of Wyatt Earp entertained readers nationwide in 1931, distracting them momentarily from the sting of the Great Depression. It was the first time most people outside Tombstone had ever heard of the Earps.

Western movies, "My Darling Clementine" and "Gunfight at the O.K. Corral," forever established the (erroneous) site of the event. A popular television series, "The Life and Times of Wyatt Earp," continued the legend.

Tombstone, "the town too tough to die," did not. It entered the public's fancy, never to depart.

In accordance with his wishes, Ed Schiefellin was buried in prospector's clothing, with a pick and a canteen alongside. Mining became his life's work, but he had initially been sent with fellow soldiers to Arizona Territory on a surveillance mission concerning Chiricahua Apache, camped only twelve miles from the future site of Ed's mines and Tombstone, where numerous murders had occurred. The Chiricahua were led at times by Cochise, Geronimo, and Victorio.

In World War I, Tombstone mined manganese for the U.S. Army; in World II, the essential ore was lead.

One-half million people a year put on a Western face as they visit Tombstone.

"Your invention of the alphabet is worth more to your people than two bags of gold in the hands of every Cherokee."

Sam Houston

THE GIFT

"Talking leaves."

That's how Sequoyah described the papers he observed his customers reading and writing.

Scarce records tell little about Sequoyah's background and parentage, though most people have heard his name.

Sequoyah is believed to have been born in Tennessee about 1770 to Wuh-the, daughter of a Cherokee chief, and a half-breed father named Nathaniel Gist or Guess. The child's English name appears to have been George Guess.

Impoverished, illiterate, and hampered by a damaged knee joint, Sequoyah (S-Si-Qua-Ya) nonetheless was a self-taught silversmith and blacksmith who constructed his own equipment (forge, furnace), tools (bellows, hammers, files, engravers, saws), and designs.

His Cherokee brothers believed writing was sorcery, but Sequoyah's quick perception that the marks on white men's mysterious sheets stood for *words* led him to believe he could make a way for his Native friends and relatives to "talk" on "leaves" of paper, as well.

The task consumed twelve years and several false starts. Sequoyah's first efforts assigned a different character for every *word*, but the overwhelming number of words proved that idea untenable. Then he tried designs for *ideas*, but these were vague and countless, as well. Finally, Sequoyah realized that his language, like others, was made up of recurring sounds in *syllables*.

That was it! Using a discarded English book in which letters and symbols were much simpler than his own designs, he put together 85 characters in a list of syllables known as a *syllabary*.

The individual syllables could be used in combinations to make many different words. Easy to write, easy to recognize, quick to read.

Not surprisingly, he was maligned as "Crazy Sequoyah," in the pattern of inventors and outside-the-box innovators verbally pilloried through the ages.

With not a speck of luck teaching the syllabary to his prejudiced and superstitious tribesmen, he took a bold, but logical, step. He enlisted his young daughter Ayoka as an enthusiastic and teachable partner.

Threatened with death for evil practices, Sequoyah and Ayoka were interrogated by a "court" of fiery young warriors, some of whom wore war paint at all times in preparation for a fight.

As a test, Sequoyah and his daughter were placed in separate rooms, where they happily "conversed" by writing and reading notes shuttled back and forth between their locations by messengers. It was a speedy and understandable communication.

Eyes opened, the warriors tossed aside their dire threats and pleaded for instruction in the syllabary. Within a week they became literate. "A whole nation at school" was one writer's description of the bombshell effect of Cherokee children, parents, and venerable grandparents mastering the process in a handful of days.

"The immediate results have no parallel in history," noted John B. Davis. "Not a school house was built and not a teacher was hired, but, within a few months, a nation of Indians called 'savages' by their enemies rose from a condition of illiteracy to one of culture, unaided save for one man."

John F. Wheeler, a printer, and missionary Samuel Worcester assisted the Cherokee in acquiring printing type-plates and presses, with the admirable result that ancient songs, stories, rituals, charms, and other fragments of cultural history were recorded for all time. In 1828, *The Cherokee Phoenix* emerged as the first Native-American newspaper. (At the time, it was the only Native document of any kind in print.) The Cherokee publication was initiated in New Echota, Indian Nation (Georgia). Revived recently in Tahlequah, Oklahoma, *The Phoenix* offers print and online versions.

As well, thousands of pages of Bible translations, tracts, and laws in the Indian language began to pour from the print shop.

The Cherokee Syllabary emerged as the sole written language developed by a Native-American tribe, and Sequoyah remains the only known individual to produce such a language singlehandedly.

> "[Sequoyah] brought our people literacy and the gift of communication through long distances and the ages..."

In 1917, a statue of Sequoyah was placed in Statuary Hall of the

U.S. Capitol in Washington, D. C.

Petitioners lost their bid to give Oklahoma the state name "Sequoyah," but the sweet-sounding word has endured, often spelled "Sequoia," as an honorific for giant redwood trees, a zoo, various parks, a county, a light aircraft, a WW I patrol boat, a U.S. Navy ship, and a Toyota sport-utility vehicle.

When the Cherokee were re-located by the U.S. government to Oklahoma Territory, Sequoyah built a log cabin in Sallisaw, which still exists and is open to the public.

Intricate pieces of silver dating from Sequoyah's time and place have been found, but his work remained unsigned. Regrettably, none can be authenticated as his art.

"...friend to white man and protector to the Indian alike..."

Denver Tribune, 1880

OURAY AND CHIPETA

On a clear winter's evening bright with meteor showers, Ouray was born in 1833 near Taos, New Mexico and given the name "Arrow" for the display in the sky.

His mother was Uncompahgre Ute and his father, Jicarillo Apache.

The young Ouray was raised in the Taos Valley, speaking Apache, Spanish, and English, while working with local sheepherders and battling rival Sioux and Kiowa.

After the death of his wife Black Mare, Ouray married a young maiden, Chipeta, "White Singing Bird." Born about 1843 and the only survivor of an attack on her Kiowa Apache village, Chipeta was taken to safety by Tabeguache Utes and raised as one of their own.

Gracious and lovely, she was wedded to Ouray at 16, becoming his helpmate and confidante, the only woman ever to sit on a Ute council. Skilled in beading, hunting, and music, Chipeta was hospitable to whites and Natives alike, without discrimination. Not known to have borne children of her own, she cared for Ouray's son until the lad was kidnapped by Sioux (and, sadly, never seen again). Chipeta may have helped raise at least four other youngsters.

Ouray's leadership qualities were obvious from an early age. He relocated to Colorado's San Juan Mountains, where Utes soaked in hot-water mineral springs known as "uncompahgre." Early Spanish explorers may have named the medicinal waters, but the surroundings were too rugged for them to remain. Not so for white men, whose intrusion increased dramatically after the discovery of gold, silver, and zinc in the San Juans.

Composed of seven tribal bands who met infrequently, the Utes consistently refrained from choosing a single leader, though they looked to Ouray in troubling times to shield their lifestyle from outside threats.

It was the U.S. government that designated Ouray, at age 27, "Chief of the Utes," thus authorizing him to negotiate on the Indians' behalf. It was an arbitrary appointment – a title that stranded Ouray in an awkward middle position as protector of his nation and, at the same time, principal mediator with the white man's government. His style of dress in Washington illustrated that dual persona; he never cut his long hair, but typically wore the buckskin clothing of western frontiersmen.

"The white man's friend" description of Ouray was not considered a compliment by angry Utes who felt he was beholden to Washington, and some turned against the leader they did not choose. That Ouray was compensated by the government as an interpreter and negotiator merely amplified the resentment directed against "the chief" by his Native brothers. Perhaps they recalled, as well, that their de facto representative was half-Apache, with an Apache wife.

Blessed with patience, forbearance, reason, and restraint, Chief Ouray met with federal officials for two decades in an attempt to work out mutually-beneficial treaties, but the chances of a stable relationship between white men and Natives vanished like the morning mist on a hot summer day.

At Ouray's side, in an era when women of both Native and white cultures were expected to stay off the stage of public policy, Chipeta moved serenely between two worlds. With often-contentious tribal brothers and sisters at home or among stubborn politicians in Washington, where she lobbied in Congress on behalf of the Utes, she nourished an enduring hope of a good outcome for "The People."

Ouray and Chipeta were realists, perceiving that the best approach was to convince the Utes that cooperation – and cooperation only – with a sovereign United States meant survival, even as tribal lands were being reduced in Colorado. Ouray was pressed to recognize U.S. authority; he had witnessed the might of the nation's army as a youth – in America's capture of Santa Fe and suppression of the Taos Revolt during the Mexican War. And he had observed the sheer numbers of that population to the east of his domain.

The lure of "striking it rich" attracted hopeful miners worldwide. A few ore diggings were made around the 1850s, but the discovery of valuable minerals opened the floodgates of intrusion into the area, which included Ute reservation lands, beginning in 1869. "Sourdoughs" and settlers arrived in droves with their equipment and home goods. New trails beat down the forests and glens, railroad crews cut down trees for crossties, and confrontations between two cultures became nasty.

> "We do not want to sell a foot of land; that is the opinion of our people. The whites can go and... come out again. We do not want them to build homes on our land."
> Chief Ouray

In 1873, the Brunot Agreement opened 3.7 million acres of the Utes' reservation property to mining. While there was an annual payment to the Natives, who retained hunting rights contingent upon peaceful behavior, much of their dominion fell under government control. Deteriorating relations between the two nations resulted in the forcible removal of the northern band of Utes to Utah in 1881. Ten years later, trains and roads crisscrossed the region.

> "He sought peace among tribes and whites and a fair shake for his people, though Ouray was dealt a sad task of liquidating a once-mighty force that ruled nearly twenty-three million acres of the Rocky Mountains."
>
> Joey Bunch

Even in tumultuous times, a compassionate Ouray often came to the aid of the white man, notably Alferd Packer and the hapless prospectors who summarily rebuffed the chief's good counsel and generous offer of shelter during a bitter mountain winter. (The party moved out into the hills; five perished in a blizzard-bound valley and Packer lived the rest of his days branded a murderer.)

Chipeta's goodness of heart has been noted, as well. Upon learning that a raiding party was about to attack her white neighbors, she forded the swollen Gunnison River on horseback to warn the families. Another time, the chief's wife rode four days and nights to help rescue (and shelter in her own home) white women and children held by the Utes after the tragic Meeker Massacre.

Still mediating to protect the Utes, Chief Ouray died of kidney disease at age 46. He is buried in Ignacio, Colorado.

> "Although one of the 'savages' of America, Ouray would have taught the czar and kings of Europe much to their interest and the happiness of their subjects."

> "[He was] a model in habits, for he never chewed tobacco, [he] abhorred whiskey, took but a sip of wine in company when it was offered, and then only as a matter of courtesy; never swore or used obscene or vulgar language."
> Sidney Jocklink

Throughout life, Chipeta and Ouray mourned the death of his son and only heir, Paron ("Apple"). They came to hope that the youth was dead rather than raised by the enemy to fight his own people. The kidnapping was a heinous act by the Sioux, but U.S. government officials, equally unconscionable, used the Utes' grief to their advantage by repeatedly feigning a search for Paron in return for favors from the Natives. Felix Brunot, of the land-takeaway Brunot Agreement, was a particularly heartless opportunist.

After Chief Ouray's death, Chipeta lived four more decades exiled in Eastern Utah. Still practicing her Episcopalian faith, she died in 1924 and was buried in a simple dirt mound. Years later, her remains were re-interred in Montrose, Colorado.

> "...and write on the whitest of God's white clouds Chipeta's name in blue."
> Gene Field

Mostly, the story of the "Queen of the Utes" appears in reports and records compiled by white men. How she actually felt about persons and events swirling about her family is, of course, speculation, but she once spoke that "our ancestors would have preferred to have kept their land." Amazingly, Chipeta added, "Never have I had an unkind feeling or unkind thought toward the government and Washington."

Ouray's name retains its fascination. For one thing, many stumble in its pronunciation, which is "Yoo'-ray." Those who study these things mostly agree that the meaning is "Arrow." The chief himself stated that the name came from his first word as a baby, "Uri" (main pole of tipi) or "Uur" (arrow).

Chief Ouray signed his name "U-ray" on an 1863 treaty; in 1868, he wrote "U-re" on another agreement, and, on an amended form of the document, "Ouray."

It's believed that Ouray was a member of the Methodist Church; an unknown source identified Ouray as "a firm believer in the Christian faith." President William McKinley said of Ouray: "He was the most intelligent man I have ever conversed with." Chipeta is believed to have visited with President William Howard Taft during one of her stays in Washington.

Today, Uintah-Ouray (Northern) Utes, numbering about 3500, have a reservation in Utah, and 1500 Southern/Uncompahgre Utes have title to 300,000 acres in southwestern Colorado, headquartered at Ignacio. In modern times, a modest amount of land has been returned to the tribes, along with millions of dollars in financial settlement. The original vast array of the native acreage is gone forever, the Northern Utes having taken the biggest hit since their reservation land was in the heart of mining country.

Chipeta was inducted into the Colorado Women's Hall of Fame in 1985.

Utes and Apaches had no written language, so we must rely on reports from Anglo writers or stories passed down through descendants of the Natives.

"I've been looking for the rest of the leg ever since."
John Perrott

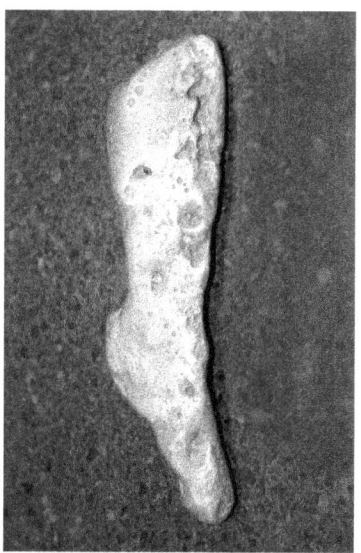

POTATO CREEK JOHNNY

"Our history is stranger than fiction."
Mary Kopco

The Black Hills Gold Rush in Dakota Territory began amid the Custer Expedition of 1874, when two experienced miners in the group found small amounts of placer gold – bits and pieces hidden in mud and caught in rocks – along Deadwood and Whitewood Creeks.

A couple of years later, four prospectors located the mother lode, source of the placer particles. The Homestake was the largest and deepest gold mine in North America, located at Lead, about four miles from Deadwood, South Dakota. For 125 years, 10% of the world's gold supply came from that vein; it closed in 2002.

John Eli Perrott, a lowly gold-panner, had no part in the Homestake bonanza. He arrived in America from Wales at age 17 and made his way to the Black Hills, where he held odd jobs and picked up small bits of placer gold in streams like Potato Creek. There he staked a modest claim, toiling forty years with the simplest of mining tools.

In a quirky turn of events, Perrott picked up one of history's largest nuggets, weighing 7 ¾ troy ounces. Jealous townspeople clambered to see the phenomenon, but scorned the treasure as no more than several smaller pieces melted or welded together – a theory that was never proven. Equally curious was the leg-like shape of the nugget. Well, it resembled *part* of a leg.

John Perrott, "Potato Creek Johnny," was an instant and enduring tourist attraction in Deadwood. His appearance fit the standard perception of a grizzled prospector. Long gray hair and beard. Floppy hat. Baggy overalls and worn-out boots. Wire-framed eyeglasses worn low on the nose. Gruff personality softened by an impish grin. And... that nugget! Visitors were amused at his claim to be "looking for the rest of the leg ever since." Kids loved him; he was about their size.

A local businessman named Adams bought the nugget for $250, placed it in a safe at his museum, and exhibited a replica on the counter out front. But there's more.

Johnny's *actual* nugget is now on permanent public display in the museum. In the best of small-town traditions, Deadwood auctioned the old replica and sponsored other fundraisers to purchase a first-rate security system for Johnny's treasure. Half the proceeds benefited wounded American soldiers, and the remainder went to the museum display. Potato Creek Johnny would be proud.

John Perrott died at age 77. At his funeral, the Adams Museum bell in Deadwood rang 77 times and a hymns burst forth from distant carillons. A headline in the *Black Hills Pioneer* read, "Potato Creek Johnny Crosses the Divide."

Lead, South Dakota, is pronounced "Leed."

Johnny's surname may have been spelled "Perrett." With his father and sister, the young man sailed to New York, took a train to Nebraska, then a stage to Dakota Territory, where an uncle was a blacksmith.

Experts have authenticated Johnny's nugget as legitimate and the largest single piece ever uncovered in the Black Hills. In 2010, the "Icebox" nugget, weighing 5.7 troy ounces, was found by prospectors.

Currently, another type of search is underway at the Homestake. With its 370 miles of tunnels and 8000' depth in places, the mine provides a noiseless and stable environment to study the workings of the universe. The project, led by the Sanford Underground Research Center, works with the U.S. Department of Energy and several science-oriented universities.

"Justice. Integrity. Service."

THE U.S. MARSHALS SERVICE

Vital to the country's interests as settlers moved westward was the cadre of U.S. Marshals and their deputies who wrangled order from chaos and justice from degradation on the raw frontier. Frequently, marshals were the sole authority of law in fresh-born little towns without any lawmen of their own. Marshals helped fill that great gap between a federal government humming along in Washington, D.C. and the vast ungoverned backcountry.

A five-point star, the oldest emblem of federal law enforcement, represents the U.S. Marshals Service, created under the Judiciary Act (1790) of the U.S. Congress that first convened in 1789. The original 13 agents were appointed by President George Washington.

The Constitution's plan for a federal system, dividing power between one central government and many state governments, was, after all, a new concept. State and local entities, accustomed to their own systems, were reluctant to yield fully to what they perceived as heavy-handed authority, especially where taxes were concerned, in Washington, D.C.

An unexpected and potentially-serious incident occured in 1794, when a marshal was endangered while serving a federal writ to protesting farmers in western Pennsylvania. A new excise tax to relieve the nation's debt after the Revolutionary War fell heavily on small, remote farms where freight on rye and corn was so exorbitant that farmers distilled the grain into liquor – more cheaply preserved and shipped, but heavily taxed under the new law.

President Washington sent a militia of soldiers from four states to protect the marshal and quell the Whiskey Rebellion. (Washington himself may have led marshals to the conflict; if so, he almost certainly was not exposed to danger.)

The unique concept of laws, including taxation, enacted by *elected* officials, may have been misunderstood by the growers, or they may have focused on their own dilemma. While the federal militia's put-down of the illegal rebellion confirmed the government's taxation powers, the farmers' plight was considered and the tax was later rescinded.

U.S. Marshals are, in effect, local representatives of the national government, serving as a bulwark of security for the federal justice system, embracing the safety and integrity of federal courts and every aspect of a federal judicial procedure.

"Justice" covers much ground, and marshal assignments through the years have run the gamut from protection of civil rights to safeguarding foreign athletes. Often, marshals are assisted by deputies, and, out of necessity, they routinely formed posse groups in the old days, when U.S. Marshals were suffering high casualty rates. From 1870 to 1896, one in four agents perished in the line of duty.

Frontier challenges have encompassed border integrity, pursuit of gangs and desperadoes, management of the Oklahoma land rush, weeding out violence in Indian Territory, and day-to-day law enforcement where there is none other. They made life difficult for

Jesse James, Billy the Kid, Belle Star, the Dalton Gang, Butch Cassidy, Sundance, and countless other outlaws.

U.S. Marshals in the Old West boast a long list of well-known personalities: Bill Tilghman, Bass Reeves, the Earp Brothers (Wyatt, Virgil, Morgan), Benjamin McCulloch, Dallas Stoudenmire, Bat Masterson, and Cal Whitson. Whitson was a one-eyed lawman portrayed as Rooster Cogburn in "True Grit," a popular movie starring John Wayne as Cogburn. Marshal Whitson served in Oklahoma Territory.

In modern times, marshals continue to protect and support judicial procedures. Other responsibilities include apprehension of federal fugitives, security and emergency operations, protection of government officials, and procedures involving asset forfeiture. The struggle for justice nowadays extends to thwarting illegal drug trade and murderous gangs. Marshals are "the federal government's manhunters," observes Jake Gibson.

The Federal Bureau of Investigation, as its name implies, investigates, while the mandate of the U.S. Marshals Service is that of *order* in our nation.

A new U.S. Marshals Museum is currently under construction in Fort Smith, Arkansas.

"commerce of the Plains"

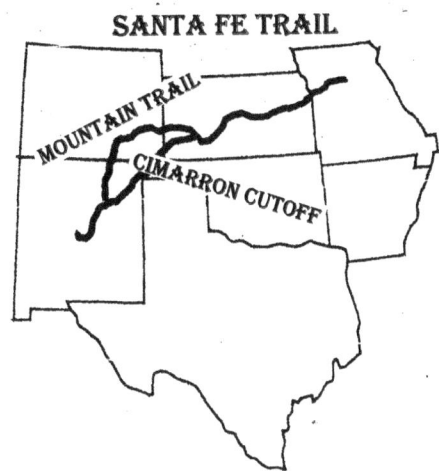

THE FIRST TRAIL

William Becknell was bankrupt.

The Missouri businessman hoped a trade enterprise in the old, yet isolated, town of Santa Fe would improve his financial situation. And that's how our nation's first international "highway" came into being.

America had possessed the Louisiana Territory, backed up against the Rockies, since 1803. Lewis and Clark's discovery voyage had traveled to the Pacific Ocean and back. Fur traders and mountain men roamed the woods and streams of the wilderness, yet no defined roadway existed into the western frontier. Spain had exerted almost full control of the Southwest since Cabeza de Vaca's unplanned exploration in 1528 and Coronado's official claim in 1540.

In 1821, Becknell laid out the 900-mile Santa Fe Trail. It was a risky move. Once he crossed the Arkansas River, the international boundary, he and his traders would be subject to the harsh policies of

Spanish hegemony, especially in the 200-year-old village of Santa Fe.

Good fortune smiled upon the Becknell group of seven on November 13, when, deep in New Mexico, the traders with their freight-laden animals encountered Captain Pedro Ignacio Gallego and 400 Mexican dragoons. Gallego informed the Americans that the Spanish grip on Mexico had at last been crushed. That newly-triumphant nation welcomed commerce in Santa Fe.

The Old Santa Fe Trail started in Franklin, Missouri, and wound its way westward along the Arkansas River into what is now eastern Colorado, at which point the route took a southerly turn, crossed the river, rose over Raton Pass, and terminated in Santa Fe. Through wicked weather, rough passages, snakes, and Native raids, pack mules loaded with trade goods made the trip in six to ten weeks, moving 18-21 miles per day. Mexicans paid for American goods with silver coins and bars. The enterprise was so profitable that, a year later, Becknell replaced the mules with heavily-loaded *wagons* of items for sale, such as stoves, lumber, and iron tools.

Because the original Mountain Trail proved too rigorous for the weighty conveyances, Becknell devised an alternate route, the flatland Cimarron Cutoff. Saving 100 miles, the cutoff parted from the Arkansas River in Kansas Territory and, after a tortuous 50 miles of dry ground (Jornada del Muerto, or "Journey of Death"), it followed the elusive Cimarron River across Indian strongholds in tiny snips of Colorado and western Oklahoma Territories. Through northeastern New Mexico Territory, the way led to its terminus in Santa Fe.

Though popular, the Cutoff smacked travelers with punishing heat, lack of dependable water sources, and increasing vulnerability to savage attacks; in one of these encounters, mountain man Jed Smith was murdered, his body never found.

The better-known Oregon, California, and Mormon Trails, while vital to the opening of the West, were principally pioneer passages, basically one-way emigration roads to a new life on the frontier. On the other hand, both branches of the Santa Fe Trail supported back-and-forth traffic for sixty years, even after New Mexico Territory became a part of the United States, till the completion of a railroad to Santa Fe in 1880.

Bent's Old Fort anchored the Mountain Trail. The secure trading post and cultural gathering-site was located on the Arkansas River, where the route swung southward near today's La Junta, Colorado, the "junction" of commerce lanes and Indian paths. Briefly an Army staging area during the Mexican War, Bent's Fort remained a private facility.

Designated a National Historic Trail by Congress, the initial Santa Fe Trail, in the words of the National Park Service, "stirs the imagination as few others can, influencing economies and bringing together a cultural mosaic of people who cooperated, sometimes clashed, and were forever changed."

Several modern highways rest on the old ruts, including stretches in Missouri and, in Kansas, over the entire trail route. Continuing the historic road are U.S. 350 between La Junta and Trinidad, Colorado, and a length of Interstate 25 from that city southward into New Mexico. The trail's final steps lie underneath a narrow main street in Santa Fe, leading directly to the city's central plaza.

"Where the cows cut the wood"

CHIPS

What? No trees?

It must've been quite a shock to westward-bound travelers as they entered the Great Plains, an enormous swatch of country with nothing taller than waving grass. A 200-mile stretch along the Platte River, for example, lacked wood of any kind.

The dearth of shady, majestic forests notwithstanding, the pioneers found themselves sorely-pressed for cooking fuel for their campfires. Not to mention light, warmth, and housing.

Bison to the rescue! Dried "ruminant manure" was found to make a dandy fire, once folks got over thinking about its source. Plains Indians had made use of this natural product probably as long as they had roamed on those Plains.

The dried "buffalo" chips offered more advantages than one could imagine.

No cutting or hauling of wood. Millions of bison moving over the Plains provided a steady and fresh supply of their leavings strewn along the ground. It was simply a matter of picking 'em up. People walked alongside their slow-moving wagons, sacking chips by the hundreds. It's said that mules got in the habit of stopping *on their own* beside a sizable pile.

You wouldn't think of it, but there was a total lack of sparks flying from fires stoked with cow chips. Especially in areas where water was scarce, folks couldn't afford to have bedding, clothing, or the prairie catch fire.

Rather dubious was the common belief that cooking with dried animal matter canceled the need for pepper. (The reason has not yet been explained.)

Nor has the reported *medicinal* use of the fodder. Mentioned in journals is the application of chips for snake bite, hiccups, sunburn, and re-attachment of severed limbs. Hard as it is to "swallow," the cow patties contain undigested residue of plant matter that is rich in minerals. Sure thing.

Fastidious pioneer women accustomed to cooking in spotless kitchens faced a sharp learning curve in their new homesteads on the treeless Plains. Baskets of "meadow muffins" became part of the scullery décor, likely just one more thing to endure.

What the cows or buffalo themselves ate sometimes became a determining factor for the quality, if you could call it that, of their chips. Animals devouring autumn plums produced chips containing the pits (seeds) of the fruit, which, in turn, guaranteed hot, long-burning fires.

> "We Soddies will remember
> No fuel could be found.
>
> "Those cows, they must have wondered
> Why we followed them around."

The fascination with dried manure seems never to end. Popular today are cow-patty tossing contests in festivals across the country.

"the place that always was"

SKY CITY

One can imagine that Acoma, atop a tall mesa in western New Mexico, was planted as surety against enemy aggression, though its panorama must have awed from the start.

At 365 feet above the desert floor, the oldest continuously-inhabited settlement in America dates from about 1100 A.D., even though ancient Pueblo culture in the Southwest – Anasazi, Mogollon, and Hohokam – potentially stretches backward to much earlier times.

The Pueblo people evolved over the ages from nomadic hunting clans to long-standing cultural villages surrounded by their own fields. "Pueblos" were built for defense and situated miles from neighboring encampments. Groupings vary in language and customs, but the societies maintained economies centered on agriculture, particularly corn of many varieties, and trade.

Desert topography necessitated the use of mud and stone for the construction of village buildings. Some of the early hamlets were like underground pits. Later in time, stacked apartment-style structures such as the Taos Pueblo were created, typically with no windows or doors. The flat roofs were covered with grass, sticks, soil, or branches; holes in the rooftops provided ventilation and access to rooms. Entrance to the pueblo was gained by ladders (easily yanked up when threats appeared) on the ground outside and on each floor.

Acoma's arrangement, nevertheless, is striking. A series of 300 steps cut by hand on the exterior stone wall and through cracks in the rock moved traffic up and down at the city on a mesa. Heaped at the top was a pile of large stones, ready for rolling down the already-precarious stairway to repel unwanted visitors.

> "They made water and agriculture the center of their spiritual universe...celebrated the seasons of planting and harvest, sought balance and harmony in their lives... cherished the sense of belonging...in their clan, which they identified by names taken from familiar animals and plants...
>
> ...As the centuries passed, the people of Acoma and their village became an expression of Mother Earth, with lives attuned to the rhythm of the seasons, as natural and enduring as the wind on the mesa top. They felt secure here, in this natural fortress. They could set their spirits free here, in their home in the sky."
>
> Jay W. Sharp

The peaceful, self-sustaining society could not have imagined the trauma that lay ahead.

In 1528, Spanish explorer Cabeza de Vaca, wandering aimlessly through the Southwest, was credibly the first white man to view Acoma, and, while he is not known to have threatened the Pueblo, the discovery nonetheless set off a tragic chain of events. Officials in Mexico City believed de Vaca's report required further investigation.

Spain, ever interested in new acquisitions, sent an exploratory party in 1539. A priest in that group, Friar Mendoza, oblivious to any standard of truthfulness, swore that he'd observed "seven cities of gold" among the pueblos. Mendoza told officials exactly what they wanted to hear.

Within a year, Francisco de Coronado set out on his far-reaching, but fruitless, expedition in search of the treasured cities. The mythical places, of course, were never found, but Coronado's soldiers made a brief stop at Acoma. One of his captains admitted, "We repented climbing to the top." An artilleryman man agreed:

> "...the greatest stronghold ever seen in the world. The Natives came down to us peaceably, although they might have spared themselves the trouble and remained on the rock, for we would not have been able to disturb them in the least."

Lured elsewhere by a passion for riches and reputation, Coronado did not pursue further scrutiny of the "sky city."

Greed for "easy" treasure kept Acoma on Spain's agenda, though, and Sky City was not spared fifty years later. King Philip II, goal-driven for conquest, religious zeal, precious metal, slave labor, and crops, sent Juan de Onate and heavily-armed troops with superior weapons – cannon, muskets, daggers, and swords – to overcome a hapless group greater in numbers, but defended solely by arrows, spears, and clubs.

Over eight decades, soldiers and state-supported priests brutally abused the Acomans. Hundreds were slain or taken to Mexico. Spanish swords lopped off the feet and legs of captive men. Younger males lost hands; women and girls were enslaved.

At times, a remnant of the Pueblos would find a way back to their ancient home on the mesa. Whether by force or in gratitude to a charismatic healer priest, surviving Natives spend 11 years constructing a massive Catholic church, San Esteban del Rey, at Acoma. Ponderosa pine was hauled by foot from mountain forests 40 miles away; dirt, stone, and water were hand-carried up the precarious staircase.

In those troubling years, Acomans coped in various ways. Some adapted to foreign customs, even marrying Spaniards. The Pueblo people were introduced to horses, donkeys, cattle, and sheep. They learned to use metal tools and weapons. Others quietly resisted, waiting for a chance to cast out Spanish conquerors and return to their own traditions.

By 1680, the tide of Spanish oppression was turning. Quietly, a prophetic and crafty Tewa religious leader named Pope (or Popay) from the San Juan pueblo secluded himself at Taos to devise plans for a bold and risky rebellion – the first Native-American rebuttal against Spanish oppression.

The Great Pueblo Revolt grew into the largest and most successful uprising of its type in the history of North America.

Popay's unique contribution was binding together a coalition of scattered cultures and doing it in total secrecy. To his advantage, the myriad of adobe settlements and nomadic tribes separated by distance, language, and varying traditions had, over many centuries, established "webs of trade and understanding."

Through commerce, war, peace, and simply the circumstances of shared environment, the connection among Southwestern cultures proved better than tenuous. Puebloan people likely knew something about events far away from their isolated desert. It's believed they were aware of the fall of Tenochtitlan (now Mexico City) to the Spaniards in 1521, LaSalle and Marquette's explorations for France, and the founding of Santa Fe in 1610.

To overcome problems in simple communication, Popay sent out messengers carrying knotted ropes with instructions for the recipients to untie one knot each day until no knots remained. Then the revolution would begin. It did – on August 11, 1680.

With the Pueblo people united as a single force, Spanish troops were routed within three weeks. Santa Fe fell; some Spanish were allowed to leave without harm, but twenty-one Franciscan priests were murdered. Churches were ransacked and religious icons smashed. What Ramon Gutierrez described as the "imposed theocratic utopia" of the brutal Spanish regime was gone. Puebloans returned to the sacred practices of ancestral times, though often in secret.

The 1700s were fairly calm for the Puebloans despite occasional troubles with intrusive Apache, Ute, and Comanche. Smallpox epidemics occurred as a result of outside contacts, but Natives and Hispanics intermarried and created a unique New Mexican culture. When the Spanish returned, it was with a different agenda. France and Great Britain's presence in America rapidly diluted the old Spanish dreams of conquest in the vast spaces of the West. One writer noted that "zealotry slackened into routine business" as Spain opted to view the Puebloans of New Mexico as *partners* in resistance to the new threats.

Wicked, deceptive, or rational, the new accommodations failed miserably. In 1821, Spain lost *all* its claims in Mexico and the Southwest. In turn, Mexico and the United States dominated Pueblo lands – but, for the most part, peace returned to Acoma.

> "There could be no complete return to how Pueblo people had lived prior to the Spanish conquest. But if the rebels' purpose was to reassert their own ways in a new setting, the rebellion succeeded, because Acoma and places like it survive on terms their people set for themselves."
>
> Edward Countryman

Today, Acoma Pueblo covers 70 square miles and 400,000 acres.

4800 tribal members are scattered across the reservation, but a few families continually reside on the mesa itself, using the old houses and maintaining the San Esteban mission built by their ancestors so long ago. Many of the modern Pueblos are Catholic, but a substantial number have returned to their traditional religious practices, as evidenced by ancient kivas resting alongside the chapel.

> "The Acomans, who must share the universal human yearning for something permanent, enduring, without shadow of change – they had their idea in substance. They actually lived upon their Rock; were born upon it and died upon it... a place to go back to."
> Willa Cather

In the National Statuary Hall of the U.S. Capitol stands a statue of Popay crafted from Tennessee marble.

In a "tribute" to those hundreds of Acoma men who'd had their feet cruelly amputated by Juan de Onate's troops, the conquistador Onate himself "lost a foot" 400 years later. The 1998 anniversary of the Spanish assault on Acoma (which had been led by de Onate) featured a bronze sculpture of the conquistador. One dark night, protestors armed with an electric saw crept up to the visitor center and lopped off the statue's right foot.

Navajo, Apache, and Hopi groups were largely safe from Spanish conquest due to their nomadic traditions and the simple fact that their populations lived mostly beyond the range of the Spanish troops.

There existed no single "Pueblo" culture, but the term generally includes those of similar lifestyles in a common environment. Even with language differences, evidence points to centuries of trade and communication among Puebloan people of the Southwest.

St. Augustine, Florida, is the oldest *continuously-inhabited city* in America. While much older, Acoma is rated as a *settlement civilization* rather than an organized city. Two other Western communities join Acoma on the "oldest" list. Santa Fe, New Mexico, is the oldest *territorial capital* in the United States. San Diego, California, is the oldest *city on the West Coast*.

Acoma and other active pueblo villages are recognized today as self-governing entities – not local units of the state government of New Mexico.

Though Coronado's quest for golden cities failed miserably, his campaign was the first exploratory party to view buffalo and the High Plains. Led by Hopi guides, one of his men, Garcia Lopez de Cardenas, first beheld the Grand Canyon.

The following observation by David J. Weber spells out the significance of events long past, in this case the 1680 revolt. "The Pueblo Revolt is gone. It lives only in oral tradition, in the written words of those who witnessed it, and in the work of scholars who try to reconstruct it."

"Eastward I go only by force, but westward I go free."
Henry David Thoreau

THE LONG LOOK WEST

"We proceeded on..." appears numerous times in journals of Lewis and Clark's expedition, highlighting the group's resiliency coupled with determination to carry out their mission successfully for the country and President Jefferson.

From youth, Thomas Jefferson was intrigued by the unknown West – encouraged by his father, his tutors, a wide array of reading material, and lively discussions. We might say that Jefferson himself had "proceeded on" (in his ideas and plans, at least) a full two decades before the famous explorers headed west.

Jefferson recognized that any claim to the American Northwest, which was emerging as the "world's hotspot" at the time, rested upon a physical presence there. Great Britain, dominating the fur trade in the region, appeared to be on the cusp of attaching the continent's west coast, or parts of it, to its empire. Spain claimed territory as far north as Anchorage; Russia was operating fur-trading outposts in the Aleutian Islands.

The Corps of Discovery led by Meriwether Lewis and William Clark was not Jefferson's first endeavor to explore and claim the unknown West. A weak effort in 1783 found Jefferson, a new member of Congress, seeking to recruit renowned military leader George Rogers Clark for an expedition beyond the Mississippi. The idea dissolved when Clark declined.

While Ambassador to France in 1786, Jefferson bolstered the fantastic proposal of a sea-otter trader named John Ledyard. Starting in Europe, Ledyard planned to traverse on foot the breadth of Russia, cross the Bering Strait as Ice-Age hunters had done, and end up on Vancouver Island. From there, he would seek a water passage across the American continent. Not unexpectedly, he was halted in frozen Siberia by Empress Catherine the Great's soldiers and summarily expelled.

In 1793, Jefferson, then U.S. Secretary of State, partnered with the American Philosophical Society to dispatch a highly-respected French botanist, Andre Michaux, up the Missouri River on what was disguised as a scientific mission. Michaux got only as far as Kentucky before Jefferson discovered he was part of a French scheme to undermine Spanish interests in Louisiana Territory.

Success at last in 1803. As President, Thomas Jefferson acquired the Louisiana Purchase from France and promptly authorized the explorers to set out the next year. (George Rogers Clark had recommended to the President that his brother William join the group.)

The official mandate of the Corps was to explore the Purchase, encompassing land drained by the Missouri River and western tributaries of the Mississippi.

However, the President privately authorized exploration onward to the Pacific Ocean. His bold instructions demonstrated an eagerness to put in motion a course of action securing this nation's stance in the

West and, importantly, its ownership of an outlet to the Pacific that would facilitate American trade in the Far East. (It was an early and bold example of Manifest Destiny, as yet unidentified or named.)

The President desired "the most direct and practical water communication across the continent," and he hoped for a juncture of two great rivers, the mighty Missouri on the east side of the Rockies and the newly-discovered Columbia, on the west side. The Missouri, via the Mississippi and the Gulf of Mexico, eventually spilled into the Atlantic Ocean. The Columbia had been found to empty into the Pacific. What lay in between the two was a mystery, but the Lewis and Clark expedition was optimistically outfitted for a crossing of the continent solely by water.

Though sailors from several countries had spotted what would later be known as the Columbia River, none had explored or claimed it. A mere twelve years before the Corps of Discovery set out westward, British sea captain George Vancouver and an American captain from Boston, Robert Gray, stumbled upon the river and compared notes. Vancouver mistakenly judged its inlet too narrow for commercial use and discounted the waterway. Gray saw it differently, and the Columbia River (named after Gray's ship) became an American possession. Though Gray followed the river only a brief distance inland, his description indicated a course of considerable breadth and length.

That information encouraged speculation that the river's inland source could possibly be located very near the headwaters of the Missouri. Explorers going upriver on the Missouri might be able to move easily to the Columbia and proceed to the ocean.

Three months into Lewis and Clark's journey, though, Captain Lewis stood on a high pinnacle of the Continental Divide and was dismayed to discover no water connection at all – only lofty mountains as far as the eye could see. Without a doubt, then, his explorers would be moving over the Divide in search of the Columbia's headwaters.

The expedition was forced to ditch and bury the river craft at the head of the Missouri and cache extra supplies, all to be retrieved on the return trip to St. Louis. Horses and mules were purchased through negotiations with the Shoshone, Sacagawea's people. After a grueling 70-day, 220-mile portage over range after range of the Rockies, the horses were entrusted to the care of cooperative Nez Perce. Hastily-constructed dugout canoes conveyed the ecstatic explorers down the Columbia to the Pacific.

America. Coast-to-coast. East-to-West.

Thomas Jefferson's fourth attempt at exploring the West proved a success without precedent. Forever known as "The Great Expansionist," the third President ultimately earned a likeness on Mt. Rushmore.

The Louisiana Purchase territory did not extend past the Rocky Mountains. The massive mountain range, source of the Missouri and its tributaries, formed a natural western boundary.

ODDMENTS

JIM BRIDGER COULDN'T READ A LICK...

Trapper, guide, trader, driver of horses, scout – but he never learned to read. Happily, Bridger found others to read *to* him. On long winter nights at Fort Laramie in the winter of 1862-1863, Captain J. Lee Humfreville read aloud the classic, Hiawatha, to his trusted guide. Dazzled by the story, Bridger asked the captain which book he would judge the grandest of all.

Humfreville replied, "I told him Shakespeare's was supposed to be the greatest. Thereupon he [Bridger] made a journey to the main road, lay in wait for a wagon train, and bought a Shakespeare copy from some emigrants, paying for it with a yoke of cattle. He hired a German boy at $40 a month to read from his treasured book, Richard III.

"Bridger took great interest in reading, listening most attentively for hours at a time. It was amusing to hear Bridger quote Shakespeare. He could give quotation after quotation. Sometimes he seasoned them with a broad oath, so ingeniously inserted as to make it appear to the listener that Shakespeare himself had used the same language."

...AND KIT CARSON COULDN'T SPELL

Kit Carson's formal education ceased early, as well. Said he, "I was a young boy in the schoolhouse when the cry came, 'Injuns!' I jumped to my rifle and threw down my spelling book, and thar it lies."

AT THE RENDEZVOUS

Named by French Canadian fur traders, the Rendezvous was the mountain men's "vacation," a time of high-spirited fellowship –

eating, drinking, dancing and singing, target-shooting, racing, and, finally, gearing up for another lonely year in the hills, streams, and forests of the West. Many showed up with Indian wives and children; Natives traded buffalo hides for coffee and sugar. All welcomed the company of others and a month's carefree days of rest.

Some few, like Jed Smith, were teetotalers, but most unabashedly drank till they dropped, including Joe Meek. At the Green River Rendezvous of 1833, Joe kept his sense of humor when a rabid wolf visited camp several nights and bit some of the mountaineers.

> "[Meek said], had a wolf bitten *him*, the alcohol in his blood would have killed [the wolf] for sure... "
>
> Mike Stamm

The first Rendezvous was assembled in 1825, organized by prominent fur trader William Ashley to corral his many employees and "settle up" after the season of hunting. Pelts were thicker in cold weather; late fall and early spring were the prime hunting times, as the beaver retired to their lodges in the dead of winter. At the summer fest, furs were sold and supplies were bought; trading with outsiders allowed trappers to remain in the mountains year around.

By 1840, trapping became unprofitable as both the demand and the supply for beaver fur sharply declined. And soon there appeared all those settlers in wagons headed to Oregon and California. The Rendezvous was no more.

A FULL HOUSE

In 1875, the Kitchen family left North Carolina and settled near the Lampasas River in Central Texas, where Mr. Kitchen planted a large field of corn. A couple of years later, he sold some of his crop to Captain J.F. Chaffin, who lived a fair distance westward.

While the corn was being ground at a mill, Kitchen became interested in the captain's description of his property at Waldrip near the Colorado River (south of Brady, Texas) and the good prospects for purchasing land. Kitchen made the return trip west with Chaffin's party to look over the country and, finding it satisfactory, made plans for relocation. Captain Chaffin kindly offered the Kitchens a room in his log cabin until they could construct a home of their own.

Already, the three-room place was a full house. Captain Chaffin, his wife and four children. The captain's aged father. Mrs. Chaffin's bachelor brother. Her unmarried sister. A Mr. Safford with three motherless children. A nephew. A Negro family of five. That's <u>nineteen</u> inhabitants.

The Kitchen bunch added five more, for a total population of <u>twenty-four.</u>

The Kitchens' new abode was built within two weeks. There's no mention of an abundance of helpers, but it's likely there were plenty of 'em, hoping to get the thing finished in a hurry. No palace itself, the log house boasted one room, one door, one chimney, no windows, flat rocks for flooring, and a roof of dirt over logs.

That left the original 19 in the Chaffin house, and who knows how long that lasted!

BOSE AND BRITT
This duo of Black men never met, but each is a notable character in nineteenth-century Texas.

Born a slave of Milton Ikard in Mississippi, Bose came to Texas with his master and ended up in 1866 as a "hand" on the first cattle drive of Charles Goodnight and Oliver Loving. (Some say he was sold to Loving for $1000 in cows and calves.) It was a fortunate turnaround for all involved.

"He never shirked a duty or discharge order. He surpassed any man I ever saw in endurance and stamina. There was a dignity, a cleanliness, and a reliability about him that was wonderful. He was my detective, my banker, and everything else in the wild country. I have trusted him further than any living man."
Charles Goodnight

Bose Ikard was the model for Deets, a major character in the movie, "Lonesome Dove." He is buried near Oliver Loving in Greenwood Cemetery, Weatherford, Texas, and his gravestone displays a tribute from rancher Goodnight.

The slave of Moses Johnson, Britton (Britt) Johnson kept his own cattle and enjoyed a large amount of freedom in his role as ranch foreman. But life took a nasty turn when the Elm Creek raid by 700 Kiowa and Comanche in 1864 resulted in his son's death and the kidnapping of his wife and two daughters. (The Natives needed more people than they could produce, so they raided at will due to the lack of a military presence in Texas during the Civil War.)

For months, with permission and monetary support from Moses, Britt roamed the wild country of the Llano Estacado in search of his loved ones. The family was reunited the next year, due to ransom, negotiation, or both.

There are reports that Johnson searched for other captives, as well. It's mainly speculation, though, that his adventures are portrayed in a movie, "The Searchers." The author of the book-behind-the-film explained that he combined features from dozens of Indian raids for his story. Britt Johnson perished in an 1871 attack.

STAGECOACH ETIQUETTE

In 1877, the *Omaha Herald* offered handy tips for a successful journey by coach.

"Don't growl at food stations or smoke a strong pipe inside in the early morning."

"Bathe feet in cold water before starting; wear loose overshoes and large gloves."

"Don't swear or lop over on your neighbor when sleeping".

"If you have anything to take in a bottle, pass it around. A man who drinks by himself in such a case has lost all human feeling."

"Don't discuss politics or religion, nor point out places on the road where horrible murders have been committed."

"Don't grease your hair before starting out, or dust will stick there in sufficient quantities to make a 'tater patch.' "

"If a team runs away, sit still and take your chances. If you jump, nine times out of ten you will be hurt."

"Spit on the leeward side of the coach."

"Don't imagine for a moment that you are going on a picnic; expect annoyance, discomfort, and some hardships. If you are disappointed, thank heaven."

"PRUNES"

A burro was typically the only "forever" companion of a lonely prospector. The sturdy little beasts of burden hauled equipment and supplies (and, as Linda Nagy adds, "whiskey and dynamite") and pulled heavy carts of ore and gravel. Steep mountainsides and rough trails posed no obstacles to burros, and they were amazingly long-lived.

In 1885, Rupe Sherwood, a miner in the high country near Fairplay, Colorado, paid two retirees $10 for the little animal that ended up serving over 50 years. Prunes also carried grocery lists, secured on his harness, to town, where shopkeepers loaded up the requested items.

Burros are vegetarians, and it was observed that Prunes preferred... prunes. Folks joked that he could read, since he sidled right up to that fruit in the stores.

Prunes and Sherwood at last retired in Fairplay, where the burro is said to have "panhandled" a bit at the doors of friendly humans. Prunes was 63 years old when he became trapped in a shed during a blizzard; he was in poor shape when found. Though the ladies tenderly fed him flapjacks, Prunes died in the spring. Townsfolk promptly installed a monument with his collar enclosed in glass. Sherwood mourned his friend, saying he "would trust Prunes ahead of any man."

A ROLLING DARKROOM

In 1879, the Army Corps of Topographical Engineers completed its scientific surveys of the West. Then the photographers came and captured images, presenting to a skeptical public the awesome features and massive scale of the frontier. An old trick was used to portray what had been described verbally by the mountain men and trailblazers. Placing humans in the pictorial scene (standing on a rock formation, beside a waterfall, at the base of a mountain) helped "provide an admission of human insignificance in this vast land." (Bill Gilbert)

Today's tourists seem to do the same. Could there be a photo of California's giant Redwoods without a grinning person nearby?

WHEN COWBOYS WEREN'T TRUE "COWBOYS"

The Cochise County Cowboys were notorious hoodlums, not working cowboys on the range. The rustlers and murderers, in particular the McLaury and Clanton families, fastened onto the "cowboy" name. Their bunch welcomed the likes of Johnny Ringo, "Curly Bill" Brocius, Billy Claiborne, "Buckskin Frank" Leslie, and Pony Diehl.

The *San Francisco Examiner* tagged the Cochise County Cowboys "the most reckless class of cowboys in that wild country."

In some old writings, the word was spelled "cow-boy."

WILD ABOUT TEXAS

Historical marker in San Saba, Texas: "First Methodist Church, Organized 1856 in an area so untamed that church gave the missionary (pastor) a $50 revolver and a $125 horse."

PLAINS PAPER

"When the Indians robbed houses, they invariably took all the books they could find, using the paper to pack their shields. They knew, as well as we did, the resistance [that] paper has against bullets... more resistance than anything to be had upon the frontier, unless it was cotton. The Indians knew this and stole all the books and paper they could find.

"I once shot an Indian down on the Quitaque. I did not kill him, but he dropped his shield. Between the folds of hides was a complete history of Rome... ."
        Charles Goodnight, *Panhandle Plains Revue*, 1928

MOUNTAIN MEN

"Why did men subject themselves to hair-raising danger, periodic starvation, exposure to the elements, isolation from civilization, and financial uncertainty?"asks western writer Mike Stamm, Why indeed?

The mountain men made their living in the American West after the explorations of Lewis and Clark and on through mid-century of the 1800s. These hardy souls' solitary existence in the wild centered around trapping beaver, hunting, fishing, and, later, scouting and guiding. Fondly calling each other "old coons," they were pathfinders, always wondering what was around the river's bend or over the next hill. "Civilization" hemmed them in; only advanced age, declining health, or death could stop the wanderlust.

Kit Carson owned a ranch in New Mexico, but preferred escorting pioneers and fighting Indians; Joe Walker *tried* to be a lawman. Bill Williams didn't stay long at his store in Taos. Jed Smith lasted less than a year in the settlements and resumed his guide services, only to be killed by Indians. Even Jim Bridger often wandered from his popular trade post at Fort Bridger. Steven Hall Meek's investments soured, and he "was compelled to take to the mountains to secure a livelihood."

William T. Hamilton departed his affluent lifestyle to move westward in the 1840s and never looked back. "My answer has always been that there was a charm in the life of a free mountaineer from which one cannot free himself after he once has fallen under its spell." Jed Smith reminisced, "My dreams were not of gold or ambitious honors, but of my distant, quiet home of murmuring brooks and of cooling waters." John Robertson said he had become "lazy" in the mountains and "do not believe I could go to work [elsewhere]."

But it *was* work – hard work – as rugged survival always is. In the course of that everyday struggle, mountain men became "at one" with the places they found. Those who followed in later years (miners, settlers, engineers, photographers, surveyors, military, and the rest) were amazed at the exactness of location and sharpness of detail the mountain men "carried in their heads."

DEER VS. TURKEY

Pioneer Texan Noah Smithwick told a story about a farm woman living near Columbus, Texas, who was accustomed to buying deer and wild turkey from the nearby Tonkawa Indians. She asked one of the Tonkawa why he offered so many deer and so few turkey. His reply:

"Oh, turkeys too hard to kill. Injun crawl along in the grass. *Deer* [look up and] he say, 'Maybe-so Injun, maybe-so stump', and then he go on eat. Injun crawl a little closer and shoot deer. *Turkey* look and say, "Injun by God," and he duck his head and run."

Smithwick had witnessed such a scene firsthand, watching "an Indian crawling upon [a] deer, holding his head just far enough above the grass to watch the motions of the game, and whenever the deer threw up its head, instead of ducking his own, the Indian would remain perfectly still, while the quarry gazed suspiciously at him for a few minutes until apparently reassured, then put down its head and went on feeding; but let a turkey catch sight of a suspicious object, he didn't wait to investigate; it was 'Injun, by God' and he was off!"

SKEETERS

Mosquitoes were a pesky distraction to pioneer life – and dangerous, as well. Decades would pass before it was proven that mosquitoes are disease vectors, exposing their victims to malaria and yellow fever. The despised insects have likely plagued mankind for half a million years. Old-time remedies were not very sophisticated – smoky fires, netting, hog-lard repellent. For relief, Native Americans mixed various plants with grease from animals such as bears or raccoons. Those who found underground crude oil covered their bodies with the greasy stuff.

Corps of Discovery's William Clark had a lot to say in his journal about the pests. Not the best of spellers, Clark used 19 variations of "mosquito" and never once got it right – muskeetors, musqueters, misquitors, and so on.

Easy to see where the mosquitoes "bugging" the Lewis and Clark expedition hatched. The Missouri River's backwaters and swampy pools were ideal breeding grounds. At times, the men couldn't shoot because of swarming mosquitoes around their faces; they ate mouthfuls of them. It's almost certain that many, if not most, western travelers, including the Corps of Discovery, at some time endured mild (or serious) forms of malaria or ague.

However, in preparation for the campaign, Meriwether Lewis had purchased 15 pounds of Peruvian cinchona-tree bark, which contains quinine. (Jesuit missionaries in Central and South America had learned about the bark in the late 1500s.) The Corps is sure to have utilized it, for no expedition member died from malaria, with the unlikely exception of Lewis himself, who mysteriously succumbed just three years after the completion of the journey. Some believe he had distributed the bark to others and stuck to Dr. Ben Rush's laxative pills himself, with the unfortunate result of fatal poisoning from malaria, wine, mercury, laudanum, bark, or some combination of them. Others believe he committed suicide or was murdered. Sad, whatever the cause.

On a cheerier note, there are some clever depictions of mosquito miseries. An emigrant on the Oregon Trail joked that mosquitoes were "smaller than hummingbirds, but larger than crickets." Joe

Meek, with a group in Kansas, bragged, "Though I heard a report of mosquitoes as big as turkeys, the biggest I ever saw was no larger than a crow."

OLIVER'S CASKET

Charles Goodnight and Oliver Loving opened a cattle trail through West Texas to New Mexico and Colorado Territories. In 1867, Loving was gravely wounded in a Comanche attack near the Pecos River. The injury in his arm was survivable, but, without antibiotics, gangrene took his life. (Reportedly, a local doctor refused to attempt amputation, as he was not experienced in surgery.)

Goodnight fulfilled his friend's last request to be buried in his home cemetery at Weatherford, Texas. First, the body was buried temporarily while Goodnight and his cowboys finished the drive. Then a tin casket was made of empty, flattened oil cans soldered together. The wood box containing Loving's body was placed in the container, powdered charcoal was added, and the metal lid was sealed.

DUTCH OVEN

The single most indispensable piece of survival gear in the Old West was the Dutch oven. Lewis and Clark carried one. In trail-driving days, chuck-wagon cooks wouldn't have fared as well without the pots that cooked their beans, biscuits, beef, and cobblers. Pioneers, mountain men, explorers, miners, and travelers would agree.

The hardy design was a technique of the Dutch in the late 1600s. In 1710, Englishman Andrew Darby traveled to the Netherlands to observe the process, whereupon he returned home and began production of the pots, which eventually immigrated to America, where Paul Revere made some of the first in this country.

The quintessential Dutch oven is a cast-iron kettle or pot with high sides and a tight-fitting rimmed lid. The pot is designed to be hung over a fire or a bed of coals; sometimes the entire vessel is buried underground in the hot coals.

Stacked one over the other, the ovens benefit from rising heat. A Dutch oven is equally serviceable on a stovetop or in a stove oven. The lid can be turned upside-down to make a griddle.

INDIAN PONIES

Across the wide spectrum of Western Native Americans, the typical and favored horse was the pony. The smallness of ponies was a sort of "classified matter" of knowledge for the Indians, who observed that larger horses and mules fare poorly when feeding is sparse in quality or limited in time. Bigger animals need more food for their larger builds, and, when feeding is compromised due to any number of reasons, the bigger animals cannot consume enough for maximum nourishment.

> "The shabbiest Shawnee pony you can pick up will answer your purpose better than the finest horse you can take from the stable."
>
> John M. Shively

On the other hand, the more massive horses and mules could carry and pull more weight, but that was not the purpose of Indian ponies, was it?

MANIFEST DESTINY

"[It is] our manifest destiny to overspread the continent allotted by Providence for the free development of our yearly multiplying millions." So pronounced John O'Sullivan, a New York editor, in 1845. He said it; they did it.

GTT

Carved into the bark of a tree. Posted on the front door. Hanging on a fence. "GTT" ("Gone to Texas") meant the residents had skipped out and headed west. Maybe those runaways of the 1800s had broken a law or were debt-ridden with no hope of straightening out their finances. Maybe they simply wanted a fresh start.

Not so anonymously, David Crockett announced his intentions to Tennessee voters before the 1835 Congressional election. "...I told the people of my district that, if they saw fit to re-elect me, I would serve them faithfully, as I had done; but, if not, they might all go to hell and I would go to Texas."

He lost the election; he went to Texas.

A BRIDGER-BRIGHT IDEA

The final Mountain-Man Rendezvous in 1840 foreshadowed the end of the once-profitable fur trade in the mountain streams of the West. The beaver population was close to extermination; it was just as well, because changes in sartorial fashion in Europe led to a preference for *silk* rather than *felt* hats.

Observing the rise of westward movement by emigrant families, Jim Bridger gave up his beaver traps and opened a trading post on the Black's Fork of the Green River, not far from the old Rendezvous site, in 1843. He thus described his enterprise and customers: "Coming out, they are well-supplied with money, but by the time they get here, they want all kinds of [provisions]. I have established a small fort with a blacksmith shop and a supply of iron along the emigrant road." Indians picked up on the travelers' trade, as well, offering robes, moccasins, and dressed venison.

Rough by the standards of another Wyoming post, Fort Laramie, Bridger's simple structures nevertheless offered a spot of relief for travel-worn families at a landmark spot along the Oregon Trail.

In later years, Jim's property was tossed about between the Mormons and the U.S. Army, ending up in the hands of a successful sutler (a civilian selling supplies to the Army). During the rest of the century, the fort monitored emigrant trails, served as a station on routes of the Pony Express and Overland Stage, and peddled provisions for construction workers on the transcontinental railroad. Location, location, location!

Bridger's investment at last was restored to his family years after his death. Today Ft. Bridger is a Wyoming Historical Landmark. Jim Bridger is considered by many to have been the "Daniel Boone of the West."

FOR THE LOVE OF BOOKS

Nelda Holder writes a heartwarming remembrance, not of the West, but from the cotton-and-tobacco country of eastern North Carolina. Somehow the tenor of the story reaches to all those lonely, book-starved folks who found themselves deep in the western wilderness.

Nelda's mother, a little girl with a big passion for reading, found few pages to devour in their sharecropper's home, but down the road lived a wealthy lawyer who, having discovered the child's desire to read, placed his extensive home library at her disposal – to come and go and borrow as many books as she wished.

By the time Nelda herself was growing up, the bookmobile, "that blessed vehicle of countryside salvation," was coming around each month. Nelda and her brother walked down the dirt road to visit with the "book angels" in "the mobile sanctuary" and load up enough reading matter to last till next time.

In Tombstone, Arizona, individuals offered small rental libraries and reading clubs; perhaps the goal was to counteract the effects of the notorious town's drinking, gambling, and violence. By 1885, a central library facility had been funded by social events featuring dancing and lemonade.

The next year, pioneer women in Howard, Dakota Territory, saw to it that a library, the territory's first, was opened, though it was simply a bookcase in a corner of Mr. Boles' general store. A volunteer librarian opened the doors of the treasured collection twice a week. After a fire destroyed the store, the library rose up like a phoenix, starting anew with the 11 books that had been in the hands of borrowers the day of the blaze.

The citizens of Butte, Montana, a rich and rowdy mining town, opened a public library in 1893 in a bold attempt to promote culture in the unlikeliest of places. While still a territory, Washington State transported its first books by steamer around Cape Horn.

Soldiers and families in Nebraska Territory welcomed a library at Fort Atkinson, the first army post built west of the Missouri River, in 1819. Kansas City's first library contained only an encyclopedia set.

In Cordova, Alaska, Episcopalian missionary Eustace Ziegler felt workingmen and families needed a place to meet. Its color derived from paint donated by the railroad, The Red Dragon clubhouse stayed open till midnight and featured a 600-volume library near a large stone fireplace. On Sundays, an altar was lowered from the rafters for church services.

Naturally, it was easier for larger cities to jump onto the reading bandwagon, but the novice facilities often were humble in style. Denver's "center of public happiness" started in empty rooms of a school building. Salt Lake City had the volumes, but no space; its 11,000 books were crammed together on the top floor of a city-county building. In Houston, Texas, the 100-book library of 1854 was associated with a debate society.

The West benefited enormously when over two thousand free Carnegie public libraries were established from 1883-1929 across the nation. The facilities were funded by the fortune of Scottish-American steel magnate Andrew Carnegie, who recalled a gentleman from his childhood, Col. James Anderson, and his encouraging practice of allowing any working boy to use his personal library.

Today, Little Free Libraries, thousands of them, have appeared in neighborhoods, public parks, and business locales in America and around the world. Their signs invite, "Take a book; leave a book." It was Todd Bol's idea. The Hudson, Wisconsin, resident honored his book-loving mother by re-styling an old garage door into a box resembling a schoolhouse, filling it with volumes from her collection, and placing it in his front yard in 2009. The goal is to "use these seeds to plant good things," in lockstep with the ambition of those old and simple libraries on the frontier.

NO BARRIERS

"Neither snow nor rain nor gloom of night shall stay these couriers from the swift completion of their appointed rounds." The memorable line appears on the James Farley Post Office building in New York City.

Beautifully put, but it's not the motto of the United States Postal Service. (The USPS has no motto or creed.) Professor George Herbert Palmer of Harvard University translated from Greek literature a statement by the ancient historian Herodotus praising the efficiency of mounted postal carriers in Persia about 500 B.C. Centuries later, the same could be said for those brave, intrepid souls risking life and limb while delivering mail in backwoods America and on the frontier.

RAGTAG TEXIANS BLAZED A TRAIL!

Any reader of Western history is bound to stumble across this trio of terms from time to time.

That **ragtag army** – who fought to the death in the Alamo, were brutally murdered at Goliad, and soundly defeated Santa Anna at San Jacinto – was routinely described as "riffraff, untidy, disorganized, and shabby." Granted, the Texians may have been unimpressive in appearance and training. "Ragtag" loses its punch, however, when considering the lasting legacy of those patriots' selfless bravery.

Americans in Texas were known as **Texians** from early Anglo settlement until statehood in 1845, when today's term "Texans" came into prominence. The word *tejas* (*tayshas, texias, techas*) was in use by Indian tribes of East Texas, chiefly the Hasinai, long before newcomers were on the scene, and it meant *friends*, particularly *allies against the Apache*.

The original sounds of the word *tejas* suggest that *Texas* might properly be pronounced *Tex-ahs* or *Tex-oss*. Performers in the outdoor musical "Texas" in Palo Duro Canyon sing it that way; so do Texas A&M University's Singing Cadets.

Blazing a trail literally means to make a notch or mark (a "blaze") on a tree to mark a path. An early use of the phrase appeared in *The Helena Independent,* a Montana newspaper, in 1883. "The merchants, desirous of securing the trade of the new mines, offered the stranger $100 if he would blaze a trail through and afterward it could be cleared... for pack animals to pass through."

OURAY, COLORADO

This scenic mountain town continues to draw visitors, even as it was irresistible to Uncompahgre Utes traveling in summer to soak in "sacred miracle waters." Indeed, therapeutic minerals lie beneath much of the village and appear as "uncompahgre," or "hot-water springs."

Prospectors arrived in 1875. The first gold veins were found in Gertrude and Una, mines that were being worked for lead, copper, and zinc in Imogene Basin. At the height of activity, there were 30 active mines. Many of today's popular high-country trails were once miners' access routes and, before that, Indian paths.

Chief Ouray loved the little place that took his name. He lived in a small cabin, soaked in the springs, and met with white officials and fellow Natives.

WHAT $15 MILLION BOUGHT... THEN AND NOW

The United States paid France **$15 million** for 828,000 square miles of land, the Louisiana Purchase, in 1803, under direction of President Thomas Jefferson. That equals **529,920,000** acres at <u>three cents per acre</u> (actually, 2.83 cents).

In 1777, Jefferson bought an estate in Virginia for his farming operations and built his magnificent home, Monticello. The acreage included Montalto ("High Mountain"), which overlooks Monticello ("Little Mountain") below. Six years after his death, Jefferson's heirs sold the Montalto property, thus excluding Monticello from any control of the vast hill.

In recent years, the Jefferson Foundation has participated in negotiations to protect the estate's integrity by regaining the original property in order to halt commercial and/or residential development that appeared imminent, towering over the beautiful and historic Monticello.

By 2004, an agreement was reached allowing the Foundation to purchase **330** acres on Montalto – for **$15 million**, or $45,454 per acre (actually, $45,454.50).

LOUISIANA: FROM "TERRITORY" TO "PURCHASE" TO "STATES"...

Louisiana Territory was claimed by French explorer LaSalle in 1682, but France lost the vast property to Spain 80 years later. When Spain ceded the Louisiana Territory back to France in 1800, America anticipated an abrupt end to its free use of the lower Mississippi River and the Port of New Orleans. There was even talk of taking the city by force.

President Jefferson sent Robert Livingston to negotiate with French minister Charles Talleyrand for outright purchase of New Orleans or simply a guarantee of unhindered access to its seaport. When James Monroe joined Livingston in France to help with the discussions, he was forced to sell his valuable collection of silverware and china to finance the journey overseas.

In a surprise move, France, due to its terrible financial burdens, offered to sell the entire Louisiana Territory to the United States. Livingston and Monroe couldn't take a chance on a lengthy wait for Congressional approval, so they hastily made the sales agreement on April 30 and signed it May 12, 1803.

The arrangement was so unprecedented that Jefferson admitted the Constitution "was stretched till it cracked" and one Senator griped that "we are to give money of which we have too little for land of which we already have too much." The purchase was approved, though, in October and possession was taken in December, 1803.

The United States paid France a little over $11 million for Louisiana Territory and forgave $3.5 million in French debt. Bargain that it was, America had to borrow a portion of the money at 6% interest. Once the loan was repaid, the price had advanced to about $23 million. It was a "steal" at any price.

Louisiana was the first state created from the Purchase in 1812. In total, nine states and parts of six others were formed from Louisiana Territory.

A LIFESAVER

It was not unusual to see Old Westerners like William Bent chomping down on raw bison liver dipped in bile. Supplementing the meat's nutritive value, the innards helped conquer those twin dangers of thirst and dehydration.

> "Buffalo fresh, buffalo dried,
> Roasted, boiled, stewed, or fried.
> Buffalo serves in every stead
> For poultry and pastry, for meat and for bread"
>
> David Lavender

DOCTOR SUE

"Do you want to be simply called " 'one of those Indians' or do you want to go to school and be somebody in the world?" Taking up her father's rather harsh challenge, Susan LaFlesche (Picotte), an Omaha born in Nebraska Territory in 1865, went on to study at Women's Medical College of Pennsylvania. The first American Indian M.D., Dr. Sue treated whoever needed her services within a broad swath of the Great Plains. She advocated sensible precautions such as school hygiene, screen doors on houses, avoidance of alcoholic beverages, and the use of individual, not shared, drinking cups. Unhailed until recent years, Dr. Sue implored, "Help us climb higher. Give us a chance."

WELLS FARGO

With no railroads in California at the time and a vigorous gold-rush business requiring safe and dependable delivery of valuables, Henry Wells and William Fargo launched the famous Wells Fargo and Company stagecoach enterprise in San Francisco in 1852. The business spread to mining towns and growing cities. Along with express transport, the firm offered banking services and mail delivery using horseback, ships, and rails (as available) in addition to their iconic stage wagons.

While there was local postal service in California by 1844, many customers came to prefer mail delivery by express companies; it was cheaper and faster. Wells Fargo charged six cents per letter; the government's charge was 25 cents. Both private and public mail services were common in the 19th century. Before a United States mint was established in San Francisco in 1854, Wells Fargo transported gold from the Philadelphia mint to that city.

Armed guards "rode shotgun" on the stages, but brazen robberies were an ever-present hazard until the strongboxes were bolted to floors of the coaches. Shipping clients never sustained any loss in the thefts; Wells Fargo covered it all, resulting in an enormous public trust in the company. (Black Bart was one of more than 200 robbers halted by the company's security employees.) It's said that miners swore "By God and Wells Fargo."

Beginning in 1857, Wells Fargo served as banker and prime lender for the Overland Mail Company. Since the Overland prohibited the transport of valuables, some Wells Fargo coaches remained in service to accommodate those shipments. Delivery of mail and goods by land or sea declined precipitously once trains ran coast to coast. Wells Fargo, though, did not immediately halt its deliveries on smaller routes.

In 1908, the company threw down its last strongbox from a Concord stage on the demand of robbers. The thieves were pursued by *automobile*! The final cargo on a horse-drawn Wells Fargo stage ran between Tonopah and Manhattan, Nevada, in 1909.

Transportation and banking were the dual services offered from the outset of the Wells Fargo enterprise. Eventually, the company's financial services evolved into Wells Fargo Bank and its cargo transport became Railway Express.

"CALIFORNIA OR BUST"

"The farmers have thrown aside their plows, the lawyers their briefs, the doctors their pills, and the priests their prayerbooks, and all are now digging gold."

Reverend Walter Colton

An energetic and optimistic America, fresh from victory in the Mexican War, looked to the gold fields of California as a new and grand adventure. President James K. Polk pronounced that the mines appeared "more valuable than supposed... [and] of extraordinary character."

Hopeful dreamers traveled overland across America, through Mexico, around Cape Horn or through the Strait of Magellan by ship, across tropical jungles in Panama and Nicaragua by boat, mule, and, eventually, rail. Most American shipping worldwide was redirected to the West Coast; whalers and cargo ships were re-styled for passengers. Boatloads sailed from Europe and the Far East. Between 1848 and 1854, 300,000 newcomers arrived. By 1850, 92% of the new state's population was male.

"California presented to people a new model for the American dream – one where the emphasis was on the ability to take risks, the willingness to gamble on the future."
Samuel Brannan, 1848

(Samuel was waving a bottle filled with gold dust at the time.)

CAPTAIN AND CAPTAIN

President Thomas Jefferson commissioned Meriwether Lewis as captain of the U.S. Army's Corps of Discovery. Lewis promptly chose rifleman William Clark as a partner in leadership. Said the delighted assistant, "I cheerfully join you and partake of the dangers, difficulties, and fatigues... "

Though the title of "captain" was never formally offered to William, Lewis consistently referred to his fellow guide as "Captain Clark."

LI'L BRAVES 'N' COLTS

Rev. Samuel Parker described "a lifetime on horses" among Indian youngsters.

"Small children not more than three years old are mounted alone, generally on colts. They are lashed upon the saddle to keep them from falling. When they go to sleep... they recline upon the horse's shoulders, and when they awake, they lay hold of their whip, which is fastened to the wrist of their right hand, and apply it smartly to their horses.

"Children still younger are put into an encasement of board and wicker... covered with cloth inside and out... or dressed skins... [and] carried upon the mother's back [on a horse] or suspended from a high knob upon the fore part of their saddles..."

The Flatheads were observed placing other riders near the young ones, to "enclose the horse where danger was, as horses dislodging the children."

(Rev. Parker, a Presbyterian, was one of the first Christian missionaries in the Northwest. The minister made his way to the frontier in 1835, vividly detailing his journey, which roughly followed Lewis and Clark's route.)

MEEKER MASSACRE

A disastrous event in 1879 led directly to the removal of the Uncompahgre Utes from their ancestral lands in Colorado. The Meeker incident started as a pushing and shouting match between white men and Natives. Nathan Meeker, an over-zealous Indian agent, was stubborn in his insistence that the Utes give up hunting and turn to a settled lifestyle of farming. It was mostly a heated argument until Meeker recklessly plowed up a Native race track to prepare a field for the crops he had mandated. The Indians balked. Meeker called in the military, an act of war in Native eyes.

Meeker and eight others were murdered; his wife, daughter, a friend, and two children were captured and held 23 days by the Utes. A Colorado militiaman, aided by Chief Ouray and Chipeta, rescued the prisoners. Ouray had ordered the Utes to halt their rampage, but his command was ignored due to a perception of their leader's divided loyalty.

The massacre marked the end of negotiating power with the Utes. *Harper's Bazaar* famously declared, "The Utes Must Go," and they did. The equitable Ouray patiently explained the forcible removal to his people; some were relocated to another site in Colorado and the remainder, to Utah. The good chief continued his struggle to mediate between Utes and white men until he died the following year.

SHERIFF OR MARSHAL?

Who was in charge? There is understandable confusion about the lawmen in the Old West. (Take Marshal Dillon, for example.)

A sheriff was elected county-wide, or thereabouts, and served only in his jurisdiction. Often, he appointed deputies to help.

A town marshal was like a chief-of-police and his hired deputies were like cops.

A U.S. (federal) Marshal was directly appointed by the authority of the President and could serve a wide geographic area, with deputy marshals hired by the U.S. Marshals Service.

The television series "Gunsmoke" featured James Arness as Matt Dillon, a fictional U.S. Marshal serving in Dodge City, Kansas.

CATTLE DRIVES

Longhorns came to Texas during the Spanish attempts to establish missions among the Indians. Early trail drives began with the demand for beef in the gold fields of California, frontier forts, and Indian reservations.

After the Civil War, the export-by-trail of Texas beef expanded rapidly to rail lines leading to large cities in the Northeast or markets in the West. The Chisholm Trail ended in Abilene, Kansas. Other major end-points were Sedalia, Missouri (Sedalia/Shawnee Trail), Ogallala, Nebraska (Western Trail), and Cheyenne, Wyoming Territory (Goodnight-Loving Trail).

Although their meat tended to be tough and stringy, longhorn steers fared best on the drive because of their tolerance of buffalo grass and sporadic watering. Steers moved faster, but mixed herds proved less likely to stampede; moreover, the cows provided milk and fresh beef for the trail table. Drives started after roundups in early spring; grass was tender, and delivery was expected to be completed before winter set in.

Responsible for the lengthy parade was a trail boss, accompanied by a dozen or more cowhands. At the head of a straggly line of 1500 to 3500 cattle, many from different owners, was the "lead steer," directed by a pair of point riders. Swing and flank riders were stationed at both sides, and a drag or "tail" rider had the unenviable job of bringing up the smelly and dusty rear. Wranglers managed the horses, including the remuda of "spares," and the whole procession inched forward at 10-15 miles a day.

The era of long trail drives lasted only twenty years. Expanded rail lines and refrigeration stamped out the need for overland removal of cattle; barbed-wire fences rendered it impossible. Like the Pony Express, the trails brought forth a unique and simple solution to the challenges of a wide-open, growing nation – and an endless fascination with the characters that made it happen.

TEJANOS

Tejano/Tejana literally means "Texan" in Spanish. During the time Texas was a colony of Spain, the term referred to Spanish settlers in Texas, including the families of Jose Antonio Navarro, Francisco Ruiz, and Juan Seguin. Navarro and Ruiz were the only native Texans to sign the Texas Declaration of Independence on March 2, 1836. Juan Seguin served throughout the Texas Revolution, including leadership of the Tejano unit at the Battle of San Jacinto. After the victory, he held various political positions in the Republic of Texas.

Also signing Texas' Declaration was Lorenzo de Zavala. Of Spanish descent as well, he was born in Mexico and was politically active in that country, including participation in Mexico's struggle for independence from Spain. He continued to serve his native country until its leader Santa Anna chose the path of dictatorship, whereupon Zavala cast his lot with the Texians and Tejanos. He helped draft the Constitution of the Republic of Texas and acted as the republic's ad interim Vice President until formal elections were held in the fall following Santa Anna's defeat at San Jacinto.

While Texas was part of Mexico, **Tejano** identified a citizen of Mexican descent who was living in Texas, and that usage continues today. (Anglo-Americans who moved to Texas were "Texians," while Mexicans in Texas were "Tejanos.") Today, **Tejano** is in wide usage culturally, including music, "vaquero" cowboy tradition, and Tex-Mex food.

AIN'T THAT THERE "BUFFALO" REALLY A "BISON"?

The mighty animals roaming in the millions across the Great Plains, commonly called "bufflers" by the old-timers, must properly be identified as "bison." Buffalo are native only to Asia (water buffalo) and Africa (cape buffalo). American and European bison have large heads and shoulders, while buffalo heads are much smaller on more-evenly- proportioned body structures.

When it comes to horns, the Asian and African beasts' massive horns win the prize, at three-to six-feet across. Bison have smaller horns, two feet or less, that are sharp and useful for fighting. Living in the rugged environment of the Plains, bison require a heavy fur coat, which is shed in summer months. The coats of cape and water buffalo are much thinner. Both buffalo and bison are ruminant, cloven-hoofed bovids.

Perhaps 60 million bison once populated the Great Plains, but near-extinction occurred late in the 19th century. Drought, disease, competition with horses for grass, range fires, railroads, predators, the market for hides, and the hunting practices of humans all played a part. Conservation programs have salvaged the breed, with half a million now on the Plains or in fenced pastures.

Charles and Mary Ann Goodnight saved for future generations a small herd of southern bison on their spread in the Palo Duro Canyon. Descendants of those animals now range on hundreds of acres in the Caprock Canyon State Park. The Texas State Bison Herd, in a class by itself, remarkably carries three unique genetic markers identifying Southern Plains Bison.

Though the Bison Act of 2016 designates the bison as America's first national mammal, old names and songs of the West celebrate the buffalo. It's hard to imagine...

> "O give me a home, where the *bison* roam..."

> "*Bison* gals, will you come out tonight and dance by the light of the moon?"

> "Bison Bill" Cody

"FIRST LADIES"

Narcissa Whitman and Eliza Spaulding were the first white-American women to cross the Rockies. With their husbands Marcus and Henry, the ladies went west in 1836 as missionaries to the Cayuse of (present-day) Washington and the Nez Perce of (present-day) Idaho, respectively. The Whitmans' wagon, a wedding present from Narcissa's parents, was one of the first wheeled vehicles known to pass over the Rocky Mountains, and traveled farther that any wagon had gone in the West.

Sadly, the Whitmans and 12 others were murdered in 1847 by Cayuse during a prolonged measles epidemic. Though the whites remained unaffected, the disease was new and virulent among the Natives, who did not understand the concept of immunity. Uneasy after the attack, the Spauldings relocated to Oregon. Their mission endeavors ended, but Henry served as a church pastor and school commissioner; Eliza taught at a small school which eventually became Pacific University. In his later years, Mr. Spaulding was able to resume his ministry among the Nez Perce.

MISSOURI RIVER
"Too thick to drink, too thin to plow."

That's what Mark Twain had to say about Big Muddy, the river of the Lewis and Clark expedition and gateway to the West. The Missouri River, longest in the United States, originates at Three Forks, Montana, where a trio of mountain streams (Jefferson, Madison, and Gallatin, as named by the Corps of Discovery) converge. The Missouri flows 2300 curvy miles to join the Mississippi at St. Louis, and the combined duo glides onward 1500 miles to the Gulf of Mexico as the longest river *system* in the world.

The river that carried Lewis and Clark was the water highway for countless others during our nation's expansion to the Pacific. At its juncture with the Mississippi, Mighty Mo was the departure point of the major western wagon-train trails – Oregon, Santa Fe, California, and Mormon. The Pony Express rode toward the setting sun from that point, as well.

The river has nurtured wildlife and humans over a span of 12,000 years. For much of that time, nomadic natives lived along its shores or in its watershed. In modern history, the river was discovered by French explorers Marquette and Joliet in the seventeenth century. "Missouri" came from *Quemessourita*, a Sioux word for "having dugout canoes." The Louisiana Purchase of 1803 ended European claims to the Missouri and its environs.

Mandan, Hidatsa, and Arikara built "bull boats," often copied by early trappers and fur traders. Native women used green willow limbs to make a frame, over which buffalo bull hides were stretched, with the fur outside. One hide carried a single person; 6 or 8 people fit in a bull boat of several hides. The round craft were hard to steer, but lightweight enough to be carried on a person's back. The tail was left attached to the hide as a strap to pull the boat out of the water, and, possibly, to mark the back of the boat to indicate proper placement in the stream. Bull boats were dragged onto shore at night to prevent rotting.

As its name indicates, the Missouri floated many a dugout canoe. Even Lewis and Clark relied on canoes at times, along with their keelboat and pirogues. Then, for twenty-odd years, Mackinaw flatboats hauled furs; those sturdy craft yielded to paddle-wheel steamboats as technology improved. By century's end, rail transport mostly replaced river freighting, though the use of gasoline-packet craft extended into the 1930s.

William Clark logged in 1804: "The water we drink of the common water of the missourie [Missouri] at this time contains half a wine glass of ooze or mud to every pint." Another western conduit, the Platte River, was likewise described as unfit to drink or plow!

The Missouri indeed carries silt, mostly sand, which, in the floodplain and in slow places, forms bars and mud flats. When Mo joins the Mississippi just above St. Louis, it takes several miles for the mud to blend in with the "Father of Waters." Today, with six dams upriver, along with dikes and levees, the Missouri is less prone to overreach its banks and, as a bonus, its sand load is much lighter.

More optimistic about the Missouri, Rev. John Clark reflected in 1841: "I looked up its mighty channel and thought of its sources two and three thousand miles distant, amid those mountains whose tops are covered with eternal snow."

ONE BAD DUDE

John Wesley Hardin killed anywhere from 27-42 men in his 42 years (1853-1895). Unfortunately named for Methodism founder John Wesley, Hardin was a gambler and cattle rustler who murdered randomly and often. Said to have killed six men for snoring, Hardin piously corrected the record: "I only killed *one* man for snoring."

Once, though, wounded and restless in the Cherokee County jail, he asked to be put on trial for his past crimes to "clear the slate." When Sheriff Richard Reagan recited the long list of his murders, Hardin changed his mind and sawed his way out of the cell.

Having served 17 years for the murder of a deputy sheriff, Hardin was released and settled in El Paso. Eighteen months later, he himself was slain, shot from behind during a card game.

SOUTH PASS

No doubt about it! The Rockies were a formidable barrier in the settlement of the West, but South Pass, a gentle mound of only 7550 feet (near present Lander, Wyoming), surely evoked expressions of relief for weary caravans. Having summited the pass, they would finish their journeys going downhill.

Discovered (too late for Lewis and Clark) in the early 1820s by mountain men Jed Smith and Thomas Fitzpatrick, South Pass was of supreme importance in the settlement of Oregon, Utah, and California, thereby firming-up America's interests toward the Pacific. Emigration would have been delayed, if not prevented, without easy passage over the great obstacle of elevation. By 1843, deep ruts from countless wagons, still visible today, marked the most-celebrated of all mountain passes.

THE "GREAT AMERICAN DESERT"

Not *that* kind of desert. Early explorers and settlers found the grasslands of the High Plains barren of trees and water. Government surveyor Stephen Long first used the term "desert" and many others agreed, including President Thomas Jefferson and Zebulon Pike ("not a stitch of timber and innumerable herds of buffalo").

Settlers seeking agricultural meccas passed as quickly as possible through the Plains en route to the "greener pastures" of Oregon and California. What was deemed so unfavorable to farmers nevertheless suited the railroad industry, because the "worthless" land of the Plains could be easily acquired for tracks and right-of-way.

Tentative steps toward settlement on the Plains in mid-eighteenth century led to the discovery of a vast underground reservoir, the Ogallala Aquifer, one of the world's largest, dating from the Ice Age. Windmills supported irrigation, barbed wire proved superior to wood fences, and train tracks led to markets. Not a desert after all.

HOW MANY?

The number of travelers on Lewis and Clark's Corps of Discovery expedition is a bit confusing. Simply stated, there were a few more on the first leg of the journey and a few less on the last part.

Early on, in August, 1804, Sgt. Charles Floyd died, apparently due to a ruptured appendix, a condition doctors would not be able to treat for decades afterward. Two members were dismissed for insubordination. From the first winter camp, a return party was sent back to Washington on the keelboat, bearing messages, journals, and natural specimens for President Jefferson. That 1804 dispatch was the last communication with the explorers until their arrival in St. Louis in September, 1806.

Sacagawea and Toussaint Charbonneau joined the group during the first winter; shortly, Sacagawea's baby added one more. There were no other deaths or departures until the return trip, when Sacagawea, Toussaint, and baby Jean-Baptiste ("Pomp") stayed at Fort Mandan.

The "permanent party" reaching the Pacific in 1805 totaled 33, plus one baby. Unofficially, make that 35. We must not overlook Seaman, "our dogg [sic] of the Newfoundland breed."

This was a military expedition. There were 2 captains, 3 sergeants, 23 privates, five civilians, an infant, and one canine.

COWS AND CLIFFS

One might understand why Richard and Charley allowed their strays to wander a little while longer on the large *mesa verde* of their Southwest-Colorado ranch.

Half-blinded by a winter snowstorm, the fellows suddenly spotted, across a wide canyon, a multi-room cliff village of three levels, clinging to a sheer wall below a massive and protective rock overhang. Pottery sat intact on the floors; stone implements appeared ready to use. Friendly Utes in the area knew about the "magnificent house" of their Ancient Ones, but avoided the site due to its sacred aspect; whites are not known to have stumbled across the phenomenon until the cows ran away on December 18, 1888.

Richard Wetherill and Charley Mason, brothers-in-law, had just discovered Mesa Verde, an Anasazi dwelling complex constructed late in the centuries-old sojourn of ancient Puebloans in the Four Corners area. A national park since 1906, Mesa Verde has yielded a treasure trove of artifacts and an amazing view of cultural adaptation. The cliff dwellers are believed to have lived out on the open mesa until some threat of danger led them to carve out their hideaway early in the 13th century. There they remained until an abrupt departure around the year 1250, possibly due to a prolonged drought or infighting among themselves.

Richard's archeological fire was lit! Joined by brothers Al and John, Wetherill made further discoveries resulting in 3 national parks and 2 national monuments in Utah and Colorado. Admittedly an amateur, Richard championed the idea of soil depth in correlation with prehistoric age. That's *stratigraphic* exploration; in a dig, each layer downward indicates an earlier period of time.

For example, a site in Utah revealed a shallow layer of pottery shards, tools, and human skulls flattened by head-binding. Several plain-soil layers downward, there rested a totally-different strata holding not a single pottery sliver, but a large quantity of spear-throwing atlatls, tightly-woven baskets, and rounded human skulls. Guess which lifestyle is older in time. Richard Wetherill's studious and meticulous work debunked the idea of a uniform culture in the Southwest.

Al Wetherill is believed to have spotted the Mesa Verde complex a year or so before its discovery by his brother Richard and Charley Mason. Reportedly, he thought he "was seeing things" and didn't mention it. There are scattered claims about earlier sightings of the cliff houses, but the Wetherill group is credited with the find. Other Anasazi sites discovered or studied by the men include Kiet Siel and Rainbow Bridge in Arizona, Betatakin and Chaco Canyon in New Mexico. These ranchers pushed Anasazi exploration far beyond Mesa Verde.

TURNTABLES, ROUNDHOUSES, AND WYES

Steam locomotives basically had one direction – forward. Backwards, there was not much control. Large *turntables* allowed trains to be turned around in a small amount of space to travel in the other direction. *Roundhouses* enclosing the turntables served as workshops for repair, maintenance, and storage for the engines. The first such structures date back to Derby, England, in early years of the railroad industry. A *wye* (shaped like Y) junction guided one train off the main track to allow another to proceed.

Today, some of these innovative designs have been built or repaired to accommodate restored steam locomotives.

THE MIGHTY THREE-AND-A-HALF

Narrow-gauge railroads meet the challenges of steep, rocky hillsides and skinny valleys. Three feet and 6 inches make up the width of a typical narrow-gauge, while standard gauge is 4 feet, 8 ½ inches. Though we envision ore-bearing trains on narrow-gauge tracks clinging to hacked-out ledges of mountains, those rails are useful, as well, for recreational areas, industrial settings, and in service to isolated hamlets.

Sometimes smaller is better! The narrow tracks are cheaper to build and maintain, with lighter-weight materials and smaller-radius curves. Add to that the advantages of smaller bridges, tunnels, train cars, and locomotives.

The Durango and Silverton (Colorado) route of the Denver, Rio Grande, and Western Railroad is the most popular tourist-travel narrow-gauge in America. The slogan of the DRG&W in the old days of serious rail transportation was "Though the Rockies, not around them."

"GO WEST, YOUNG MAN...

...and grow up with the country."

> "Do not lounge in the cities. There is room and health in the country away from the idlers and imbeciles. Go west before you are fitted for no life but the factory."

> "The best business you can enter you will find in your father's farm or in his workshop. If you have no family or friends to aid you and no prospect open to you, then

turn your face to the great West and there build up your home and fortune."

Who said it? Horace Greeley? John B.L. Soule? In the era of Manifest Destiny, such sentiments grew in popularity, though industrialists in the East worried about losing myriads of workers to the call of the hinterland. Greeley, founder of the *New York Tribune*, supported an orderly westward movement, if it was to be inevitable.

The New Yorker proclaimed in 1838: "If any young man is about to commence the world, we say to him, publicly and privately, 'Go to the West.' " Thomas Fuller deemed that advice the motto of the 19th century. Trappers-turned-farmers settled in Oregon Territory, followed by missionaries and wagon-train families in the 1830s.

GHOST TOWNS

Though abandoned towns exist worldwide, there's something magical and mysterious about ghostly villages in the Old West. What happened to make these once-lively communities turn into piles of crumbling buildings lining dusty streets?

"Boom and bust" characterized many a mining mecca, but other ruinous factors doomed small communities. Natural disasters, such as floods, wildfires, drought, and tornadoes. Economic woes caused by the shutdown of mills, logging operations, oil and gas activity, and business enterprises. In "more cases than you can shake a stick at," communities bypassed by a rail line or, in today's world, a major highway, sadly watched their lifelines disappear.

It's encouraging that some ghost towns find new life. Terlingua, Texas, curtailed its mercury production, but gained a world-famous chili cook-off. Old mining meccas like Virginia City, Nevada, Tombstone, Arizona, and Cripple Creek, Colorado, now rely on tourism for a vigorous revival. These "towns for which the reason for being no longer exists" (Lindsey Baker) happily discovered new (and perhaps more sustainable) methods of chasing away the ghosts.

SALT

Salt (sodium chloride) has been used for food preservation and flavoring over centuries of time; modern industrial and medical uses alone number 14,000 or more. In ancient history, salt was taxed, traded and used as currency. Battles were fought over it; cities and roads were located near its known sources. *Salzburg, salary, salami, salad* and *soldier* derive from *sal*.

America's westward-bound pioneers knew the mineral's value in the preservation of meat they hunted for food. Salt greatly improved the taste of wild animals and bitter greens; at the same time, it replenished natural salts lost from the human body. President Thomas Jefferson, intrigued by rumors of a great salt mountain near the Missouri River, strongly hinted to Lewis and Clark that their expedition (1804-1806) should search for the site and claim its product, as valuable as gold, for the United States.

They never located that source, but luckily found a small salt lick near a creek that fed the Missouri River. The deposit yielded enough for the time being, and a portion was cached for their return to St. Louis.

During the long winter of 1805-1806 near the mouth of the Columbia River, three of the explorers who were familiar with evaporation methods successfully processed two kegs (20 gallons) of salt from the Pacific Ocean. That generous amount served through the season, and there remained the cache to be recovered downriver on the homeward journey.

In June of 1811, Major George C. Sibley, guided by Sans Orielle of the Osage, came across the long-sought treasure on a tributary of the Arkansas River in (today's) northwestern Oklahoma. Not a mountain, it was a vast plain of salt, in places 16 inches thick. Though it was located in Comanche territory, many a future wagon train left the Santa Fe Trail to collect the precious mineral. Some years later, the Great Salt Lake was "discovered" in Utah, but it was already familiar to Natives and a few early trappers.

WINNING THE WEST

Innovation and invention might be labeled "the twins of change," the results of which are strikingly apparent in the settlement of the Old West. Barbed wire. Winchester rifle. Prairie schooner. Bowie knife. Windmill. Steel plow. Mechanical reaper. Colt revolver. Pick your own "top three."

Credit Joseph Glidden (barbed wire, 1874), Oliver Winchester (repeating rifle, 1866), prairie schooner (a modified Conestoga wagon, Santa Fe Trail, 1821), James Bowie or unknown others (Bowie knife, perhaps 1827), Daniel Halladay (modern wind pump, 1854), John Deere (steel plow, 1837), Cyrus McCormick (reaper, 1834), and Samuel Colt (revolver, 1836).

THE FRONTIER CLOSES

A "frontier" is described as an area with a population of less than two people per square mile. The "frontier line" is the point beyond which that description fits.

In 1890, the U.S Census Bureau officially announced that America's western frontier was no longer in existence. Farms, ranches, towns, and cities were thriving. Natives no longer roamed and raided. Roads, telegraph and telephone systems hummed with activity. The continent's territories, save Oklahoma, New Mexico, Arizona, Alaska, and Hawaii, had become states by century's end.

Oklahoma gained statehood in 1907, Arizona and New Mexico in 1912, Alaska and Hawaii in 1959.

Unpalatable to many, government support nevertheless boosted the process of taming the frontier – from the Corps of Discovery, commissioned by President Jefferson, onward to military operations, communication and transportation systems, exploration, mapping, and conservation.

New frontiers come naturally to the American spirit. Alaska followed the Old West as an earthly frontier; John F. Kennedy touted "a new frontier" in space travel. In our time, fresh horizons swirl from land to ocean, from cyberspace to outer space.

"The experience of the frontier was what distinguished America from Europe, observed noted historian Frederick Jackson Turner. He celebrated the "practicality, individualism, and energy of the American character," as shown in the growth of the West and its part in the development of our great nation.

BIBLIOGRAPHY

Ahert, Gerald T. <u>Butterfield Overland Mail Company: Coaches and Stage Wagons Used on the Southern Trail</u>. Tucson, AZ: Westernlorepress, 1999.

"A Journey to Denver on the Overland Dispatch." www.legendsofamerica.com. March 10, 2010.

Aker, Andrea. "The Legend of Red Ghost." www.arizonaoddities.com. March 10, 2010.

Allred, Pauline. Osage Nation Museum and Library, Pawhuska, Oklahoma. Personal interview, February 15, 2015.

"A Man of Peace." *Native American Legends*. www.legendsofamerica.com . January 8, 2016.

Ambrose, Stephen E. <u>Undaunted Courage: Meriwether Lewis, Thomas Jefferson, and the Opening of the American West</u>. New York: Simon and Schuster, 1997.

"American Mountain Men and the Western Fur Trade." *Travel Montana*, 2007.

Anderson, Gerald, editor. <u>Biographical Dictionary of Christian Missionaries</u>. New York: Macmillan and Co., 1998.

Anderson, Greta. <u>More Than Petticoats: Remarkable Texas Women</u>. Guilford, CN: Twodot/The Globe Pequot Press, 2002.

Anderson, H. Allen. "Big Die-Up." www.tsha.com. April 17, 2016.

Anderson, Robert. "Barbed-Wire Fences Were the First Rural Telephone Systems." www.knowledgenuts.com. January 17, 2016.

"Andrew Carnegie." *America's Story*. www.americaslibrary.gov. May 7, 2015.

"Arrival of the Donner Relief Party." Drawing, as described by William G. Murphy, Feb. 18, 1847. www.wikipedia.org/wiki/Donner-Party. April 29, 2016.

Arteaga, Raul H. "El Paso was the Midpoint of the Overland Mail Service." El Paso Community College, 1999.

Aubry, Francois (Francis) Xavier. "Exploring Southwestern Trails," The Journals of Philip St. George Cooke, William H.C. Whiting, and Francois Aubry. Ralph P. Bieber, ed. Glendale: Arthur H. Clark and Co., 1931-1943.

Austin, Damien. "Bison Restoration." www.americanprairie.org. October 14, 2016.

Avey, Tori. "The History Kitchen." www.toriavey.com/history-kitchen. May 31, 2013.

Baker, T. Lindsey. Ghost Towns of Texas. Norman: University of Oklahoma Press, 1991.

Bancroft, Hubert Howe. History of Arizona and New Mexico 1530-1888. San Francisco: The History Company, 1889.

Banks, James E. The Alferd Packer Wilderness Cookbook. Palmer Lake, Colorado: Filter Press, 1969.

Baum, Doug. "The Ghost of Camels Past: From Winsome to Weird." *American History Texas*, June 17, 2015.

Beck, Glenn. Being George Washington. New York: Threshold Editions/Simon and Schuster, 2012.

Becker, Cynthia. Chipeta: The Peacemaker. Palmer Lake, CO: Filter Press, 2008.

Becker, Cynthia and P. David Smith. Chipeta: Queen of the Utes. Lake City, CO: Western Reflections Publishing Co., 2003.

Bellis, Mary. "The History of Blue Jeans." www.inventors.about.com. January 6, 2014.

Bender, Nathan E. "Perceptions of a Mountain: John "Jeremiah" Liver-Eating Johnson." *The Rocky Mountain Fur Trade Journal*, 2007.

Bender, Nathan E. "The Abandoned Scout's Revenge: Origins of the Crow-Killer Saga of Liver-Eating Johnson." *Annals of Wyoming*, WY State Historical Society.

Benge, Janet and Geoff Benge. Theodore Roosevelt: An American Original. Bingley, West Yorkshire, England, UK: Emerald Books, 2004.

Bennett, Marilyn. It Happened in San Antonio. Summit, PA: Rowman and Littlefield Publishers, Inc., 2006.

Biesele, Rudolph L. The History of German Settlements in Texas, 1831-1861. Austin: Von Boeckman-Jones, 1930.

Bittman, Mark. "Everyone Eats There." *New York Times*, Oct. 10, 2012.

Blazer, W. Paul. "Chief Ouray." *History Blazer*, January, 1995.

Bone, Corey. "Osage Oil." *Encyclopedia of Oklahoma History and Culture*. www.history.org. February 9, 2015.

Bourasaw, Noel V. " 'Go West, Young Man': Who Wrote It? Greeley or Soule?" *Skagit River Journal*, April 17, 2007.

Brabner, Wendy, ed., Texas Characters Datebook. Austin: Texas Monthly Press, 1884.

Breihan, Carl W. Lawmen and Robbers. Caldwell, Idaho: The Caxton Printers, Ltd., 1986.

Brinkley, Douglas. "The Great Bear Hunt." *National Geographic*, May 5, 2001.

Brister, Louis E. "Adelsverein." *The Handbook of Texas*. Texas State Historical Society.

Broday, Linda. "Early Canned Foods in America." *Petticoats and Pistols* Newsletter. June 11, 2013.

Buchanan, Minor Ferris. Holt Collier: His Life, His Roosevelt Hunts, and the Origin of the Teddy Bear. Jackson: Centennial Press of Mississippi, 2002.

Bunch, Joey. "Chief Ouray: Broken Heart Helped Settle the West." *The Denver Post*, August 13, 2012.

Burns, Louis F. "Osage (Tribe)." *Encyclopedia of Oklahoma History and Culture*. www.history.org. February 9. 2015.

Burroughs, Raymond Darwin. The Natural History of the Lewis and Clark Expedition. East Lansing: Michigan State University Press, 2nd edition, 1995.

Burton, Art T. Black Gun, Silver Star: The Life and Legend of Frontier Marshal Bass Reeves. Lincoln: University of Nebraska Press, 2006.

Burton, Art T. Black, Red, and Deadly: Black and Indian Gunfighters of the Indian Territory. Austin: Eakin Press, 1991.

Burton, Art T. <u>Marshal Bass Reeves</u>. Lincoln: University of Nebraska Press, 2008.

"Butterfield's Overland Mail Company." www.legendsofamerica.com. February 9, 2015.

"California Gold Rush." www.shmoop.com/california-goldrush-quotes.html. December 30, 2016.

Calverly, Dorthea Horton. "History is Where You Stand; A History of the Perce." Dawson Creek, British Columbia, Canada.

"Camel Cavalcade of the American Deserts." www.legendsofamerica.com. February 11, 2015.

Carroll, Jeff. "Meet Bet-a-Million Gates." www.legendarytexas.com. February 14, 2015.

Cartaxo, Joseph and Pauline Holdsworth and Alan Jalowitz. <u>Stetson: The Hat That Tamed the West</u>. University Park, Pa: PA Center for the Book, 2010-2011.

"Cattle Drives and Cowboys: What It Was Really Like." www.tripsinhistory.com. February 1, 2017.

"Chief Ouray: A Man of Peace." www.legendsofamerica.com. February 4, 2017.

"Chipeta and Chief Ouray." Colorado Historical Marker, Grand Junction, CO.

Clark, Rev. John. <u>Gleanings By the Way</u>. Philadelphia: W.J. and J.K. Simon, 1842.

Clarke, Charles G. The Men of the Lewis and Clark Expedition. Lincoln: University of Nebraska Press/Bison Books, 2002.

Cleere, Jan. More Than Petticoats: Remarkable Nevada Women. Guilford, CN: TwoDot/Globe Pequot Press, 2005.

Clifton, Robert T. Barbs, Prongs, Points, and Stickers. Norman: University of Oklahoma Press, 1970.

Colorado County (Texas) Historical Commission. Colorado County Chronicles, Vol. 1: From the Beginning to 1823. Austin: Nortex Press, division of Eakin Publications, Inc., 1986.

Connally, E. L. The Crash at Crush: Famous Duel of the Iron Monsters, Waco, TX, 1896. Waco: Texian Press, 1960.

Coppedge, Clay, "Britton Johnson: The Truth That Inspired the Legend." *Country World*, January 21, 2014.

Corbett, Christopher. Orphans Preferred. New York: Broadway Books, 2003.

Corbett, Christopher and Russell Alan Spreeman. "Pony Bob Haslam." *Cowboys and Indians*, October, 2011.

Corbett, Christopher. "The Pony Express: Riders of Destiny." *Wild West*, April, 2006.

Cordier, Mary Hurlburt. School Women of the Prairies and Plains: Personal Narratives from Iowa, Kansas, and Nebraska. Albuquerque: University of New Mexico Press, 1992.

Countryman, Edward. "The Pueblo Revolt." *History Now* 28, Summer, 2011. The Gilder Lehrman Institute of American History. www.gilderlehrman.org. June 14, 2015.

Couture, Lisa. "The History of Canned Foods." Slideshow. Johnson and Wales University, Providence, RI. www.scholarsarchive.jwu.ed. April 28, 2010.

"Cowboy Hat." www.ed.wikipedia.org/wiki/Cowboy_hat. April 18, 2015.

"Cowboy Hats in History." www.cowboyhathistory.com. April 18, 2015.

"Cow-boy Nuisance in Arizona." *The Tombstone Epitaph,*" September 16, 1881.

Cox, Mike. "Lady Doc." *Texas Tales.* September 1, 2005. www.texasescapes.com. April 20, 2015.

Cox, Mike. "Ranger History in Brief Form." Waco: Texas Ranger Hall of Fame.

Cox, Mike. "Silver Stars and Six Guns." Waco, TX, Convention and Visitor Services.

Cox, Mike. Texas Ranger Tales: Stories That Need Telling. Austin: Republic of Texas Press, 1997.

Crookes, David. Redcoats. Queensland, Australia: Big Indian Pty, Ltd., 2010.

Crutchfield, James A. and Bill O'Neal, Dale L. Walker. Legends of the Wild West. Lincolnwood, IL: Publications International, Ltd., 1995.

Curtis, Mabel Rowe. "The Coachman Was a Lady." Pajaro Valley Historical Society, 1959.

Dajani, Laika. Black Bart: Elusive Highwayman and Poet. Manhattan, KS: Sunflower University Press, 1996.

Dale, Edward Everett. Frontier Ways: Sketches of Life in the Old West. Austin: University of Texas Press, 2010.

Davis, John B. "The Life and Work of Sequoyah." *Chronicles of Oklahoma.2222*, Oklahoma Historical Society. Online. www.okstate.edu. Accessed 8-25-2014.

Dean, Lynn. "John Bet-a-Million Gates." Online. www.discovertexas.com. November 4, 2014.

Deda, Pauline. "125-Year-Old Jeans Sold for $100,000." Fox News online, May 26, 2018.

Deeringer, Martha. "Dr. Sofie Herzog." *Cowboys and Indians*, January, 2012.

"Denim by Occasion." Video. *Harper's Bazaar*, November 12, 2015.

Denison, Jennifer. "The Pony-Express Paradox." *Western Horseman*, September, 2006.

DePlato, Justin. The Cavalier Presidency: Executive Power and Prerogative in Times of Crisis. Lanham, MD: Lexington Books, 2014.

DeVoto, Bernard. The Year of Decision. New York City: St. Martin's Griffin, 1943/2000.

Diehl, Daniel and Mark F. Donnelly. Eat Thy Neighbor: A History of Cannibalism. Charleston, S.C.: The History Press, 2012.

Dobie, J. Frank. The Voice of the Coyote. Boston: Little, Brown, and Co., 1950.

Dobie, J. Frank. *Up the Trail From Texas*. New York: Random House, 1963.

"Dodge City Ruts: Santa Fe Trail, 1821-1880." Santa Fe Historical Trail, NPS.

"Donner Party Tragedy." www.legendsofamerica.com. September 16, 2014.

Douglas, C.L. *The Gentlemen in the White Hats*. Austin: State House Press, 1992.

Downey, Lynn. "The Blue Jean Story: A History of Denim." *New International*, June, 1998.

Durham, George and Clyde Wantland. *Taming the Nueces Strip*. Austin: University of Texas Press, 1982.

Dyer, John Lewis. *The Snowshoe Itinerant: An Autobiography of Rev. John L. Dyer, Familiarly Known as Father Dyer of the Colorado Conference, Methodist Episcopal Church*. Cincinnati: Cranston and Stone, 1890.

Dyer, Robert L. "A Brief History of Steamboating on the Missouri River With an Emphasis on the Boonslick Region." *Boone's Lick Heritage*, Vol. 5, #2, June, 1997, Boonslick Historical Society, Boonville, MO.

Earp, Virgil. Untitled news article in the *Arizona Daily Star*, May 30, 1882.

Eckhardt, C.F. "Before Maw Bell: Rural Telephone Systems in the West." May 8, 2008. www.texasescapes.com. Accessed 10-6-2014.

Elliot, Mark and Melissa Durr. "Schools in South Dakota: An Educational Development." Prepared for South Dakota Historic Preservation Office, Pierre, SD, 1998.

Ellis, E.R. "Barbed Wire, Barbaric Backlash." *Texas Co-op Power*, January, 2014.

Emmett, Chris. Texas Camel Tales. Mockingbird Books, digital edition, 2012 (originally published 1933) and San Antonio: Naylor Press, 1932.

Everett, Edward. Sketches of Life in the Old West. Austin: University of Texas Press, 2010.

"Explore the Santa Fe Trail." Santa Fe Trail Interpretive Center, Las Vegas, NM.

Fagan, Jim. "Snowshoes, Saloons, and Salvation." www.snowshoemag.org. December 2, 2004.

Fairchild, Carolyn. "Does Levi Strauss Still Fit America?" *Fortune Magazine*, September 18, 2014.

Fanselow, Julie. Traveling the Oregon Trail. Lanham, MD: Roman and Littlefield Publishers, Inc, 2001.

Farney, Henry F. "The Song of the Talking Wire." Painting, 1904. Taft Museum of Art, Cincinnati, Ohio.

Faulk, Odie B. The U.S. Camel Corps: An Army Experiment. New York: Oxford University Press, 1976.

Feister, Mark. Look for Me in Heaven: The Life of John Lewis Dyer. Boulder, CO: Pruett Publishing Co, 1980.

"Fencing the Great Plains: the History of Barbed Wire." Homestead National Monument, Beatrice, NE, National Park Service.

Fenwick, R. W. <u>Alferd Packer – The True Story of Colorado's Maneater</u>. Denver: *Empire Magazine of the Denver Post*, 1963.

Fielder, Mildred. "The Story of Poker Alice." South Dakota History Archives, SD Historical Society, The Roosevelt Inn, 2006.

Fifer, Barbara. "Pierre Cruzatte, Pilot of the Boats." *Journals 2 & 3*, Moulton, ed., Lewis and Clark Fort Mandan Foundation.

Fine, John Christopher. "Biggest Nugget in the Black Hills." *True West*, Oct. 9, 2014.

"First Transcontinental Railroad." www.ducksters.com. March 3, 2014.

"First Transcontinental Railroad Facts." www.softschools.com/facts. March 3, 2014.

Fischer, Ron W. "Bass Reeves Set a Timeless Example." *The Tombstone News*, May 19, 2006.

Fisher, David. <u>Bill O'Reilly's Legends and Lies: The Real West</u>. New York: Henry Holt, 2015.

Flanagan, Mike. <u>The Complete Idiot's Guide to the Old West</u>. Indianapolis: Alpha Books, 1999.

Fleming, Walter L. "Jefferson Davis' Camel Experiment." *Popular Science Monthly*, February, 1909.

Flint, Richard and Shirley Cushing Flint. "Fred Harvey: Civilizer of the West." April 6, 2015.

Fowler, Gene. "Cowboy Hatters." *Texas Co-op Power*, April, 2016.

Fox, Randee. "The Cowboy Hat." *American Quarter House Journal*, June 26, 2013.

Frangos, Steve. "Philip Tedro: A Greek Legend of the American West." *Greek-American Review*, October, 2006, updated November, 2007.

Franks, Kenny Arthur and Paul F. Lambert. Oklahoma: The Land and Its People. Norman: University of Oklahoma Press, 1997.

Fried, Stephen. Appetite for America: Fred Harvey and the Business of Civilizing the West – One Meal at a Time. New York: Bantam/Random House, 2010.

Friggens, Myriam. Tales, Trails, and Tommyknockers: Stories From Colorado's Past. Boulder, CO: Johnson Books, 1979.

Froman, Robert. "The Red Ghost." *American Heritage Magazine*, Vol 12, #3, April, 1961.

Frost, H. Gordon and John H. Jenkins. I'm Frank Hamer: The Life of a Peace Officer. Austin: State House Press, 1968.

Gabel, Skyler. "Liver-Eating Johnson." Student essay. Cody, WY, 2008.

Gamble, James. "Wiring a Continent." *The Californian*, 1881.

Gant, Paul H. The Case of Alferd Packer, the Man-Eater. Denver: University of Denver Press. 1952.

Gard, Wayne. The Chisholm Trail. Norman: University of Oklahoma Press, 1954.

Geohegan, Tom. "The Story of How the Tin Can Almost Wasn't." *BBC News Magazine*. April 21, 2013.

Gibson, Jake. "U.S. Marshals Yesterday and Today." Fox News, April 16, 2018.

Gilbert, Bill, writer. <u>The Trailblazers</u>. "The Old West" series. New York: <u>Time-Life Books</u>, 1973.

Glischinski, Steve. <u>Santa Fe Railway</u>. Minneapolis: Voyageur Press, 1957.

Goldthwaite, Carmen. <u>Texas Dames: Sassy and Savvy Women Throughout Lone Star History</u>. Mt. Pleasant, SC: The History Press, 2012.

"Goodnight." *Panhandle Plains Review* article, 1928.

Goodyear, Dana. "Excavating the Donner Party." *The New Yorker*, April 17, 2006.

Grattan, Virginia. "Mary Colter: Builder Upon the Red Earth." Grand Canyon Natural History Assn., 1992.

Gray, Tom. "Teaching with Documents: The Treaty of Guadalupe Hidalgo." DeRuyter Middle School, DeRuyter, New York.

"Great American Desert." www.wikipedia.org/Great American Desert. March 3, 2017.

Greene, A.C. <u>900 Miles on the Butterfield Trail</u>. Denton: University of North Texas Press. 2006.

Greever, William S. <u>Bonanza West</u>. Moscow, Idaho: University of North Idaho Press, 1963.

Groneman, Bill. Alamo Defenders. Austin: Eakin Press, 1990.

Grove, Lloyd. "Just How Many Democrats Did Alferd Packer Eat? George Washington University Professor Digs into the Legend." *The Washington Post*, June 8, 1989.

Guinn, Jeff. The Last Gunfight: The Real Story of the Shootout at the O.K. Corral and How It Changed the American West. New York: Simon and Schuster, 2011.

Gunn, LaDonna. "Colorado Springs History." www.oldcolo.com. January 8, 2014.

Gunn, LaDonna and Dave Hughes. "Colorado City: Life and Lore." www.oldcolo.com. January 8, 2014.

Hale, Edward Everett. Frontier Ways: Sketches of Life in the Old West. Austin: University of Texas Press, 2010. (original printing: 1959)

Hall, Daniel. M. "The Strange Life of Charley Parkhurst," *Metro Santa Cruz*, March 5-12, 2003.

Hallowell, John. "Camels at Camp Verde." John Hallowell, Vol. 2, 2012, *Texas Hill Country* ezine. www.texas-hill-country.com. April 23, 2015.

Hamilton, Allen E. "Train Crash at Crush." *American West*, July-August, 1983.

"Harvey Girls." Kansas State Historical Society. Feb.19, 2014.

Hawkins, Vince. "The U.S. Army's Camel Corps Experiment." U.S. Army History Center, 1784-1860.

Hegarty, Stephane. "How Jeans Conquered the World," 28 February, 2012. BBC World Service. www.bbc.com/news/mag. April 23, 2015.

"Helpful Hints for Stage Coach Passengers." *Silver Thread Scenic and Historic Byway*. Summer, 2016. (Original Source: *Omaha Herald*, 1877)

"He's a Bad Indian." *Arkansas Gazette,* April 29, 1890.

Heu, Charlotte. "Frazier is More than a Building." *Las Vegas Sun*, Nov. 21, 2007.

Hill, Fern J. Charley's Choice. Amazon Digital Services, 2008.

Hiller, Jennifer. "Barbed Wire Presentation Changes American West." *San Antonio Express- News*, Feb. 20, 2015.

Hills, Christopher. "John Perrott: Potato Creek Johnny." *History, Legends, and Lore*. Black Hills Visitor Center.

"History of Howard Public Library." Document. Personal interview with Deborah Roden, Howard, South Dakota, Public Library director.

"History of the Pacific Railroad Through Missouri," www.thetrailsend.org. June 17, 2016.

Hodge, Frederick Webb and Theodore H. Lewis, eds. Spanish Explorers in the Southern United States 1528-1543. New York: Scribner, 1907.

Hoeper, George. Black Bart: Boulevardier Bandit. Sanger, CA: Word Dancer Press, 1995.

Holder, Nelda. "Did You Hear the One About the Lawyer?" Asheville, NC: *Citizen-Times*, June 1, 2015.

Holley, Joe. "Tejanos Played a Key Role in the Texas Revolution." *Houston Chronicle*, April 18, 2014.

Holmberg, Jim. "Monument to a Young Man of Much Merit." *We Proceeded On*. August, 1996.

Holmberg, Jim. "Seaman's Fate?" *We Proceeded On*, February, 2000.

Holmes, Bob. "Wired Wild West Cowpokes Chatted on Fence-Wire Phones." *New Scientist*, December 31, 2013.

"Homestake Mine, South Dakota." www.wikipedia.com November 11, 2015.

Hopkins, A.D. "Maude Frazier." *Vegas Review-Journal*, Feb. 7, 1999.

Horgan, John J. and Bruce A. Berg. Criminal Investigation. New York: McGraw Hill, 1974.

Horn, Jonathan C. "Brunot Agreement." www.coloradoencyclopedia.org. January 9, 2017.

Houghton, Eliza Donner. The Expedition of the Donner Party and Its Tragic Fate. Original Script, 1911. Project Gutenberg, 2004. www.gutenberg.net. Feb. 17, 2012.

Howard, Kathleen and Diana F. Pardue. Inventing the Southwest: Fred Harvey Company and Native American Art. Flagstaff, AZ: Northland Publishing Co., 1996.

Huler, Mary. "Big Boost for Little Free Libraries Announced in Austin." *Austin American-Statesman*, March 10, 2016.

Humfreville, J. Lee. <u>Twenty Years Among Our Hostile Indians</u>. Mechanicsburg, PA: Stackpole Books, 2002.

Hunt, Katrina Brown. "America's Coolest Ghost Towns." www.travelandleisure.com. March 8, 2017.

Hunter, Frances. "Lewis and Clark vs. the Mosquito." American Heroes Blog, January 7, 2010. www.wordpress.com. May 7, 2013.

Huser, Verne. <u>On the River With Lewis and Clark</u>. College Station: Texas A&M University Press, 2004.

"Index of Trail Blazers, Riders, and Cowboys." www.legendsofamerica.com. May 22, 2015.

Indian Pueblo Culture Center. www.indianpueblo.org. January 18, 2013.

Inman, Colonel Henry. <u>The Old Santa Fe Trail</u>. Minneapolis: Ross and Hames, Inc., 1966. (Original date of publication: 1897)

Isaacs, Sally Senzell. <u>Stagecoaches and the Pony Express</u>. Chicago: Heinemann-Raintree, 2004.

Jacobs, Jane, ed. <u>The Story of Hannah Breece, a Schoolteacher in Old Alaska</u>. New York: Vintage Press, 1997.

James, Ramon. <u>Come and Get It: The Story of the Old-Time Cowboy Cook</u>. Norman: University of Oklahoma Press, 1952.

Japenga, Ann. "Tracking Down the Truth of What Happened to the Donner Party." *Los Angeles Times*, May 11, 1986.

Jenson, H. Bert. "Chipeta: Glory and Heartache." *The Outlaw Trail Journal*, Salt Lake City, UT, Oct. 30, 1979.

"Jeremiah Johnson's Body to Be Moved." *The Evening Independent*, Masillon, OH, May 28, 1974.

Jocklink, Sidney. "Searching for Treasure." *Independent Press-Telegram*, Nov. 16, 1968.

Judd, A.N. "The Story of Charley Parkhurst: Recalling a Romantic Character of the Early Days in California." *The Pajaronian, Santa Cruz Surf*, October 4, 1917.

"Judge Isaac Parker." National Historic Site, National Park Service, Fort Smith, Arkansas.

Kaska, Kathleen, "Crash at Crush." *Texas Highways*, July, 2012.

Kaufman, Polly Welts. Women Teachers on the Frontier. New Haven and London: Yale University Press, 1984.

Kesner, Mason, Media Director, U.S. Marshals Museum. Personal interview, 12-18-2015.

King, Gilbert. "The History of the Teddy Bear – From Wet and Angry to Soft and Cuddly." *Smithsonian Magazine*, December 12, 2012.

King, Irene E.: John O. Meusebach: German Colonizer in Texas. Austin: University of Texas Press, 1967.

King, Joseph A. "Luis and Salvador: Unsung Heroes of the Donner Party." *The Californians*, Vol. 13-2, 1996.

King, Randy. "How to Cook a Wolf." *Boise Weekly*, March 7, 2002.

Kitchen, Gladys. Pawnee Historical Society, Pawnee, Oklahoma. Personal interviews: February 25, 2015; March 5, 2015; Osage Tribal Museum, Pawhuska, OK. April 2, 2018.

Knights, Blue with Lt. Dan Marcou. "Was U.S. Marshal Bass Reeves the Real Lone Ranger?" www.policeone.com. August 24, 2013.

Knowles, Thomas W. *They Rode for the Lone Star: the Saga of the Texas Rangers, Vol. 1*. Bryan, TX: Lone Star Publishing, 2009.

Koon, David. "Deputy U.S. Marshal Bass Reeves Haunted the Nightmares of Desperadoes in Indian Territory." *Arkansas Times*, August 22, 2013.

Krantz, Rachel and Elizabeth A. Ryan. *The Biographical Dictionary of Black Americans*. Facts on File, New York, 1992.

Krudivig, Vici Leigh. *Hiking Through Colorado History*. Englewood, CO: Westcliffe Publishing, 1998.

Krystek, Lee. "The Great Texas Train Crash at Crush." The Museum of Unnatural Mystery. www.unmuseum.org. March 6, 2014.

Kushner, Ervan. *Alferd G. Packer, Cannibal Victim?* Frederick, CO: Platte Press, 1980.

Lake, A.I. *Pony Express*. Vero Beach, FL: Rourke Publications, 1990.

Lang, Walter R. *The First Overland Mail: The Butterfield Trail, St. Louis to San Francisco 1858-1861*. Washington, D.C., 1940.

Latimer, Rosa Walston. *Harvey Houses of Texas*. Charleston and London: The History Press, 2014.

Lavender, David. *Bent's Fort*. Lincoln, NE: University of Nebraska Press, 1972.

Least-Heat Moon, William. *A Voyage Across America*. Farmington Hills, MI: Cengage Gale, 2000.

Lederer, Rich. "The Toy Story of Teddy Roosevelt and the Bear." *Union Tribune San Diego*, September 27, 2014.

Lee, Hilde Gabriel. <u>Taste of the States: A Food History of America</u>. Charlottesville, VA: Howell Press, 1992.

Leonetti, Shannon Moon. "Charley's Secret." *American History Magazine*, Volume 32, #2, May-June, 1997.

"Levi Strauss." *Biography, A&E Television Networks*. 2014.

"Levi Strauss." www.shmoop.com/california-gold-rush/levi-strauss.html. February 24, 2014.

Lindmeier, Tom and Steve Mount. <u>I Can See by Your Outfit: Historic Cowboy Gear of the Northern Plains</u>. Glendo, WY: Hi Plains Press, 1996.

"Living in La Plata County." Southern Ute Tribes General Administration, Colorado Commission of Indian Affairs, published by Southern Ute Tribe and La Plata County.

Lord, Walter. <u>A Time to Stand</u>. Lincoln: The University of Nebraska Press. First edition, 1978.

Loving, Solon Ollie. "A History of the Fisher-Miller Land Grant." Master's Thesis, University of Texas, 1974.

Lowe, Sam. <u>Red Ghost – Mysteries and Legends of Arizona: True Stories of the Unsolved and Unexplained</u>. New York: Globe-Pequot Press.

Madigan, Tim. "Iconic Stetson Hat, Produced in Garland, Defines Cowboy Style." *Fort Worth Star-Telegram*, April 15, 2015.

Maguire, Jack. Talk of Texas. Austin: Shoal Creek Press, 1980.

Mansfield, Leslie. "The Lewis and Clark Cookbook: Historic Recipes From the Corps of Discovery." Lewis and Clark Bicentennial Guide, 2003. www.L&CTrail.com. April 17, 2013.

Marcou, Dan and Blue Knights. "Was U.S. Marshal Bass Reeves the Real Lone Ranger?" www.policeone.com August 24, 2013.

Marcy, Randolph B. The Prairie Traveler: A Handbook for Overland Expeditions. Published by the authority of the War Department, 1859.

Marsh, Graham. From Cowboys to Catwalks: A History of The World's Most Legendary Fabric. London: Aurum Press, 2005.

Mattei, Eileen. "The Unbroken Peace Treaty." *Texas Co-op Power*, July, 2014.

Matthews, John Joseph. The Osages: Children of the Middle Waters. Norman: University of Oklahoma Press, 1961.

May, John D. "Walters, Colonel Ellsworth." *Encyclopedia of Oklahoma History and Culture*. www.history.org. February 9, 2015.

Mazio, Joann. "The Butterfield Overland Mil: Stitching the Country Together." www.southernnewmexico.com. April 9, 2013.

McAlister, George A. Alamo: The Price of Freedom. San Antonio: Docutex, Inc., 1990, second edition.

McAuliffe, Jr., Dennis. Bloodland: A Family Story of Oil, Greed, and Murder on the Osage Reservation. San Francisco: Council Oak Books, 1999.

McKay, Brett and Kate. "Lessons in Manliness From Bass Reeves." www.artsofmanliness.com. April 21, 2011.

McSherry, Patrick. "Theodore Roosevelt." The Spanish-American War Centennial Website. www.spanamwar.com. February 10, 2015.

Meek, Steven Hall. The Autobiography of a Mountain Man, 1805-1889. Whitefish, MT: Kessinger Publishing Co., 2010 reprint.

Michaux, Nelson Vaunda. Bad News for Outlaws: The Remarkable Life and Legend of Frontier Marshal Bass Reeves. Lincoln: University of Nebraska Press, 2006.

Miller, Daniel. Blue Jeans: The Art of the Ordinary. Oakland: University of California Press, 2012.

"Montana Ranchmen Making General Use of the Fences." *Butte, Montana, Intermountain.* 1901. (Published in *The New York Times,* June 1, 1902.

Moody. Ralph. The Old Trails West. New York: Thomas Y. Crowell Company, 1963.

Morris, Edmond. Theodore Rex. New York: Random House, 2001.

Morton, Jane. Dyer, Dynamite, and Dredges: The Story of a Breckenridge Church and a Colorado Pioneer. Breckenridge, CO: Father Dyer United Methodist Church publication, 1st edition, 1990.

Mulvany, Kieran. "What Happened at the O.K. Corral?" www.discovery.com. October 26, 2012.

Murphree, Daniel S., ed. Native America: A State-by-State Historical Encyclopedia. Westport, CN: Greenwood Publishing Group, 2012.

Myers, Laurie. <u>Lewis and Clark and Me: A Dog's Tale</u>. New York: Scholastic, Inc., 2002.

Nagy, Linda. "South Park Burros." *Colorado Life Magazine*, July-August, 2013.

Nash, Robert Jay. "Alferd Packer." <u>Encyclopedia of Lawmen and Outlaws</u>. Boston: <u>DeCapo</u> Press, 1994.

"Native American Legends: Pueblo Indians – Oldest Culture in the United States." www.legendsofamerica.com/na-puebloindians.html. February 22, 2013.

Nelson, Vaunda Michaux. <u>Bad News for Outlaws: The Remarkable Life of Bass Reeves, Deputy U.S. Marshal</u>. Minneapolis: Lerner Publishing Group, 2009.

Nussbaum, Greg. "Lewis and Clark Animal Discoveries." Nussbaum Educational Network, LLC.

Obituaries. *Ponca City, OK, News*. March 28, 1932.

Online. cavemangreg, 1-25-2011, www.paleodietandliving.com. May 9, 2014.

Online. www.indianpueblo.org April 17, 2014.

Online. "O.K. Corral Gunfight." www.legendsofamerica.com. April 7, 2014.

Online. www.paleofood.com/pemmican.htm. February 3, 2015.

Online. www.pbs.org/wgbh/theymadeamerica/whomade/strauss_ lo.html. January 1, 2016.

Online. www.pbs.org/weta.thewest/people/s-z/strauss.htm. August 3, 2014.

Online. www.phrases.org.uk. August 8, 2013.

Online. www.renotahoe.about.com/od.historicsites/a/levis/htm. October 10, 2015.

Online. www.smithsonian-magazine.com/history/the-history-of-the-teddy-bear from-wet-and- angry-to-soft-and-cuddly. November 5, 2015.

Online. www.shmoop.com/california-gold-rush/levi-strauss.html. September 8, 2015.

Online. www.tahoetopia.com/thedonnerpartytriedashortcut. April 4, 2016.

Online. www."Goodnight-Loving Trail." *Handbook of Texas*. tsha.org. July 7, 2015.

Online. "What It's Like to Wagon West on the Oregon. Trail." www.todayifoundout.com. May 6, 2015.

Online. www.txdps.state.tx.us/texasrangers. March 3, 2014.

Online. www.usmarshalsmuseum.org. March 6, 2017.

Ormsby, Walter T. "The Butterfield Overland Mail." Huntington Library, San Marino College, California, 1942.

Ornstein, Allan C., Daniel U. Levine, Gerry Gutek, David E. Vocke. Foundations of Education. Boston: Cengage Learning, 2016.

"Osage and Oil Rights." www.historyandtheheadlines. August 25, 2015.

"Ouray, Colorado." Ouray Chamber Resort Assn. Online. www.ourayco.com. August 24, 2015.

<u>Our Community: Organization and Development of Nolan County</u>. Sweetwater, TX: Watson-Focht Co., 1960.

Parham, Greg. "Diet and Living." www.paleodietandliving.com. January 25, 2013.

Parker, Rev. Samuel. <u>Journal of an Exploring Tour Beyond the Rocky Mountains in the Years 1835, '36, and '37</u>. Moscow, ID: University of Idaho Press, 1990. (original printing, 1838)

Parsons, Chuck and Marianne E. Hall. <u>Captain L.H. McNelly: Texas Ranger</u>. Austin: State House Press, 2001.

Pekar, Dotha Riggs. "Dr. Sofie Herzog." Brazoria Heritage Foundation, May, 2004.

"Pemmican Recipes Old and New." www.paleofood.com/pemmican.htm. Jan. 25, 2012.

Peters, Ruth Olson. "Santa Fe Trail History." Larned, KS: The Santa Fe Trail Center.

Petroleum History Almanac, American Oil and Gas Historical Society, 2015.

Phelan, Richard. "Tho' Battered by the March of Time, Enchanted Rock Endures." *Sports Illustrated,* April 22, 1985.

Philipkoski, Kristen. "Sorry, Freezing Your Jeans Will Not Ungross Them." www.gizmodo.com. June, 2014.

"Pierre Cruzatte: A Musical Journey Along the Lewis and Clark Trail." www.cruzatte.com. February 21, 2017.

Plafke, James, "Rural Network Was Built Using Barbed-Wire Fences." *Good Old Days,* January 2, 2013.

"Poker Alice Tubbs: Early Deadwood." www.blackhillsvisitor.com. March 19, 2014.

Poling-Kempes, Lesley. <u>The Harvey Girls: Women Who Opened the West</u>. Boston: DeCapo Press, republished 1994.

"Pony Express Debuts, 1860." This Day in History. www.this-day-in-history/pony-express.debuts. April 3, 2015.

"Pony Express: Fastest Mail Across the West." www.legendsofamerica.com. March 9, 2015 and February 3, 2017.

"Pony Express Trail National Backcountry Byway." www.utah.com. March 9, 2015.

"Pre-Territorial, 1850-1868." Wyoming State Historical Preservation Office.

Preimsberger, Duane. "Charley Parkhurst, Stagecoach 'Whip'." Temecula Valley Historical Society. Temecula, CA.

Ramon, F. James. <u>Come an' Get It: the Story of the Old-Time Cowboy Cook</u>. Norman: University of Oklahoma Press, 1952.

Ramos, Mary. "The Crash at Crush." *Texas Almanac,* 1962-1963.

Ramsland, Katherine. "Alferd Packer, the Maneater of Colorado." www.murpedia.org. August 30, 2013.

Rasmussen, Cecilia. "Trailing a Wild-West Character to His Graves." *Los Angeles Times,* August 21, 2005.

Reagan, Albert B. and Wallace Stark. "Chipeta, Queen of the Utes and Her Equally Illustrious Husband, Noted Chief Ouray." (authors' personal interviews plus Ute Agency Files, War Department Records, and Handbook of American Indians," Bureau of American Ethnology, Washington, D.C., October 12, 1912, Bulletin 30, 1-2.)

Reichenberger, Larry. "One-Room Country Schools. *The Furrow*, November, 2015.

"Rescuers Reach Donner Party." This Day in History. www.history.com. Feb. 19, 2013.

"Restoring Bison to America." www.allaboutwildlife.com. Paul Guernsey, ed., June 23, 2016.

Reyburn, Tom. Personal interview. History Day at Hinsdale County Museum, Lake City, Colorado, 2010.

Reyburn, Tom, Lake City, Colorado. Personal interview via email, September 21, 2014.

Reynolds, William and Ritch Ranch. The Cowboy Hat Book. Layton, UT: Gibbs Smith Publishers, 2003.

Rice, James E. "Remarkable Career of 'Black Bart.' " *Bankitaly Life*, December, 1920.

Richardson, Rupert N. "Some Details of the Southern Overland Mail." *Southwest Historical Quarterly*, #20, July, 1925.

Ring, Trudy, Noelle Watson, Paul Schellinger, eds. The Americas: International Directory of Historic Places. New York: Routledge, 1996.

Risjord, Norman K. <u>Jefferson's America</u>. Washington, D.C.: Rowman and Littlefield, Publishers, 2009.

Ritter, Rich. <u>The Perilous Journey: A Magnificent Episode of Seven Tragically-Entangled Lives</u>. Kindle Books Online. January 18, 2016.

Robenault, Jeffrey. "The Meusebach-Comanche Treaty." www.texasescapes.com. August 15, 2012.

Roberts, David. <u>In Search of the Old Ones: Exploring the Anasazi World of the Southwest</u>. New York: Simon and Schuster, 1996.

Robson, Alan. Personal Interview. Hinsdale County Museum, Lake City, CO. August 3, 2014.

Rohdenburg, Brad. "Traditional Trail Foods." *Backwoods Home Magazine, #81*, May-June, 2003.

Ronda, James P. <u>Voyages of Discovery: Essays on the Lewis and Clark Expedition</u>. Helena, MT: Montana Historical Press, 2002.

"Roosevelt: In Honor of a President." Theodore Roosevelt National Park, NPS, April 13, 2018.

"Roosevelt Pursues the Boat Thieves." Theodore Roosevelt National Park, NPS, North Dakota.

Roosevelt, Theodore. <u>Ranch Life and the Hunting Trail</u>. London: Pavilion Press, 2004 (reprint). First edition: New York: The Century Co., 1888.

Root, Waverly and Richard de Rochement. <u>Eating in America: A History</u>. New York: Morrow, 1976.

Rupp, Rebecca. "The Lukewarm Gluey History of Portable Soup." www.theplate.nationalgeographic.com. September 14, 2012.

Ryan, Joal. "The Secret History of the Lone Ranger." www.yahoo.com/movies. July 3, 2013.

Ryan, Susan M. "John B. Stetson: A Hatter Legacy." Presentation to the Board of Trustees, Stetson University, 2016.

Sajna, Mike. Crazy Horse: <u>The Life Behind the Legend</u>. Edison. NJ: Castle Books, 2000.

Sanders, George, ed. <u>The Trail Drivers of Texas</u>. New York: Argosy-Antiquities, Ltd., 1963.

Sanders, J.R. "Crush's Locomotive Crash Was a Monster Smash." *Wild West*, April 2, 2010.

Sando, Joe S. and Herman Agoyo, eds. "Po'pay: Leader of the First American Revolution." Santa Fe: ClearLight Publications, 2005.

"Santa Fe Trail: Highway to the Southwest." www.legendofamerica.com. September18, 2016.

Saunders, George, ed. <u>The Trail Drivers of Texas</u>. New York: Argosy-Antiquities Ltd.: 1963.

Schablitsky, PhD, RPA. University of Oregon Museum of Natural and Cultural History. www.speaking of history.com/donnerfeedback. June 8, 2015.

Schimmel, Julie. <u>The West as America: Reinterpreting Images of the Frontier</u>. Washington, D.C. and London: Smithsonian Institute Press, 1991.

Schlissel, Lillian. Women's Diaries on the Western Frontier. Brooklyn College, City University of New York, 1977.

"Seaman." National Expansion Memorial, St. Louis, MO. National Park Service.

"Sense and Nonsense." *Saturday Evening Post*, Vol. 186, Issue 1, Page 44, August 9, 1913.

"Sequoyah and the Cherokee Syllabary." www.cherokee.org. May 24, 2015.

Shapiro, Fred R. "Who said 'Go West, Young Man'? Quote Detective Debunks Myths." *CUA Magazine*, November, 2007.

Sharp, Jay W. "Acoma Pueblo: The Sky City." www.desertusa.com/desert-new-mexico/acoma-city. May 6, 2013.

Shaw, Simon, Linda S. Peavy, Ursula Smith. Frontier House. New York: Atria Books, 2002.

Shively, John. Guide to Oregon and California, 1846. Dale Morgan, ed. Lincoln: University of Nebraska Press, 1993.

Sicilia, David B. "How the West Was Wired." *Inc. Magazine* online. May 6, 2014.

Siggurdson blog. "Camels Arrive in Texas, Begin U.S. Army Experiment, April 29, 1858." *American Legion*, April 29, 2011.

Simmons, Lee. Assignment Huntsville: Memoirs of a Texas Prison Official. Austin: University of Texas Press, 1951.

Simmons, Marc. "Mesa Verde Pioneer Richard Wetherill Met a Tragic End." *Santa Fe New Mexican*, June 5, 2015.

Simpson, A.W.B. Cannibalism and the Common Law. Chicago: University of Chicago Press, 1984.

Smallwood, Karl. "...In Which Theodore Roosevelt Makes Men Everywhere Feel a Little Less Manly." www.todayifoundout.com. May 6, 2015.

Smith, P. David. Ouray: Chief of the Utes. Ouray. CO: Wayfarer Press, 1986.

Snyder, Jeffrey. Stetson Hats and the John B. Stetson Company, 1805-1890. Atglen, PA: Schiffer Publishing Co, Ltd., 1997.

Staff, Fred. Bass Reeves: Lawman. Charleston, S.C., 2015.

Staff, Fred. Judge Parker and Bass Reeves: Two-Fisted Justice. Charleston, SC, 2014.

Staff, Fred. Young Bass Reeves: The Life and Legend of Bass Reeves. Charleston, SC, 2012.

"Stagecoaches of the American West." www.legendsofamerica.com. October 17, 2016.

Stamm, Mike. HorseMuleGrizzlyIndianBuffalo: Wrecks of the Frontier West. Medicine Wolf Press, 1997.

State Historical Society of North Dakota, Museum Division. Handout 88-2: "History for Everyone."

Steele, Sam. Quotation. Northwest Mounted Police, 1874.

Stefansson, Vilhjalmur. The Fat of the Land (enl. edition of Not By Bread Alone. New York: The Macmillan Co., 1980.

Sterling, William Warren. Trails and Trials of a Texas Ranger. Norman, OK: University of Oklahoma Press, 1969.

"Stetson Life." www.stetson.com. May 26, 2014.

Stewart, George. Story of the Donner Party: Ordeal by Hunger. Lincoln: University of Nebraska Press, 1960.

Stong, Phil. Horses and Americans. New York: Frederick A Stokes Co., 1939.

"Strauss." www.pbs.org/weeta.thewest/people/s-z/strauss.htm. September 9, 2014.

Sublett, Jesse. "Lone on the Range: A History of the Texas Rangers." *Texas Monthly,* December, 1969.

Swan, Oliver G. Covered Wagon Days. New York: Grosset and Dunlap, Publishers, 1928.

Swanton, John Reed. "The Indian Tribes of North America." Bulletin #3, Smithsonian Institute, Bureau of American Ethnology. Washington, D.C.

Swearingen, Marshall. "Mining for Dark Matter in Lead, South Dakota." *High Country News,* June 17, 2013

Taylor, Elizabeth Berlin. "Origins of the Teddy Bear." The Gilderman Institute of American History. www.gilderlehrman.org. April 10, 2015.

Tchudi, Stephen. Western Technological Landscapes. Las Vegas: Nevada Humanities Committee, 1998.

"Teddy Bear." *Plaything Magazine,* October, 1906.

"Teddy Bear." Theodore Roosevelt Center at Dickenson State University, Dickinson, ND.

Terrell, Timothy. "The Real Story of the Transcontinental Railroad." *Homeschooling Today*, July-August, 2005.

Texas Historical Marker, 204 South Brown Street, San Saba, Texas, placed in 1965.

Texas Ranger Hall of Fame and Museum, PO Box 270, Waco, TX, 76702.

"Texas Rangers: Silver Stars and Sixguns." www.dps.texas.gov/Texas Rangers/silverstars.html. December 2, 2013.

"Texas State Bison Herd: Epic Journey from Near Extinction to Celebration." Texas Parks and Wildlife Dept., Sept. 7, 2011.

"The AT&SF and Fred Harvey Civilize the Southwest." *Western Trips*, September 15, 2011.

The Columbia Electric Encyclopedia, 6th edition, New York: Columbia University Press, 2012.

"The Concord Coach." Wells Fargo publication, 1999.

"The Crash at Crush." Handbook of Texas. Austin: Texas State Historical Assn., 2015.

"The Denver and Rio Grande Western Railroad: Main Line Through the Rockies." www.american-rails.com. February 11, 2017.

"The Donner Party Tried a Shortcut." www.tahoetopia.com. May 11, 2014.

"The Early Years: A Brief History of Barbed Wire." Kansas Barbed Wire Museum, LaCrosse, Kansas.

"The Earps Shoot it Out at the O.K. Corral." www.thisdayinhistory.com. October 26, 2015.

"The Earps Shoot It Out at the O.K. Corral in Tombstone, Arizona." Video. Tombstone Chamber of Commerce, 2015.

"The First Transcontinental Railroad." www.terr.com. September 9, 2015.

"The Heroines of the Western Schoolhouse." www.123HelpMe.com. June 13, 2016.

"The History of the Teddy Bear." *Smithsonian Magazine*, December 12, 2012.

"The Horses of the Pony Express." *Western Horseman*, January-February, 1942.

"The Journals of Lewis and Clark." Charlottesville: University of Virginia, n.d. web, May 2, 2013.

"The Journals of Philip St. George, Wm. H.C. Whiting, and Francois (Francis) S. Aubrey." Ralph Bieber, ed. Glendale, WY: Arthur H. Clark and Co., 1931-1943.

"The Overland Pony Express." *Harper's Weekly*, Nov. 2, 1867.

"The Pony Express Rides into History." Sheridan, WY, Heritage Center. USPS, 1970.

"The Pony Express Riders of Destiny." *Wild West Magazine*, April, 2006.

"The Real Bear Story." Theodore Roosevelt Assn., Oyster Bay, NY.

"The Real Story of How Teddy Bears Got Their Name." www.todayifoundout.com. May 16, 2015.

"The Story of Charley Parkhurst: Recalling a Romantic Character of the Early Days of California." *The Pajaronian*, October 5, 1917.

"The Story of the Fred Harvey Company." www.h2g2.com. January 5, 2014.

"The Story of the Teddy Bear." National Park Service, Theodore Roosevelt National Historic Site, New York.

"The Tragic Fate of the Donner Party, 1847." www.eyewitnesstohistory.com. March 5, 2013.

"The Voyage of Discovery: An African-American in the Corps." www.nebraskastudies.org. May 18, 2015.

"They Made America: Levi Strauss." www.pbs.org. June 28, 2014.

"Thomas, Ralph D. "Everything You Wanted to Know About Cowboy Hats, But Didn't Know Who to Ask." Tribal and Western Impressions, Georgetown, TX.

Thompson, Clay. "Fred Harvey and the Harvey Girls." *The Arizona Republic*, April 13, 2011.

Thorp, Raymond T. and Robert Bunker. The Saga of Liver-Eating Johnson. Bloomington, IN: Indiana University Press, 1983.

Tkaczyk, Flip. Alderleaf Wilderness College, Seattle, WA.

"Top Ten Schoolhouses." www.arizonaadventures.com. January 4, 2016.

Trew, Delbert. "Barbed-Wire Telephone Lines Brought Gossip and News to Farm and Ranch." *Farm Collector*. September, 2003.

Trommer, Rosemerry Wahtola. "Place Names." *Telluride Daily Planet*, Nov. 26, 2015.

Twain, Mark. Roughing It. Hartford, CN: American Publishing Co., 1872. Revised 2011 by University of California Press, Oakland.

Uldrich, Jack. Into the Unknown. New York: Amacom, 2004.

Underwood, Lamar. Tales of the Mountain Men: 17 Stories of Survival, Exploration, and the Frontier Spirit. Guilford, CN: The Lyons Press, 2004.

Underwood, Todd. "Butterfield Overland Stage Route." www.frontiertrails.com. July 6, 2015.

United States Deputy Marshals Badge. www.google.com. September 9, 2014.

"U.S. Marshals Museum." www.usmmuseum.com. September 9, 2014.

Utley, Robert. Lone Star Lawmen: The Second Century of Texas Rangers. New York: Oxford Press USA, 2007.

"Valley Railroad 3025 Turned the Wye." www.youtube.com February 11, 2017.

Vaughan, Carson. "The Incredible Legacy of Susan LaFlesche, The First Native American to Earn a Medical Degree." *Smithsonian Magazine*, March 1, 2017.

Verney, Edmund Hope. "Trails of Hope." *London's Good Words and Sunday Magazine*, May-June, 1866.

Viola, Herman J. Diplomats in Buckskin: A History of Indian Delegations in Washington City. Norman: University of Oklahoma Press, 1995.

Wade, Lelia Jeanette. Our Community: Organization and Development of Nolan County. Sweetwater, TX: Watson-Focht Company, 1960.

Wagner, Sandra and Carol Ann Wetherill. "A Tough Job." *Silver Thread Scenic and History Byway*, Summer, 2014.

Wall, Holly. "Bass Reeves: The Real Lone Ranger." *The Roundup*. www.thislandpress.com/roundup. March 1, 2014.

Wallace, Ernest. Ranald Mackenzie on the Texas Frontier. College Station: Texas A&M University Press, 1993.

Wallis, Michael. The Real Wild West. New York: St. Martin's Press, 1999.

Walsh, Tim. Timeless Toys: Classic Toys and the Playmakers Who Made Them. Kansas City, MO: Andrews McMeel Publishing, 2005.

Ward, George P. "The Crash at Crush: Texas' Great Pre-Arranged Train Wreck." Master's report: The University of Texas at Arlington, May, 1975.

Webb, Walter Prescott. The Texas Rangers: A Century of Frontier Defense. Austin: The University of Texas Press, 2nd edition, 1965.

Weber, David J., ed. What Caused the Pueblo Revolt of 1680? Boston and New York: St. Martin's Press, 1999. H-Net: Humanities and Social Sciences Online. November 5, 2015.

Weiser, Kathy. "Beale's Wagon Road From New Mexico to California." www.legendsofamerica.com. January 18, 2014.

Weiser, Kathy. "Poker Alice: Familiar Frontier Gambler." www.legendsofamerica.com. Jan. 14, 2014.

Weiser,Kathy and Dave Alexander. "Staging and Banking in the Old West." www.legendsofamerica.com. March 3, 2016.

Weiss, Jr. Harold J. <u>Yours to Command: The Life and Legend of Ranger Captain Bill McDonald</u>. Denton: University of North Texas Press, 2009.

Welborn, Amy. "Retired Katy Engineer Tells of Wreck At Crush." *Katy Employees' Magazine*, 1950.

Welker, Glen. compiler. "Sequoyah." www.indigenouspeople.net, 1993. March 30, 2013.

Wellman, Jr., Paul I. <u>The Trampling Herd: The Story of the Cattle Range in America</u>. Lincoln: The University of Nebraska Press, 1988.

Werner, Shawn. "Poker Alice: Gambler. Madam, Celebrity." *Deadwood Magazine*, August, 2009.

"What was Life Like for York, Clark's Black Slave, During the Expedition?" PBS Interview with Stephen Ambrose. Living History. www.pbs.org. October 13, 2014.

"When the Pony Express was in Vogue." *San Francisco Newsletter*, 1925.

"White Gold: The Amazing Story of Thomas Jefferson's Mountain of Salt and the Discovery of The Great Salt Plains of Oklahoma." Istonia Ministries Blog. April 5, 2017.

Whitney, Susan Lyman. "Chipeta." *Deseret News*, October 16, 1994.

"Who Invented the Cowboy Hat?" www.wonderopolis.com. February 26, 2014.

"Why Do We Call It a Ten-Gallon Hat?" www.history.com. February 26, 2014.

Wilkins, Frederick. The Law Comes to Texas. Austin: State House Press, 1999.

Williams, Glenn F. "We Found It Excellent, White, and Fine." *Army History Magazine*, U.S. Army Center of Military History.

Williams, Jacqueline. Wagon Wheel Kitchens: Food on the Oregon Trail. Lawrence, KS: University Press of Kansas, 1993.

Wilson, Terry P. The Underground Reservation: Osage Oil. Lincoln: University of Nebraska Press, 1985.

Wise, Watson W. "Lone Wolf Gonzaullas: Texas Ranger." *Petroleum History Almanac*.

Wolfe, Jen. "The Legend of Prunes: A Man and His Mule." *Southwest Characters*, Aug. 18, 2009.

Wolvern, Pat. Personal interview. Orange Empire Railway Museum, Perris/Riverside, CA. May 15, 2012.

Woodger, Elin and Brandon Toropov. "Encyclopedia of the Lewis and Clark Expedition." New York: Facts on File, 2004.

"Workers of the Union Pacific" and "Workers of the Central Pacific." American Experience. www.pbs.org. February 18, 2015.

Wright, Muriel H. "The Butterfield Overland Mail: 100 Years Ago." www.digital.library. okstate.edu..August 25, 2015.

"York." Lewis and Clark National History Trail. www.nps.gov. August 27, 2015.

Zentner, Joe. "Camels in America's Southwest: The Desert Camel Experiment." www.desertusa.com. March 3, 2013.

Zhang, Sarah. "Barbed Wire Fences Were an Early DIY Telephone Network." www.gizmodo.com. March 25, 2014.

INDEX

A

Abecedarians, 194
Abilene, KS, 41, 273
Acoma, 237-243
Adams Museum, 222
Adams, Ramon, 42
Adams, W.E., 222
Adelsverein, 187-189
Africa, 275
Alamo, 53-56, 183, 265
Alamo City, 23
Alaska Territory, 14, 201, 263
Alaska, 201, 286-287
Albuquerque, NM, 94, 97
Aleutian Islands, 245
Alexandria, VA, 103
Alferd Packer Memorial Grill, 113
Alferd/Alfred, 113
Ali, Haiji, 11
Ambrose, Stephen, 108
America, 27, 31-3, 91, 102, 106, 133, 143-5, 163, 166, 190, 198, 208, 219, 221, 237, 240-3, 246, 267, 270, 280, 285
"America the Beautiful," 195
American Airlines, 149
American Express, 144-145
American Philosophical Society, 246
Anasazi, 237, 281-282
Anchorage, 245
Anderson Col. James, 264
Andrews, T.G. 140
Anna Karenina, 79
Apache Pass, 148
Apache, 215-216, 220, 241, 242, 265
Apostle John, 4-5
Arbuckle's, 43
Arctic/Antarctic, 127
Arikara, 278
Arizona, 8, 12, 14, 81, 146, 164, 205-206, 209-210, 254, 282, 284, 286-7
Arkansas, 85, 149, 202, 227
Arkansas River, 229, 230-231, 285
Armstrong, John B. 182
Army Corps of Engineers, 2
Army Corps of Topo Engineers, 254

Arness, James, 273
"Arrow," 215
Arthur, Chester A., 209
Ashley, William, 250
Asia, 14, 165, 275
Atchison, Topeka, & Santa Fe, 92
Aten, Ira, 176
Atlantic Ocean, 247
Aubrey, Francis, 33
Austin, Stephen F., 76, 175-176
Austin, TX, 182, 184-5
Autry, Gene, 3
Ayoka, 212
Asia, 14, 165

B

Bactrian camel, 10-11
Baker, Lindsey, 285
B and O Railroad, 168
Barb Fence Co., 22
Barnes, Frank, 15
Barnum, P.T., 15
Barrow, Clyde, 182
Bartholomew, Graham, 130
Bartlesville, OK, 101
Battle of San Jacinto, 274
Battle of Vicksburg, 130
Beale, Edward F., 11-13
Beale's Wagon Road, 12-13
"Beck," 205-206
Becknell, William, 229-230
Bell, Alexander Graham, 27
Bell, Ma, 28, 31
Bell, Shannon, 110, 112
Bent, William, 268
Bent's Old Fort, 231
Berg children, 200
Bering Strait, 246
Berryman, Clifford, 115-119
Bessemer, 167
Betatakin, 282
Bible, 86, 137-8, 154-155, 171, 197, 199, 202, 205, 213
"Big Die-Up," 24
"Big Medicine Man," 163
"Big Muddy," 277

Big Nose Smith, 184
Billings, County, ND, 77
"Billy Possum, " 118
Billy the Kid, 227
Birch, Ebenezer, 171
Bird Cage Theatre, 207
Bismarck, ND, 80
Bison Legacy Act, 276
Black Bart, 130-132, 269
Black Hills 221-222
Black Hills Pioneer, 222
Black Mare, 215
Black's Fork, 261
Blackfoot/Blackfeet, 9, 48, 136
Bois D'Arc, 41
Bol, Todd, 264
Boles, Charles, E., 129-130, 132
Boles General Store, 263
Bolin, Ricky, 4
"Bond of Friendship, " 102
Boone, Daniel, 262
Boot Hill, 207
Borden, Gail, 45, 127
Borneman, Walter, 165
Bosetti, Violet, 95
Boston, 247
Boudin Blanc, 35
Boudin family, 39
Boulder, Co, 113
Bowie, James, 53-54, 286
Bowie knife, 155, 286
Brady, TX, 251
Branch, E.D., 96
Brannan, Samuel, 271
Brazil, 71
Brazoria, TX, 73-74, 76
Breckenridge, CO, 141
Breece, Hannah, 201
Breen, Patrick, 67
Bridger, Jim, 65, 70, 249, 256, 261-262
British, 157, 165
Broadwater County, MT, 108
Brocius, Wm. "Curly Bill, " 255
Brooklyn, NY, 117
Brooks, Garth, 4
Brown, Aaron, 145
Brown County, TX, 182
Brownsville, TX, 75-76

Brownwood, TX, 95
Brunot Agreement, 218-219
Brunot, Felix, 219
Brunter Brothers, 83
Buchanan, James, 11, 145
Buckskin Joe, 138
Buffalo Bill, 4, 160, 276
"Buffalo Gals, " 276
Buffalo Hump, 189
Bunch, Joey, 218
Bunker, Robert, 51
Burlington Railroad, 97
Burton, Art, 88-89
Burton, Captain Richard, 157
Bush, George and George W., 4
Butte Mountain Independent, 30-31
Butte, MT, 263
Butterfield, John, 143-150, 163-164, 169
Buzzard, S.M., 45
"By God and Wells Fargo, " 269

C

Cage of Hands, 207
Calaveras County, CA, 130
California, 8, 11, 14, 19, 39-40, 47, 57-8
    63-5, 67-8, 70, 92, 101, 129, 143-4, 147,
    149, 152-3, 155-6, 161-4, 168, 171, 173-
    4, 243, 250, 255, 269-71, 273, 279-80
California Limited, 94
California Pacific, 157
California Trail, 64-66, 230, 277
Cameahwait, 35
Camel Corps, 11-12
Campbell, Homer, 61
Campbell, William, 163
Camp Verde, 10, 12
Canada, 165
Canadian, 165, 249
Canadian Mountie, 126
Cannibal Grill and Saloon, 113
Cannibal Plateau, 112
Cape Horn, 58, 144, 263, 270
Caprock Canyon State Park, 276
Cardenas, Garcia L., 243
Carnegie, Andrew/Libraries, 264
Carson, Kit, 249, 256
Carver, Dr. Hartwell, 167
Cascades, 134

Cassidy, Butch, 227
Castaneda, General, 53
Castell, TX, 192
Cather, Willa, 242
Catherine the Great, 246
Catholic, 74, 240, 242
Cayuse, 276
Celerity Wagon, 146, 149
Cenotaph (Alamo), 55
Central America, 258
Central Pacific RR, 164, 167-168
Central Route, 145, 150, 164
Chaco Canyon, 282
Chaffin, J.F., 250-251
Charbonneau, Jean-Baptiste, 107, 281
Charbonneau, Toussaint, 35, 107, 280-281
Cherokee, 85, 211-214
Cherokee County Jail, 279
Cherokee Phoenix, 213
Cherokee Syllabary, 212-213
Cheyenne, 162, 273
Chickasaw, 146
Chief of the Utes, 216
Chinese, 40, 165
"Chinese Wall, "166
Chiricahua Apache, 205, 210
Chisholm Trail, 273
Chuck box, 41
Chuck wagon, 41-42
Cimarron, KS, 25
Cimarron River/Cutoff, 230
Civil War, 1, 12, 41, 44, 50, 71, 85, 92, 103, 130, 132, 149, 153, 157-8, 163-5, 183, 252, 273
Claiborne, Billy, 208, 255
Clanton Gang, 208, 255
Clark, George Rogers, 246
Clark, Rev. John, 278
Clark, Wm., 106, 136, 246, 258, 271, 278
Clatsop, 34, 106
Clearwater River, 134
Clinton, Bill, 108
Clyman, James, 66, 70
Cobb, Will, 203
COC & PP, 156
Cochise, 210
Cochise County Cowboys, 208-209, 255
Cody, Buffalo Bill, 4, 159-162, 276
Cody, WY, 47

Cogburn, Rooster, 227
Colbert, B.F., 146
Coloma, CA, 70
Colorado, 2, 8, 101, 109, 111, 114, 122, 141, 201, 216-17, 220, 230, 254, 259, 272, 280, 283-284
Colorado City, TX, 45
Colorado River, 189-250
Colorado Women's Hall of Fame, 220
Colt .45 Peacemaker, 86, 181
Colt, Samuel/Revolver, 178-179, 220, 286
Colton, Rev. Walter, 270
Columbia, 247
Columbia River, 107, 134, 247-248, 285
Columbus, TX, 257
Comanche, 44-45, 175, 178, 182, 87, 191, 200, 241, 252, 259, 286
Comancheria, 189, 285
Comanche TX, 182
Comstock Lode, 206
Concord coaches, 144, 146, 149, 174, 270
Concord, NH, 174
Concord, PA, 200
Conestoga wagon, 286
Confederacy, 12, 19, 92, 164
Confederate flag, 103
Constitution of Rep. of TX, 275
Continental Divide, 133, 247
Continental Oil Co./Conoco, 102, 122
Corazon, Frenchy, 111
Corbett, Christopher, 156, 159
Cordova, AL, 263
Corning, 38
Coronado, Francisco, 229, 239, 243
Corps of Discovery, 105-8, 133-4, 136, 246-7, 258, 271, 277, 280, 287
Cosden, Josh, 101
Council Bluffs, IA, 163, 167-168
Countryman, Edward, 241
Cox, Mike, 176
Cree, 125
Creighton, Edward, 162-163
Cripple Creek, CO, 284
Crocker, Charles, 165
Crockett, David, 53, 183, 261
Crookes, David, 49
Cross Cut, TX, 95
Crow, 48, 50

Crow Killer, 51
Crowder, Robert "Bob, " 181
Crush, George, 15-16, 18-20
Crush, TX, 15-16, 18-20
Cruzatte, Pierre, 133-136
Custer Expedition, 221

D

Dakota Territory, 77, 221, 223, 263
Dallas Morning News, 17, 181
Dallas, TX, 16, 177
Dalton Gang, 227
Darby, Andrew, 259
Darkey, Charlotte, 173
Davis, Jacob, 58-60
Davis, Jefferson, 9-10, 12
Davis, John B., 213
Davis, Miriam, 45
Deadwood Creek, 221
Deadwood, SD, 221-222
De Cardenas, Garcia Lopez, 243
Deep South, 26
Deere, John, 286
Deets, 252
DeKalb, IL, 25
DeLand, FL, 5
DeLand University, 5
Denver, 137, 139, 169, 264
Denver Tribune, 215
De Onate, Juan, 239, 242
Derby, England, 282
De Rojas, Lorenzo, 191
De Vaca, Cabeza, 229, 238
De Zavala, Lorenzo, 274-275
Diaz, Cameron, 60
Dickinson, Almeron/Susanna, 54-55
Dickinson, Angelina, 54-55
Dickinson, ND, 79
Dickinson, Susanna, 54-55
Diehl, Pony, 255
Dillon, Marshal Matt, 273
Directory of Deceased Physicians, 76
Dobie, J. Frank, 35, 44, 177
Dodge automobile, 201
Dodge City, KS, 41, 94, 97, 273
Dongri, India, 61
Donner, Eliza (Houghton), 68
Donner, George, 64-67

Donner, Jacob, 64
Donner Party, 66-70, 112, 128
Donner, Tamsen, 63, 66-67
Dow, Wilmot, 78, 81
Drake, Ben, 44
DRGW RR, 283
Drift fences, 24
Dromedary camel, 10-11
Duffield, Frank, 121
Duffy, Pete, 99, 100, 102
Dunaway, James, 184
Dungarees, 61
Durango-Silverton RR, 283
Dutch, 259
Duvall, Robert, 4
Dyer, Father John, 137-142
Dyer, Judge Elias, 141

E

Earp brothers, 208-209, 227
East Orange, NJ, 2
Easter/Easter Bunny, 191
Easter Fires Pageant, 191
Eckhardt, C. F., 28
Eisenhower, Dwight, 4
Elkhorn Ranch, 77, 78, 81, 142
Elks Convention, 123
Ellsworth, Elmer Ephraim, 103
El Lobo Solo, 180
Ellwood, Isaac, 22, 25
Elm Creek Raid, 252
El Paso, TX, 10, 146, 150, 279
El Reno, OK, 99
El Tovar, 96
Emmett, Chris, 9
Enchanted Rock, 178
England/English, 138, 211, 215, 259
Episcopal, 74, 219, 263
Europe, 25, 192, 246, 261, 270, 287
Evans, Dale, 4
Evans, Gus, 203
Ewing, J.R., 4

F

Fagan, James, 85
Fairplay, CO, 254
F.A.O. Schwarz, 117
Far East, 247, 270

Fargo, William, 144, 149, 269
Father Dyer Church, 141
"Father of Texas," 175
"Father of Waters," 278
Faulk, Odie, 13
FBI, 102, 185, 227
Feister, Mark, 142
Field, Gene, 219
Finnigan, 77-78, 80
Fisher, Billy, 151, 159
Fisher, Burchard, 189
Fisher-Miller Grant, 187, 189, 192
Fisher, William, 159
Fitzpatrick, Thomas, 279
Flatheads, 48, 272
Floyd, Sgt. Charles, 280
Ford automobile, 76
Ford, John S. "Rip," 178-179, 184
Fort Atkinson, 263
Fort Bridger, 64-66, 70, 200, 256, 262
Fort Clatsop, 36
Fort Hall, 64
Fort Laramie, 200, 249, 262
Fort Smith, AR, 85-87, 89, 150, 227
Fort Worth Star Telegram, 76
Fortune 500, 60
Forty-Niners, 143
Four Corners, 281
Fowler, Cliff, 3, 4
France, 39, 133-134, 240-1, 246, 266-8
Franciscan, 241
Franklin (El Paso), 146
Franklin, MO, 230
Frazier, Maude, 201, 203
Fredericksburg, TX, 188-192
Fremont Street, 208
Fremont, John C., 114
Frenchman's Gulch, 140
Frontier Battalion, 183
Fry, Johnny, 152-153
Frying Pan Ranch, 23
Fuller, Thomas, 284
Fuqua, Benjamin/Silas/William, 55
Fuqua, Galba, 53-55

G

Gadsden Purchase, 164
Gallatin (MO River fork), 277

Gallego, Captain Pedro, 230
Galveston, TX, 75
Gamble, James, 162
Garland, Judy, 97
Garrison, Col. Homer, 182
Garrison, John, 48
Gaston, John Davis, 53-54
Gates, John, 21, 23, 26
Genes, 58-59
Genoa, Italy, 58
Genoa, NV, 201
Georgia, 213
Germany, 57, 117-118, 187-192
Geronimo, 210
Gerry, Judge Melville B., 109, 111
Gertrude gold vein, 266
Gibsland, LA, 182
Gibson, Jake, 227
Giddings, Genevieve, 196, 203
Gilbert, Bill, 254
Gird, Richard, 206
Glidden, Joseph, 21-22, 25-27, 32, 286
Glidden, Lucinda, 22
Gold Rush, 130, 144, 171
Golden Rule, 203
Golden Spike, 167
Golden State, 58, 153
Goliad/Massacre, 56, 183, 265
Gonzales, TX, 53-55
Gonzales Rangers, 54-59
Gonzaullas, Manuel, 180-181, 185
Goodnight, Charles, 40-41, 251-252
 255-256, 259, 276
"Goodnight, Ladies," 29
Goodnight-Loving trail, 273
Goodnight, Mary Ann, 276
Goodwood Racetrack, 26
Goose Flats, 207
Graham, Bartholomew, 130
Grand Army of the Republic, 123
Grand Canyon, 42, 96, 243
Granite, CO, 141
Grant, U.S., 85
Graves, Franklin, 68
Gray, Robert, 247
Great American Desert, 169
Great Britain, 241, 245
Great Chute, 134

Great Depression, 96, 209
Great Oxbow Route, 145
Great Plains, 36, 233-234, 268, 275
Great Pueblo Revolt, 240
Great Salt Lake, 65, 286
Great Salt Lake Desert, 66
Great Seal of Texas, 177
Greek George, 11
Greek language, 264
Greeley, Horace, 158, 284
Greenleaf, 84
Green River, 250, 261
Green River Rendezvous, 249-250
Greenwood Cemetery, 252
Grinnell, Jack, 140
GSA, 113
Guadalupe Peak, 149
Guadalupe River, 10, 53, 188
Guess, George, 211
Guess/Gist, Nathaniel, 211
Gulf of Mexico, 247, 277
"Gunfight at the O.K. Corral," 209
Gunnison River, 218
"Gunsmoke," 273
Gutierrez, Ramon I., 241

H

Halladay, Daniel, 286
Hamer, Frank, 182
Hamilton, Sam (Billy), 153
Hamilton, William T., 256
Hangtown fry, 39
Hardin, John Wesley, 182, 279
Hardtack, 39
Harper's Bazaar, 61, 272
Harper's Weekly, 110, 143
Harrington, Col. Marion, 76
Harvard University, 264
Harvey House, 93
Hasinai, 265
Haslam, Robert "Pony Bob," 152, 155, 160
Hastings Cutoff, 65-67, 69-70
Hastings, Lansford, 64-67, 70
"Hatters," 5
Havana Harbor, 4
Hawaii, 286-287
Hays, John Coffee, 178, 179, 183, 188
Herodotus, 265

Herzog, Dr. August, 74
Hiawatha, 249
Hickok, James "Wild Bill," 159
High Plains, 243, 280
Hi Jolly, 11, 14
"Hindenburg," 61
Hinsdale, County, Co, 109-110
History of the James Bros., 79
Hohokam, 237
Holbrook, AZ, 93
Holder, Nelda, 262-263
Holliday, Doc, 208-209
Holmes, Bob, 28
Holmes, Sherlock, 89
"Home on the Range," 276
Homestake Mine, 221
Hopi, 242-243
Houghton, Eliza Donner, 68
Houston, Sam, 55, 183, 211
Houston, TX, 264
Howard, Dakota, Territory, 263
Hudson Bay, 125
Hudson, WI, 264
Humfreville, Capt. J. Lee, 249
Humphrey, James, 110
Huntington, Col Marion, 76
Huntsville, 49-50

I

Ice Age, 246, 280
"Icehouse Nugget," 223
Idaho, 113, 276
Ideal Toy Co., 117
Ignacio, CO, 218
Ikard, Bose, 251-252
Ikard, Milton, 251
Illinois, 129
Immortal 32, 53-54
Imogene Basin, CO, 266
Independence, MO, 63, 70
Independence Rock, 71
Indianola, 10
Indian Territory, OK, 85, 87, 100, 146
Interstate 25, 231
Interstate 40, 12
Iowa, 137, 163
Ipsen, Mary, 168
Irish, 165

Iron Horse, 13
Isthmus of Panama, 166
Ivers, Alice, 121

J

JA Ranch, 23
Jackass Mail, 14, 159
Jackson, Joaquin, 183
James Farley Post Office, 264
James Frank, 79
James, Jesse, 227
Jefferson Foundation, 266-267
Jefferson (Missouri River fork), 277
Jefferson, Thomas, 12, 34, 133, 245-247, 266-267, 271, 277, 280, 285, 287
Jehu, 171
Jesuit, 258
Jewish Sabbath, 58
Jicarillo Apache, 215
Jocklink, Sidney, 219
Johnson, Anna, 196
Johnson, Britt, 251-252
Johnson, Jeremiah, 47-48
Johnson, Lyndon B., 4, 147, 196
Johnson, Moses, 252
Jones, John B., 183
Jones, Kiowa, 184
Jones, Tommy Lee, 4
Jornada del Muerto, 230
J. Strauss Bros. and Co., 57
Judiciary Act of 1790, 225

K

"Kansan, " 102
Kansas, 22, 92, 95, 100, 102, 152, 230-231, 259-260, 273
Kansas City, KS, 94, 263
Kansas Pacific, 97
Karankawa, 175
Katemcy, 189
Keith County, NE, 203
Kellar, Maxine, 95
Kellogg, John B., Jr., 54
Kennedy, John F., 287
Kentucky, 106, 108, 246
Keyes, Sarah, 69
Kiet Siel, 282
Kilgore, TX 180

King, Gilbert, 118
King, Irene Marschall, 192
King, John Gladden, 55
King, Nancy, 55
KIng, William P. "Billy, 53-55
Kiowa, 215, 252
Kitchen family, 250-251
Kitchen, Gladys, 103
Knowles, Thomas, 176
Koch, Peter, 50
Kopko, Mary, 221
Ku Klux Klan, 176

L

Ladies Home Journal, 119
LaFlesche-Picott, Susan, 268-269
La Fonda, 96
La Junta, CO, 231
Lake City, CO, 109-110, 112-113
Lake, Stuart, 209
Lampasas River, 250
Lancaster, CA, 51
Lander, WY, 279
Lansbury, Angela, 97
LaSalle, 240, 267
Las Vegas, 202
Latvia, 58
Lavender, David, 268
Lead, SD, 221-223
Leadville, CO, 121-122
Leavenworth, KS, 159
Ledyard, John, 246
Leipzig Trade Fair, 117
Leslie, Buckskin Frank, 255
Levi's, 57-62
Lewis & Clark, 34, 36, 45, 133, 164, 256, 259, 279
Lewis & Clark College, 108
Lewis & Clark Expedition, 105, 108, 229, 245-246, 258, 272, 277- 280, 285
Lewis, Meriwether, 35, 105-106, 135-136, 258, 271
Liberty, TX, 55
Lighthall, Doc, 23
Lincoln, Abraham, 103, 152, 161, 163
Lipan Apache, 175
Little Free Libraries, 264
Little Missouri River, 77

Little Sunflower River, 115
Littleton, CO, 112
Liverpool, England, 91
Livingston, Robert, 267
Llano Estacado, 252
Llano River, 189
London, 26, 163
London World's Fair, 127
Lone Ranger, 3, 88-89
"Lonesome Dove," 4, 252
Lone Star State, 21
Long, Stephen, 280
Longhorn, 23
Longino, Andrew, H., 118
Look for Me in Heaven, 140, 142
Los Angeles, CA, 13
Los Pinos Indian Agency, 109-110, 113
Louisiana, 118, 268
Louisiana Purchase, 14, 133, 246, 248, 266-268, 277
Louisiana Territory, 229, 246, 267-268
Louisville, KY, 108
Loving, Mabel, 158
Loving, Oliver, 251-252, 259
"Lucky Cuss," 206
Lyman, William, 44

M

Ma Bell, 28, 31
MacDougall, Rob, 29
Mackinaw flatboats, 278
Madison (MO River fork), 277
Mandan-Hidatsa, 106, 278
Mandan Fort, 281
Manhattan, NV, 270
Manhattan, NY, 58
Manifest Destiny, 247, 284
Marcy, Randolph B. 37-38
Marquette & Joliet, 240, 277
Marshall House Inn, 103
Mason, Charley, 281
Masterson, Bat, 227
McAlister, 54
McConnell, R.E., 131
McCormick, Cyrus, 286
McCulloch, Ben, 183, 227
McDonald, Bill, 175, 177, 185
McGuffey Readers, 197

McKinley, Wm., 220
McLaury brothers, 208, 255
McLintock!, 45
McManus, Pete, 21, 23
McNelly, Leander, 183-184
McNeil's, 91
McSherry, Patrick, 81
Mediterranean Sea, 10
Medora, ND, 81
Meek, Joe, 250, 258-259
Meek, Steven Hall, 256
Meeker Massacre, 218, 272
Meeker, Nathan, 272
Memphis, TN, 150
Mendoza, Friar/Fray, 239
Menger Hotel, 21
Mercer, Johnny, 97
Mercer, T. Lillie, 200
Mesa Verde, 281-282
Methodist/Church, 25, 123, 137, 141, 220, 255, 279
Meusebach-Comanche Treaty, 190
Meusebach, John, 187-192
Mexican Cession, 14, 143
Mexican War, 48, 67, 70, 178, 183, 188, 217, 231, 270
Mexico/Mexican, 8, 53-54, 65, 76, 102, 106, 164, 175, 179, 182, 190, 230, 239, 241, 270
Mexico/MX City, 238-240, 270, 274
Meyers, Bernice, 95
MGM, 97
Michaux, Andre, 246
Michtom, Benjamin, 117
Michtom, Morris & Rose, 116-117, 119
Mid-Continent Oil/Gas Region, 101
Middle East, 10
Mighty Mo, 277-278
Military Plaza, 23
Miller, Broncho Charlie, 159
Miller, Burchard, 189
Miller, Frank, 110
Million-Dollar Elm, 101
Milton, Jeff, 184
Minnesota, 137
Mississippi, 115, 118, 251
Mississippi River, 19, 64, 153, 163, 227, 246-247, 267, 273, 277-278
Missouri, 22, 229, 231

Missouri River, 49, 107, 168, 198, 202, 246-248, 258 263, 277-278, 285
Missouri Territory, 202
Mix, Tom, 3
MKT Railway, 15-16, 18-19
Mochila, 154, 159
Mogollon, 237
Mongols, 5
Monroe, James, 267
Montalto, 266-267
Montana, 31, 41, 49-50, 108, 265
Monticello, 266-267
Montrose, CO, 219
Moody, Ralph, 160
Moore, Craig, 29
Moore, Lester, 207
Morgans, 155
Mormon Trail, 230, 277
Mormons, 165, 262
Morris, Michael, 9
Morse, Charles, 97
Morse Samuel F.B., 161
Mosquito Pass, 139, 141
Mount Rushmore, 248
Mountain Trail, 230-231
Murphy, Levinah, 68, 71
Muskogee, 87
My Darling Clementine, 195, 209
Myers, Bernice, 95

N

Nagy, Linda, 253
Napoleon, 45
National Bison Legacy Act, 276
National Historic Trail, 231
National Park Service, 158, 231
Nat'l Pony Express Re-Rides, 159
National Statuary Hall, 242
Navajo, 242
Navarro, Jose Antonio, 274
Nebraska, 203, 222, 263, 268, 273-4
Netherlands, 259
Nevada, 8, 152, 201-202, 206, 284
Nevada Dept. of Education, 201
New Braunfels, TX, 188
New Echota, 213
New Hampshire, 174
New Jersey, 48, 74

New Mexico, 8, 24, 81, 122, 146, 164, 168, 215, 230-231, 237, 241, 243, 256, 259, 282, 286-287
New Orleans, 92, 267
New York, 32-33, 44, 144, 223, 261
New York City, 57-58, 61, 74, 91, 116-117, 150, 159, 163, 264
New York Herald, 147
New York Tribune, 284
New York, 32-33, 44, 133, 222
New Yorker, The, 284
Newfoundland breed, 105, 281
Nez Perce, 134, 248, 276-277
Nicaragua, 270
Nilson, Swan, 140
Nimshi, 171
Nobel, Alfred, 166
No Name Hat Shop, 2
Noon, George, 110
North America, 14, 125, 221, 240
North Carolina, 250, 262
North Dakota, 200
North Pole, 127
Northern Illinois University, 26
Northern Route, 164
Northwest Territory, 125, 201, 245
Norwegian, 139
Nueces River/Strip, 179, 184

O

Oakley, Annie, 4
Ogallala Aquifer, 280
Ogallala, NE, 273, 280
Ogden, UT, 102
O.K. Corral, 207-209
Oklahoma, 24, 81, 85, 87, 99-100, 146, 213-214, 226-227, 230, 285, 286-7
Old Owl, 189
Old Trail Town, WY, 47
Omaha, NE, 138, 168, 268
Omaha Herald, 253
Omaha Indians, 134
"On the A., T., and the Santa Fe," 97
Oregon, 70-71, 106, 108, 167, 250, 277, 279-280, 299, 284
Oregon Trail, 37-38, 64, 164, 230, 258, 262, 277
Ormsby, Waterman, 147-148, 150
O'Rourke, P.J., 61

Osage, 22, 99-100, 102, 285
O'Sullivan, John, 261
Otero, AZ, 200
Ouray, CO, 110, 113, 266, 272
Overland Mail Co., 143, 145-150, 152, 163, 169, 269
Overland Route, 146, 149, 163
Overland Stage, 150, 162
Oxbow Route, 146, 149
Oxford English Dictionary, 61
Ozark Mountains, 202

P

Pacific Coast, 47, 60, 134, 229, 277, 281
Pacific Ocean, 107, 133, 153, 229, 246-248, 277, 285
Pacific Railway Acts, 163
Pacific Telegraph Act, 162
Pacific University, 277, 285
Packer, Alferd, 109-113, 218
Packer Memorial Grill, 113
Paiute, 67, 152, 156
Palmer, George Herbert, 264
Palo Duro Canyon, 265, 276
Panama/Canal/RR, 144, 171, 270
Panhandle, 23-24, 34, 40
Panhandle Plains Revue, 256
Parham, Greg, 127
Parker, Bonnie, 182
Parker, Judge Isaac, 85, 87, 89
Parker, Rev. Samuel, 271-272
Park View Middle School, 51
Paron, 216, 219
Pawhuska, OK, 101
Pawnee Historical Society, 103
Peary, Robert, 127
Pecos River, 184, 259
Pecos Strawberries, 42
Pemmican, 36-37
Penateka Comanche, 189-192
Pennsylvania, 226, 268
Pensacola, FL, 182
Perrott, John, 221-223
Persia, 265
Peru, 258
Petsy, 117
Philadelphia Folk Festival, 113
Philadelphia, PA, 2, 91, 269

Phillip II, King, 239
Phillips, L.E. and Frank, 101
Phillips Petroleum, 101-102
Philmont, MT, 193
Pierce, Franklin, 7
Pike's Peak, 2, 137, 138, 156
Pike, Zebulon, 134, 280
"Pilot of the Boats," 134
Pittsburgh, PA, 105
Plains, 40, 155, 229, 234, 275-6
Plains Indians, 22, 25, 64, 125, 190, 233
Platte River, 64, 233, 278
Plaything Magazine, 117
Poling-Kempes, Lesley, 97
Polk, James K., 270
Pomp, 107, 281
Ponca City, OK, 102
Pony Express, 139, 149, 151-164, 169, 262, 274, 277
Pony Express Nat'l Museum, 156
Popay, 240-242
Port Arthur, TX, 26
Porter, David D., 10
Portland, OR, 108
"Possum, Billy," 118
Presbyterian, 272
Prince Carl of Solms-Braunfels, 188-189
Prohibition, 30
Promontory Summit, UT, 167-168
Providence, RI, 171
Provo, UT, 109
"Prunes," 254
Pueblo/Puebloan, 237-243
Purvis, Hardy B. and Hardy L., 176

Q

"Queen of the Utes," 219
Quemessourita, 277
Quitaque, 256

R

Rababou/robbiboe, 127
Railway Act, 163
Railway Express, 270
Rainbow Bridge, 282
Rarick, Ethan, 70
Raton, NM, 93, 230
Raton Pass, 230

Raymond, Sarah, 200
Reagan, Ronald, 4
Reagan, Sheriff Richard, 279
Reconstruction, 183
Red Dragon club, 263
"Red Ghost," 12
Red Lodge, MT, 50
Red River, 146
Redford, Robert, 48, 51
Redwoods, 255
Reed, James, 63-67, 69, 70
Reeves, Bass, 227, 83-89
Reign of Terror, 102
Rendezvous, 249-250, 261
Republic of Texas, 188, 274
Revere, Paul, 259
Revolutionary War, 225
Rhoads, Daniel, 71
Richard III, 249
Ringo, Johnny, 255
Rio Grande, 146, 179, 184
Riverfront Plaza, 108
Robertson, John 256-257
Robinson, Tri, 51
Roby, John A., 51
Rocky Mountains, 32, 35, 107, 114, 133-134, 162, 218, 229, 247-8, 276, 279-83
Rogers, Kenny, 57
Rogers, Roy, 3
Rogers, Will, 96
Rohdenbury, Brad, 128
Rolleri, Jimmy, 131
Roosevelt, Kermit, 118
Roosevelt, Theodore, 77-81, 115-119, 142
"Rough Riders," 81
Roughing It (Twain quotes), 157, 174, 277
Route 66, 12
"Royal Flush," 26
Ruiz, Francisco, 274
Rush, Dr. Benjamin, 258
Rushkoff, Douglas
Rusk State Hospital, 181
Russell, Majors, Waddell, 153 158-159
Russia, 116, 214, 245-246

S

Sacagawea, 35, 107-198, 248, 280-281
Sacramento, CA, 153, 156, 162-163, 168

Sacramento Daily Bee, 173
Safford, Mr., 251
Saguache, CO, 109-110
Sallisaw, OK, 214
Salt Lake City, UT, 162, 169, 264
San Antonio, TX, 10, 21, 23, 43-55
San Diego, CA, 243
San Esteban de Ray, 240, 242
San Francisco, 39, 58, 63, 131, 145-7, 150, 165, 207, 269
San Francisco Examiner, 255
San Jacinto, TX, 183, 265
San Juan Mountains, 110, 113-114, 216
San Juan Pueblo, 240
San Marcos River, 55
San Pedro Valley, 205-206
San Saba, TX, 255
Sanford Underground Center, 223
Sans Orielle, 285
Santa Anna, 53-55, 192, 265
Santa Fe Railroad, 12, 92-93, 97
Santa Fe, NM, 96, 217, 229-230, 240-1, 243
Santa Fe Trail, 189, 192, 229-231, 277, 286
Santana, 189, 192
Sarvisberries, 38
Saskatoon berries, 126
Schieffelin, Al and Ed, 205-210
School Cave, 202
"School Days," 203
Scottish, 183, 264
Seaman, 105-106, 108, 281
Sears, 28
Sedalia MO/Sedalia Trail, 273
Seguin, Juan, 274
Seminole, 84
Sequoyah, 211-214
Serge de Nimes, 59
Settle, Raymond, 156, 158
Seven Cities of Gold, 239, 243
Sewall, Bill, 78, 81
Shakespeare, 53, 249
Sharp, Jay W., 238
Shawnee, 260
"She'll Be Coming 'Round the Mtn.," 195
Sherwood, Rupe, 254
Shipman, Winifred, 193
Shirkey, Mary Ann and Pauline, 7
Shively, John M., 260

Shoshone, 35, 105, 107, 134, 248
Shultz, Willabelle, 86
Siberia, 246
Sibley, Major George C., 285
Sicilia, David B., 27, 32
Sierra Nevada, 152, 159, 162, 172
Silverton, CO, 67, 140
Sioux, 49, 163, 215-216, 219, 277
Six-shooter coffee, 43
Skelly, Wm. (Bill), 102
Skidi/Skedee, 102
Smith, "Big Nose," 184
Smith, Cornelia Marschall, 192
Smith, Evan, 181
Smith, Jed, 36, 230, 250, 256, 279
Smithsonian Institution, 118
Smithwick, Noah, 257
Snake River, 134
Son-of-a-gun stew, 42
Soule, John B. L., 284
"Sourdough," 217
South America, 166, 258
South Dakota, 122
South Pass, 279
South Plains, 24
South Plains bison, 276
Southern Pacific, 168
Southern Route, 145, 150, 164
Southern Uncompahgre Utes, 220
Southwest, 26, 159, 229, 237-238, 243, 282
Spain/Spanish, 12, 159, 185, 215, 229-30, 238-242, 245-246, 267, 274
Spanish-American War, 81
Spaulding, Eliza and Henry, 276-277
Spicer, Judge Wells, 205
Spindletop, 26
Springfield, IL, 63
St. Augustine, FL, 243
St. Joseph, MO, 64, 153, 156, 162
St. Laurent, Yves, 59
St. Louis, MO, 36, 87, 92, 107, 135, 145, 147, 150, 153, 207, 248, 277-8, 280, 285
St. Louis-Brownsville-MX Rail, 75-76
Stamm, Mike, 250, 256
Stanford University, 167
Starr, Belle, 83, 227
Starrs, James E. 112
"Star-That-Travels," 99

Statuary Hall, 213
Steele, Mabel, 201
Steiff, Richard and Margaret, 117, 119
Stetson Hats, 1-5
Stetson, John B., 1-5, 141
Stetson University & Law School, 5
Stoudenmire, Dallas, 227
Strait of Magellan, 270
Stratigraphic, 282
Strauss Levi & brothers, 57-61
Stuart, Gilbert, 196, 203
Studebaker, John, 144
Sturgis, SD, 123
Stuttgart Zoo, 117
Sugarfoot, 172
Sultana, 19
Sundance Kid, 227
Supply, 10
Sutter's Mill/Fort, 65, 69-70, 143
Swallowin' Sand Burrs, 70
Swan, Israel, 110, 112
Sweetwater River, 64
Syllabary, 212
Sylph, 153

T

Tabeguache Utes, 215-216
Taft, President William H., 118, 220
Tahlequah, OK, 213
"Tales of the TX Rangers" (TV), 185
Tallack, William, 150
Talleyrand, Charles, 267
Taos, NM, 215-216, 238, 240, 256
Taos Pueblo, 238
Taos Revolt, 217
Taylor Brothers, 55-56
Taylor County, TX, 55
"Teddy" (Dodge car), 201
Tedro, Philip, 14
Tejas, 265
Tennessee, 145, 150, 211, 242, 261
Tenochtitlan, 240
Terlingua, 284
Teton Sioux, 79, 136
Tewa, 240
Texas, 7, 10-12, 22-24, 26, 41, 44, 55, 74-76, 81, 146, 149, 164, 175-185, 187, 190, 192, 250, 255, 261, 265, 273-274

Texas A&M University, 265
Texas Company/Texaco, 26
Texas Declaration of Independence, 274
Texas DPS, 177, 185
"Texas" Pageant, 265
Texas Prison System, 182
Texas Rangers, 4, 44, 86, 176-185
Texas Revolution, 53-55, 274
Texas State Bison Herd, 276
Texas State Library, 192
Texian, 54, 265
The Barb Fence Co., 22
The Cherokee Phoenix, 213
"The Great Expansionist," 248
"The Harvey Girls," 97
The Helena Independent, 265
The Homestake Mine, 221
The Life and Times of Wyatt Earp, 209
"The Nation's Attic," 203
The New Yorker, 284
Theodore Roosevelt Nat'l Park, 81
"'The People" 217
The Pony Express Rides On, 158
"The Searchers," 252
The Tombstone Epitaph, 207-208
Thoreau, Henry David, 245
Thorpe, Raymond T., 51
Three Forks of the Missouri, 277
Three Godfathers, 45
Tilghman, Bill, 227
Tipton, MO, 147, 150
Tolstoy, 79
Tombstone, AZ, 206-210, 263, 284
Tonkawa, 257
Tonopah, NV, 270
Topeka, KS, 92
"Tough Nut," 206
Toyota, 214
Transcontinental telegraph, 161-163
Travis, William B., 53-54
Treaty of Guadalupe Hidalgo, 8, 14
Trew, Delbert/Trew Ranch, 29, 32
Trinidad, CO, 231
Troy, Kansas, 152
"True Grit," 227
Tubbs, Warren G., 122
Tulsa, Ok, 100-101
Turner, Frederick Jackson, 287

Twain, Mark, 157, 174, 277
TX State Bison Herd, 276

U

Uintah Ouray Ute, 220
Una gold vein, 266
Uncompahgre, 215-216, 266, 272
Union, 12, 70, 103, 129-130, 153, 163, 168
Union Pacific, 97, 164, 166-167
United States, 23, 168, 215-17, 231, 241, 266-68, 285
University of Colorado, 113
University of Nevada, Las Vegas, 202
Unruh, John, 197
Upper MO River Bridge, 168
Upper Rio Grande Valley, 201
U.S. Army, 8, 12, 14, 127, 205, 210, 231, 262
U.S. Army Corps of Discovery, 271
U.S. Bureau of Census, 286
U.S. Capitol, 214, 242
U.S. Cavalry, 4
U.S. Congress, 5, 9, 145, 162-165, 167-168, 217, 225, 231, 246
U.S. Constitution, 225, 267
U.S. Department of Energy, 223
U.S. Federal Court, 85, 89
U.S. Hwy #350, 231
U.S. Mail, 139, 143
U.S. Marshal/Marshals Service, 273
U.S. Marshals Museum, 227
U.S. Mint, 269
U.S. Naval Hospital, 74
U.S. Navy, 48, 214
U.S. Postal Service, 264
U.S. President, 273
U.S. Secretary of State, 246
U.S. Secretary of War, 9
U.S.S. Maine, 4
U.S. Treasury Dept., 185
Utah, 8, 65-6, 70, 162, 165, 167, 218-219, 272, 279, 282, 285-286
Utes, 110, 113, 215-220, 241, 266, 272, 283

V

Vancouver, George, 247
Vancouver Island, 246
Verde Creek, 10
Verney, Edward H., 147

Vicksburg, 130
Victorio, 210
Vienna, Austria, 74, 76
Violette, Dick, 29
Virginia, 101, 121, 266
Virginia City, MT, 200; Nevada, 284
Visscher, Col. William L., 158
Von Furstenberg, Diane, 57

W

Waco, Texas, 15
Waldene, 200
Waldrip, 251
Wales, 221
Walker-Colt, 179-180
Walker, Joe, 256
Walker, Samuel, 179
Wallace, William "Big Foot," 183
Wallace, William "Braveheart," 183
Walters, Col. Ellsworth, 101-103
Wapato, 35
Ward, "Monkey," 28
Warner, Solomon, 62
Warren, Harry, 97
Wasatch Mountains, 66
Washington, D.C., 9, 89, 102, 153, 203, 213-214, 216-17, 219-220, 225, 280
Washington, George, 196, 203, 225-226
Washington Territory/State, 199, 263, 276
Watsonville, CA, 174
Wayne, Henry C., 7-8, 10
Wayne, John, 4, 45, 227
Weatherford, TX, 252, 259
Webb, Deputy Charles, 182
Webb, Jim, 85
Webb, W. Prescott, 179
Weber, David J., 243
Weiss, Harold J., 185
Wellman, Paul I., 23
Wells Fargo, 129-32, 144-5, 149, 160, 172, 269-270
Wells, Henry, 144, 269
Wesley, John, 138, 279
West, 36, 39, 45, 197-198
West Coast, 34, 36, 58, 134, 171, 243, 270
West Point, 165
Western District of Arkansas, 89
Western Trail, 273

Western Union Telegraph Co., 162-163
Wetherill, Al and John, 282
Wetherill, Richard, 281-282
Wheeler, John, F., 213
Whiskey Rebellion, 226
Whistleberries, 42
White House, 116
"White Man's Friend," 216
"White Singing Bird," 215
Whitewood Creek, 221
Whitman, Marcus & Narcissa, 276
Whitney, Ann, 200-201
Whitson, Cal, 227
Whittier, John Greenleaf, 202
Williams, Bill, 256
Winchester rifle, 115, 286
Winchester, Oliver, 286
Wisconsin, 201, 264
Wise, Watson, 181
Women's Medical College of PA, 268
Woodhawk, 48-49
Worcester, Samuel, 213
World War I, 25, 96, 102, 158, 210, 214, 218
World War II, 5, 60, 96, 102, 210
Wrangler, 61
Wright, J. George, 101
Wuh-The, 211
WXYZ radio station, 88
Wyoming, 8, 41, 47, 110, 200, 262, 273, 279

X

XIT Ranch, 23
XXXX Family Flour, 45

Y

Yerba County, CA, 130
York, 106, 108
York Island, 108
Youphes, Jacob, 58

Z

Zhang, Sarah, 31
Ziegler, Eustace, 263

www.ingramcontent.com/pod-product-compliance
Lightning Source LLC
Chambersburg PA
CBHW081453040426
42446CB00016B/3227